Stra

a

Also by Jenny Diski

Stranger on a Train

Daydreaming and Smoking
Around America with Interruptions

Jenny Diski

Picador
New York

FOR IAN

STRANGER ON A TRAIN. Copyright © 2002 by Jenny Diski. All rights reserved.
Printed in the United States of America. No part of this book may be used or
reproduced in any manner whatsoever without written permission except in
the case of brief quotations embodied in critical articles or reviews. For information, address Picador, 175 Fifth Avenue, New York, N.Y. 10010.

www.picadorusa.com

Picador® is a U.S. registered trademark and is used by St. Martin's Press under
license from Pan Books Limited.

For information on Picador Reading Group Guides, as well as ordering, please
contact the Trade Marketing department at St. Martin's Press.
Phone: 1-800-221-7945 extension 763
Fax: 212-677-7456
E-mail: trademarketing@stmartins.com

ISBN 0-312-28352-0 (hc)
ISBN 0-312-42262-8 (pbk)

First published in Great Britain by Virago press, an imprint of Time Warner
Books

10 9 8 7 6 5 4 3 2

Acknowledgements

Parts of this text have appeared in *Harper's Bazaar* (US), *The Guardian* and the *London Review of Books*.

My thanks to Marjorie and Merle Turner for time off and good company in Oregon, and for straightening me out on the rivers of the Northwest. Thanks, also, to John and Maria Phipps for oasis time. And thanks to my New Mexican hosts. I am grateful to an anonymous, virtual, but, I am assured, human librarian at the Newark Public Library for his or her helpfulness and kindness in finding and sending me the Frank Leslie quote. Frederic Tuten and Karen Marta made New York an even more vivid and invigorating place to begin and end my journey. And many thanks for everything to Ian Patterson, who changed my horizon entirely.

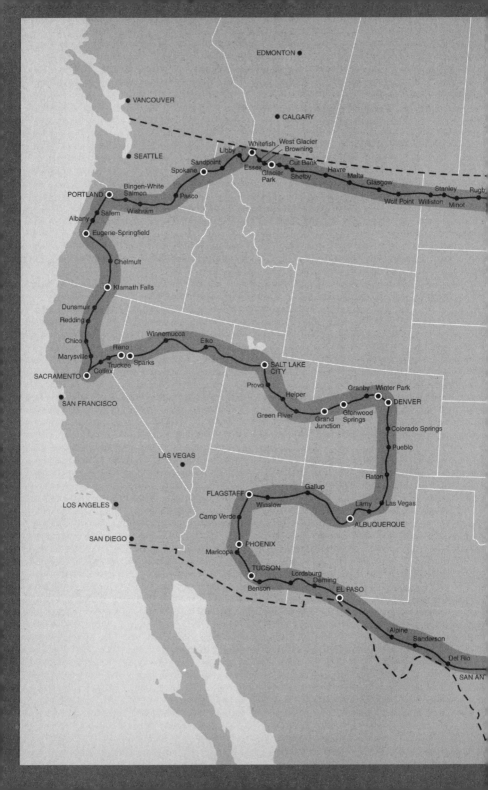

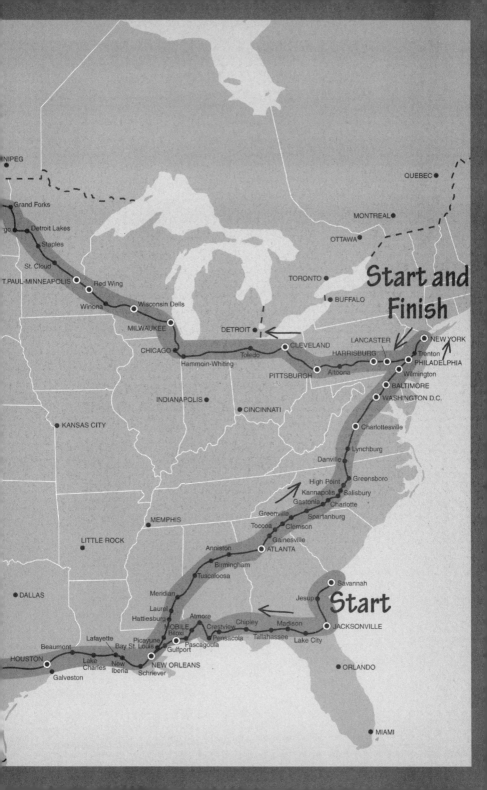

Circles and Straight Lines

Many writers have imagined that history is cyclic, that the present state of the world, exactly as it is now, will sooner or later recur. How shall we state this hypothesis in our view? We shall have to say that the later state is numerically identical with the earlier state; and we cannot say that this state occurs twice, since that would imply a system of dating which the hypothesis makes impossible. The situation would be analogous to that of a man who travels round the world: he does not say that his starting-point and his point of arrival are two different but precisely similar places, he says they are the same place. The hypothesis that history is cyclic can be expressed as follows: form the group of all qualities contemporaneous with a given quality: in certain cases the whole of this group precedes itself.

An Inquiry into Meaning and Truth,
BERTRAND RUSSELL, 1940

One month after I had started my journey around the circumference of America, I was back again where I began, on the frantic concourse at Penn Station, in Madison Square Garden, New York—

I hate neat endings. I have an antipathy to finishing in

general. The last page, the final strains of a chord, the curtain falling on the echo of a closing speech, living happily ever after; all that grates on me. The finality is false, because there you still are, the reader, the observer, the listener, with a gaping chasm in front of you, left out of the resolution of the story that seduced you into thinking yourself inside it. Then it's done and gone, abandoning you to continuation, a con trick played out and you were the mark. An ending always leaves you standing in the whistling vacancy of a storyless landscape. Any ending exposes the impossible paradox – the desire for completion, the fear of termination – which like an open wound is too tender to uncover. But neat endings are the worst; the rounded closure that rings so true and so false, the harmonious conclusion that makes sense of the beginning and of all that happened in-between, and makes a lie of what you know about the conduct of your life, a lie of you.

There are two kinds of neat endings: the satisfying circle that ends where it began, and the straight line that ends in a point. Our life, we are inclined to think, is like the latter; the world is like the former. Artifice – art, if you must – very often inscribes the circle, taking the straight line to its desired conclusion: the point becomes a metonymy for the completed circle. Artifice makes the circle the secret pattern beneath the straight line. Very gratifying, that. It is as if our brains are tuned to that wavelength, we look for completion like we look for the definitive note at the end of a symphony. And, should they wish to challenge it, all that life and artifice can do against the tendency is subvert it: to deny us what we expect, what we are disposed to want, so that what we feel is *lack*. But finally that only reminds us again of what we crave. We don't escape by exposing ourselves to subversion, we only experience our uneasiness at being deprived of what we want. We should be wary of this, aware at least that there's a covert affirmation of the status quo in volunteering ourselves for discomfort.

When I was thirteen, at weekends and during the holidays, I spent a large part of my days underground. I hated my home at that time. Having run away from my distressed and distressing mother and without anywhere else I could be, living with my father was a last resort. He had disappeared without trace over a year before and only recently been found again, living in the house of a woman called Pam. I hadn't chosen to be there, nor had they chosen to have me. Pam, it turned out later, had made a secret deal with my mother after I arrived at her house. She would do what she could to make me feel unwelcome so that I would want to leave and return to my mother. Nothing would have made me do that. The result was an epic sulk on my part. I lived inside a kind of microclimate, a dark cloud of misery and punishment. We all suffered. I spoke to no one, ate meals in silence and retreated to my room at the top of the house. Every morning when I was not at school I walked to the local library and took out three books, novels, whatever took my fancy, based on nothing but titles and covers (I read Nabokov, Somerset Maugham, Edgar Allan Poe, Nevil Shute and Margaret Mitchell with equal enthusiasm and literary innocence), and I took these to the nearest underground station, Notting Hill Gate. Notting Hill, to my great good fortune, was on the Circle Line, a London phenomenon that has been the saving of many a tramp, drunk, overcrowded writer and sulking teenager down the years. It is the only tube line that travels in a continuous complete circle, although looked at on the modern tube map it is shaped more like a bottle lying on its side. All the other lines go north–south or east–west, beginning and ending at opposite ends of the outskirts of the city. The Circle Line, depicted in bright

yellow, sits in the centre of the underground web, enclosing
within its boundaries the heart of London. It is central
London's perimeter and a route that includes most of the
major main-line stations. The point about it was that instead
of having to get off at a particular station and take another
train back, you could sit in the same plush if tatty seat and
circle endlessly all day long for just the cost of the minimum
fare to the next stop. It was the cheapest day out in London,
and the best way to keep dry if it was raining and warm if it
was cold. Anyone with time on their hands, who didn't want
to be at home, or didn't have a home to be at, could, for just
pennies, use the Circle Line as their office (it is said that
Naomi Mitchison used it to write novels) or their escape, or
even, given the ever-changing cast of characters, their enter-
tainment. If, like me, you were travelling without a
destination, or planned eventually to return to your starting
point, you could choose, when you first got on, whether to
travel clockwise or anti-clockwise; it didn't matter. In those
days I could recite the stops in order in both directions, now I
have to remind myself by looking on the map. Notting Hill
Gate, Bayswater, Paddington (for points west), Edgware Road,
Baker Street (where I went to Madame Tussaud's in the old
days with my father), Great Portland Street, Euston Square
(almost at the block of flats I grew up in until we were evicted
after my father moved out), King's Cross St Pancras (to head
up north), Farringdon, Barbican (not there in my travelling
days), Moorgate, Liverpool Street (for eastern areas), Aldgate,
Tower Hill (again, trips with my father in the old days),
Monument, Cannon Street, Mansion House, Blackfriars,
Temple, Embankment, Westminster (coming out of the City
now), St James's Park (feeding the ducks, being stopped by old
Queen Mary when I was three and chucked under the chin by

her close-laced hand emerging from her car window), Victoria (to the south), Sloane Square (into unknown chic territory for me), South Kensington (the museums on a Sunday with my father), Gloucester Road, High Street Kensington and Notting Hill Gate (home, though I never thought of it as that).

People got on, people got off. Every now and then someone else didn't get off, though you couldn't be sure they were doing the same as you until you had been a full circle, since they might just have gone round in the wrong direction. There would be a couple of flashers a day, who sat opposite you and exposed a pale worm from a slit in their trousers when the carriage was empty enough. A friend, who I met too late for my journeys, used to look at them hard and say very loud, 'Well, it looks like one, only smaller.' At thirteen, I was too embarrassed to say anything. Not distressed, but embarrassed for these pathetic adults. Also annoyed that I would have to get up and change carriages. Flashing was ubiquitous, and nothing more than a nuisance in those days. I didn't speak to anyone, nor they to me. That was inner-city travel. People wrapped up in their own thoughts, brooding about their lives, or others, about work or love or whatever people think about on the way from here to there and yet in neither place. I smoked if I had any cigarettes – we lived above Pam's newsagent and tobacconist shop, and sometimes I would sneak down in the middle of the night and steal a packet of twenty. I read voraciously. There was no need to look up to check which station we had arrived at, it made no difference to me. So I could keep my head buried (as Pam would say contemptuously) in a book. I got through my three books by the following morning unless I had chosen something I found unreadable. That was very rare. The fact that something could be read made it readable to me in those days. Books were where I lived, not because I was bookish, but because everyone has to have a place to go, and between the covers of books was mine. If I was hungry and I had any money, I could get off at a station and buy chocolate or nuts from a machine, and I bought a drink on the way to the station. The round trip, these days, is reckoned to be about forty-eight minutes. And I would go round and round all day long. I didn't count but if I rode the Circle Line from ten in the morning until five, when it was time for me to go home to eat supper and return to my room to finish my third book, while sitting smoking through the open window, I would have done the circuit nine times. The Circle Line was a salvation until I figured out a way of getting the local council to send me back to the boarding school I had been asked to leave because my mother kept turning up and screaming at everyone.

—In fact there were two American journeys, not a single, neatly planned, satisfyingly structured circular trip. The second excursion around the edge of the States was an after-thought, conceived of as the plan for a book inscribed on the geography of North America, and circumscribed by the schedule of the Amtrak rail system. The first trip was impromptu. I was going to smooth the two journeys into one, for the sake of neatness, for the sake of describing a gratifying circle. But I don't think I will, after all. On the first, acciden-tal journey I travelled, delightfully, as a stranger; with the second, planned trip my deliberate strangerness became both stranger and more familiar than I had intended. When the unexpected becomes entirely expected and known, and when the known becomes bizarre and spirit-draining, it's time to go home and wonder what you thought you were doing.

Another thing. *The plan for a book*. I am predominantly a writer of fiction. Research, which might include travelling, only comes about because of a need for detail required for the novel which essentially comes out of my head. I was once at a party where a novelist asked a journalist if he knew about the World Bank located in New York. The journalist replied that he did, and began to discuss the workings of the bank, its international role and effect. The novelist stopped him in mid-sentence.

'No, I just want to know what colour the front door is.'

That is exactly what researching a novel is like. Some things you make up, others you can read about, but there are small crucial details that have to be accurate.

A travel book is something else, if it is non-fiction. Though I'm not at all clear what. I imagine a travel writer plans a trip in order to write about it. Why, I'm not exactly sure. A film would give the curious a much better idea of the terrain, so it must be something about the act of travelling itself, adventures, encounters along the way. Travel writers must assume that adventures and encounters will occur. They must put their faith in the inevitability of incident.

I'm not much of a traveller at all. I travel in order to keep still. I want to be in or move through empty spaces in circumstances where nothing much will happen. When I go on holiday, I want a vacant beach and an uncluttered horizon. The last time I was on such a beach, I was sitting in a taverna when the Poet, my companion, put his glass of beer down on the table in front of us.

'Excuse me, that's my horizon,' I complained.

That is the trouble with travelling in company.

So going on a journey and writing a book about it is an odd thing for me to contemplate. The journey is in concept entirely uneventful, and so, therefore, is the prospective book.

'Well,' I explain to my editor, 'it will be a book about nothing happening.'

This book about nothing happening is the perfect book that I have in my head. The one I write towards but fail to reach whether what I'm writing is called fiction or non-fiction. My editor nods benevolently, going along with the notion, at least for my benefit. I would be perfectly happy to take these trips for their own sake, but I have to earn a living. I mean to say, that I am not a travel writer in any reasonable sense of the word. I do not feel compelled to bring the world to people, or meet interesting characters, or enlarge my circle of acquaintance. I just want to drift in the actual landscapes of my daydreams, and drifting, other than in the imagination, is expensive. So I concoct the idea of a book about my uneventful drifting. Eventfulness is not the mode of the fiction writer, or at any rate of my fiction writing – events just get in the way. So what a proper travel writer hopes for, I dread: incident. My ideal method of writing a travel book, I realise, would be to stay at home with the phone off the hook, the doorbell disconnected and the blinds drawn. I confess that I remain baffled that I should have put myself at such risk of incident. Baffled and very glad to be home with the blinds drawn.

As for America being the place I chose to trace my circle, well, it wasn't entirely fortuitous. As a child in fifties London, America was as distant a reality to me as ancient Egypt, yet present in my life in a way that those who had carved the remnants of mighty statuary I knew from my visits to the British Museum could never be. Distant is not quite the word. America was like the moon: its remoteness was irrelevant, what mattered was the light it bathed me in, its universal but private reach. The moon was the moon, and mine; familiar and personal, shining over me wherever I was, whenever I looked at it. America, too, was light. It beamed above my head from the cinema projection booth, particles dancing in its rays, ungraspable as a ghost, but resolving finally on the screen into gigantic images of a world I longed for, yet only half believed in. If I walked directly in front of the screen and got caught in its light, my very own shadow was projected up there with the bold and the beautiful, the lovers, the adventurers, the under-world, the mean streets, the main streets, the promising and punishing streets, the all-singing, all-dancing, all-laughing and crying world of what we then called the flicks. People in the audience shouted at me to duck down and get out of the way as if I hadn't realised what had happened, but I knew exactly what I was doing. I wanted to be in the way of all that.

JOURNEY ONE

Magic Monotony

One thing follows another. I had just spent three weeks crossing the Atlantic Ocean on a cargo ship carrying 25 tonnes of potash from Hamburg to offload in Tampa, Florida, and then doubling back round the tip of Florida to take on kaolin miles up a wriggly inlet at Port Royal, near Savannah, Georgia. I watched or felt every yard of the 6000 or so miles we travelled at a stately average of fifteen miles an hour. My capacity for staring had developed beyond even my expectations. Conrad writes of 'the magic monotony of existence between sky and water. Nothing is more enticing, disenchanting and enslaving than the life at sea.' I sat on a small deck, like a veranda, at the back of the ship, the *MV Christiane*, and watched the ocean like a vigilante as we passed over it, loath to miss a single wave or trick of the light retexturing the water, so that I had to drag my eyes down to the book on my lap, or force myself to go back to my cabin to work or sleep. Even at night, the rabble of stars demanded to be watched, and how could I ignore the effect of the fiercely shining moon, lighting up a brilliant pathway in the encircling blackness of the surrounding sea? Night-time on deck was special, like being awake in the early hours in a darkened hospital ward and seeing the night nurses sitting at dimly lit desks, or gliding silently about to check on sleeping patients. While I walked on deck, and the majority of the Croatian crew got their rest, one of the officers kept watch on the bridge, and an engineer attended to the gauges in the thudding depths of the ship's engine room. That someone is awake and keeping watch in a pool of light when night is at its blackest is very comforting.

After a very short time, when you are travelling so far at such a snail's pace, and with no urgent need (or in my case, any need at all) to get to where you are going, you become an aficionado of detail. I took on the task of witnessing the sea, as if someone, somewhere had to be constantly alert to its shifts and nuances, and here and now the job was mine. I kept an eye on the window when I brushed my teeth for fear of missing something. It was not a fear of missing dolphins leaping, or whales breaching, or a tornado five miles off withdrawing back into its cloud: though I did chance to see those events as I kept watch. It was a fear of missing all the nothing that was happening. The more ocean I watched, the more watching I needed to do, to make sure, perhaps, that it went on and on and that the horizon never got any closer. But simple witnessing is not easy, and I began to notice, with increasing irritation, my need to describe and define what I observed, when all I really wanted was for the sea simply to be the sea. I found myself constantly thinking of it in terms of something else, as if I were reading it for meaning, which was not what I thought I wanted to do at all. The sea was like shimmering mud, I heard myself think, glossy as lacquer, slate-grey, syrupy, heavy silk billowing in the breeze . . . it was like this, and then that. It's true that it did change all the time, but the most remarkable thing about it was that it was always and only like itself, though I couldn't manage to keep that thought firmly in my mind, which, being a human mind, was also like itself and probably couldn't help it.

I devoted myself to keeping track of the smallest changes in the sea, or the weather, or the progress of the incessant painting of the ship by the crew in the futile effort to impede the attack on its metal and wood by the salt, wind and water. Twice a day or more I examined the charts for the current longitude and latitude to check our progress and our exact whereabouts in the middle of the entirely featureless ocean. I wasn't bored, I was enthralled by the journeying, by the minutiae of the passage of miles and time. I watched our wake elongate behind us, like a snail's trace, disturbing the sea's own pattern into a visual account of where we had been in an environment that offered no other clue that we were making any progress at all. But always, in the distance behind the ship, the sea would close over the anomalous agitation, and return to its normal undifferentiated condition as far as the horizon. The frothy turbulence of the wake proved our movement, but the record of it was continually lost, rubbed out by the vast body of water that healed all the scars scored by whatever made its way through it.

There is never perfect solitude, I've learned.

'Always you sit reading or looking at the sea, but you are not unhappy, not lonely,' said the third engineer, as if he were asking me a question.

None of the crew could understand why the few passengers they carried would volunteer for such an existence. They were all quite clear that they were seamen by necessity. There were no jobs in post-war Croatia. Captain Bruno Kustera was a great-bellied man, entirely at the mercy of gravity. Everything about him tended downward: his belly, his chin, his jowls and the corners of his eyes and mouth. He made ruefulness his own. 'Pirate stories made me a sea captain,' he told me. 'But now it's routine. Just back and forth across the Atlantic. But what to do, there is no well-paid work at home. Always I go back and forth looking for work somewhere else. I would like to work in shipping, but on land. No one loves the sea. Do you know anyone in shipping circles in London?'

I didn't. He shrugged.

'You know, the Cold War was a wonderful thing. If you didn't like one, you could believe in the other. Now, it's all the same.'

He had been tending a pair of pigeons who came aboard for a well-earned rest, hundreds of miles out in the Atlantic. He made sure there was food and water for them on the bridge, and they lived quite contentedly up there for a couple of days, until a ship passing in the other direction, heading back to Europe, called time on their vacation and they left.

'Why don't you get a cat?' I asked, when he shook his head sadly at the loss of the pigeons. 'What about a ship's cat?'

His big eyes drooped. 'No, it is difficult. An animal has to be owned by one man. And also at sea you always find some-one crazy. That one would torture the cat.'

Towards the end of the trip we waited in a flat desert of sun-blasted water for the local pilot to come and tow us up a creek through the torrid desolation of an alligator-infested swamp to the improbably named Port Royal in South Carolina. Captain Bruno joined me at the rail. There was nothing in sight but the utterly still greenish water, no wind,

and the only sound, with the ship's engines off, was a humming of the saturating heat. I had been marvelling silently
that I had at last found myself truly up shit creek without a
paddle.

'This looks like the end of the universe,' I murmured.

He smiled with mock appreciation at the emptiness on
every side of us, and launched into a sardonic hymn to his
existence.

'Our bosses, they are experts at finding wonderful places for
us to go. I expect you never dared to dream in your life that
you would come to Port Royal. Nor did I. *Port Royal*' – he put
his fingers to his lips as if extolling an exquisite rare vintage –
'these Americans. You will see what is there. Nothing.
Nothing but the Last Chance Saloon. No, it is true. You will
see it at the end of what they like to call the harbour. We are
in a dream, or a nightmare. This is Gabriel Garcia Marquez's
Moranda. The lost land. You see, they have a very special
kind of kaolin in Port Royal. We will take two holds back to
Europe of Port Royal kaolin, and the six holds of the ordinary
kind we loaded in Tampa. It is best not to get them mixed up.
We are specialists in not getting our kaolin mixed up.'

'You must be very proud,' I laughed.

'Oh, very proud,' growled Captain Bruno, repeating it
diminuendo as he turned and made his weighty sweat-soaked
way back to the relative comfort of his cabin.

I had no trouble at all living with the melancholic irony of
these men as I kept watch on the passing minutes and miles.
They were, in spite of their dissatisfactions and landlubber
dreams, real seamen, understanding and even appreciating the
necessity for the tedium that meant they were making it safely
to the next port. Freighters can be very old and are lost at sea,

I was assured by a well-wisher before I left, at a rate of several a month. Apart from the officers, the crew dined together on a large wooden table on the lower deck at the back of the ship, joking, or being quiet, accepting the particular ways of each other, drinking moderately, because they knew their lives depended on working and living well together, and being alert. They cleaned and oiled the machinery, sanded and painted parts of the ship, replaced worn cables, and checked the emergency supplies on the lifeboats with attentive concentration. They worked because the work they were doing was essential. They spruced the ship, washed and ironed their clothes, scrubbed down the decks, kept everything stored and stashed, because orderliness was the only way to survive months at sea in a confined space with thirty or so other people. It was an education in institutional living. They fully understood the purpose of all this. The sea is dangerous; a ship full of potential for lethal accident. They took care of the ship and of each other. If there was a cat torturer among them, it was not obvious who it might be. Which, of course, doesn't mean there wasn't one.

About two hundred miles south of Bermuda, in the Sargasso Sea, in sweltering June (it was in the mid-30s Celsius by seven in the morning), I was woken at 5 a.m. by a terrible noise. The screaming of metal breaking up had something hellish about it, as if Neptune and all his sea imps were tearing the ship apart. There were sounds of shouting, men calling to each other, and trainers thumping along the corridor past my cabin. I wondered alarmed but sleepily if they were not shouting 'Abandon ship' in Croatian, but I'd had a heatwave headache the night before and taken a sleeping pill. I decided I'd rather go down with the ship than abandon it at such an hour. It turned out that the air-conditioning fan had catastrophically loosened, got out of line and one shaft had smashed irreparably. They did not, the chief engineer explained at breakfast, have a replacement fan on board. It was too hot for the loss of the air-conditioning system to be merely inconvenient. The day before I had been down to the engine room. It was like descending into my own headache, deep in the centre of the ship. The heat and airlessness were stunning, and the ubiquitous drumbeat deepened into a deafening roar down by the line of giant pistons pumping power to the massive screw that drove the propeller. It was not, however, entirely oppressive. The engine room was a fantastically clean, pale green cathedral as well as a fiery furnace; a vast space that soared up from the bowels of the ship to the open hatches, four decks above, through which the sky could be seen. In the middle of the day the engine room was reaching a temperature of 48 degrees Celsius. They would just have to make a new shaft for the fan.

'Can you?' I asked.

'We'll have to,' he said.

The chief engineer and half a dozen crew members worked all day around a brazier on the lower deck, straightening the remains of the broken shaft and forging a new piece of metal to fit it. By the early evening they were setting it in place. The screaming began again almost as soon as they turned the air-conditioning plant on. They returned to the deck and the makeshift forge. I slept fitfully in the suffocating heat. The next morning I woke to a cool air-conditioned cabin. At breakfast I learned that they had worked all night, and the chief engineer, glowing with pride, waved sleepily as he went off to bed for the first time since five the previous morning. The crew radiated heroic achievement, wafting their hands triumphantly around the cool air in the corridors as I passed them. I applauded

appreciatively. They bowed. It was, of course, a welcome challenge in the general tedium of caring for an ageing ship at sea.
The energy of having solved a problem that had looked impossible gave the whole company an air of gaiety for several days.
For a while they seemed quite contented with their seafaring lot.
Even the lugubrious Captain Bruno ('They are a good crew.
They work hard. No, I do not tell them. I write to them when
the trip is finished.') expressed his appreciation at the job they
had done by declaring a fishing fest the following evening after
we had entered the Gulf of Mexico.

I woke from a late afternoon nap into an uncanny silence,
and it was a moment before I realised the ship was still. The
incessant throb of the engines had stopped ('Ah, the music of
the engine room,' crooned Captain Bruno). It was like a death.
Heart failure. When I looked down from the small deck by my
cabin, I saw below me most of the men, twenty-five or so
crew and officers, side by side along the rails at the back of the
main deck, dangling lines into the sea, shouting and joking to
each other. Marco, the bullet-headed second engineer, wearing
a great yellow sun across his mammoth stomach and baggy
shorts that ended in the middle of his calves, a brute in boy's
clothing, waved at me.

'Come and fish.'

The deck itself, usually immaculate, always cleaned and
washed down daily, was bloody carnage. Everywhere there
were buckets and tubs full of small silvery fish, the ones on
top writhing and flapping in the drowning air. The deck was
alive with a plague of gasping fish that had used their last
energies flopping themselves out of their containers to achieve
no more than a solitary death, or been unhooked and flung
down by the fishermen so that not a minute of fishing was
wasted. The young cabin boy slithered around picking up the

slippery arching creatures and throwing them into the buckets, before running off to find new containers for the great haul. Hundreds and hundreds of fish lay around, dead and dying, waiting for their turn to be gutted by the smiling, patient cook and his assistant. The cook sat on an upturned bucket and wielded his knife like a sushi chef, with just a thrust or two removing what had to be removed, throwing the bloody intricate waste down on the deck where his assistant eventually scooped the mounting pile of entrails into a bucket. Every now and then one of the men called out to him, and he stopped preparing the fish for long enough to cut more strips of the squid he had defrosted for bait. His task was impossible, there was no keeping up, but he smiled and worked on. The men were catching three or four fish on each line every few seconds, and the fish in these parts appeared to be suicidal.

'You see,' Marco said, seeing the look of horror on my face as I picked my way through the corpses. 'They love to be caught. It is their destiny.'

Marco handed me his line – generously, because this was an informal competition between the men who trumpeted out their current score to each other. The out-and-out champs were Marco and the second mate, who fished unsmiling like a man possessed, pulling in his catch and casting again immediately in case any fish whose destiny it was to be caught by him was lost. Marco showed me how to throw the line out away from the side of the ship, and in a moment there was a tug and I yelped my ambivalence while Marco instructed me on the correct technique for pulling in the line. Three fish dangled and danced on the hooks. I was paralysed. I'd never fished before, and when Marco told me to manoeuvre the fish off the hooks I wailed my misery at being the cause of such misery. I was hopelessly squeamish about grasping the desperate, dying fish and having to wrench them off the hooks. Marco was disappointed. So was I. We both had higher hopes of me. Did I like fishing, Marco asked. Yes, I did, but I didn't care for actually catching fish. Nevertheless the men all congratulated me at having pulled three fish out on my first try. I accepted being patronised as what I deserved and gave up my fishing lesson to sit on an upturned bucket amid the dying fish and watch the men relaxing and goading each other, just enough, not too much.

Only Marco appeared contented with his sea life. At home he had a wife, a cat and a son who is in the Croatian water polo first team. He seemed proud of all of them, especially the cat. And of the crew. Not a brute after all, almost a sentimentalist was Marco. 'You see how well the men get on? They have fun now, but when there is problem, everyone serious. Everyone pay attention. I like this life. Peaceful.' It seemed to be Marco's job, with his Sun King outfit and his grunting comments, to make people laugh. 'I never eat chicken,' he bellowed at Franju the steward, dismissing the plate he was being offered at dinner (all the men disliked chicken; it was often all there was to eat during the war. It was the food of desperation). 'They are too stupid. I don't eat stupid things. Don't eat egg, also. What more stupid than an egg? In a few hours it becomes a small chicken, then a few more hours, big chicken. That's all.' He shrugged dismissively. He ate fish though. Soon the barbecue was hot and the first fish were laid on it. Out of the sea and into the frying pan. About as delicious, these fish ('What kind of fish are they?' 'They are fish.'), as anything I'd ever eaten. However squeamish I was about catching and killing them, I had no trouble eating these nameless creatures. Marco explained the difference between America and Croatia as he continued to pull fish out of the water and I watched.

'In Croatia the food is fresh, the wine is domestic, the

women good. In US the women are unloved, the flowers have
no scent and the food is tasteless.' His favourite film was *One
Flew Over the Cuckoo's Nest*. 'The Indian,' he said with a
smile. 'The Indian.'

As I said, a sentimentalist.

They had all been through the war with Serbia, but no one
wanted to talk about it much. There was a small deep pool
that was filled every morning with sea water. One day, I swam
in it with one of the crew who had just come off duty. He was
a quiet man, who I had noticed looking at me from time to
time with a shy interest. We talked, treading water. He was in
his forties. I asked him about the war. He winced.

'I fought for three years, but what for? Now no money, no
job, no food in Croatia. Tudjman,' he shook his head in disgust. 'I had to fight. I got woman and three children. But I
don't hate anyone. I went to school, and learned engineering,
geography and history. Then I get a letter telling me I have to
pick up a gun and kill people. I like people. Tito was good.
Serbs and Croats lived together before the war. Will live
together after the war. When Croatia was part of Yugoslavia
we were not independent, but we had jobs. Can we talk about
something else? Something we can smile about?' We were
silent for a bit.

'You are beautiful. Would you like to drink tea when I come
off duty at midnight?'

I declined. He nodded that it wasn't a problem. He left the
pool after a while and I lounged in the water with my back to
him. Suddenly, he called out. I turned towards him. He was
standing by the edge of the pool holding up one of his shoes,
size 15, and one of mine, size 4. He smiled slightly.
Nostalgically, perhaps. Sadly. Wistfully.

'Look,' he said.

Back in London before I left, a woman acquaintance had looked horrified when I told her about the trip I planned.

'But aren't you frightened about being on your own spending weeks and weeks isolated with so many men?'

They were after all *men*, and three weeks without a woman but with one in sight would, she supposed, turn them into ravening beasts. But the same rules for surviving in an enclosed community were applied to women as to living with each other and caring for the ship. They took care (as I did) not to disturb the balance of the group. There were surreptitious looks from some of the men, not those long aggressive stares that can become anything, or downright invitations, but glances I would sometimes catch that I had not been supposed to see, thoughtful, interested, but not to be acted on. And there was a kind of comradely flirting between Marco and myself that we both kept well below critical level. The invitation to take tea was slightly shocking in the careful atmosphere, but my refusal was taken as lightly as it was made. It even had a touch of old-fashioned romance about it. On other occasions when we met in the mess, my friend would tell me about his life, his hopes of setting up a small engineering factory, the music he liked. He smiled at me a lot, and bought me a beer from time to time. He would often be in the pool when I was swimming. And he asked me about myself and my life. It was clear that I could have chosen to intensify the contact if I wished, but I think he trusted me not to, at least until the end of the journey. There was a pleasing formality about my relations with the crew, as if we were all capable of living in earlier times, when these things were better ordered. It seemed we all knew how to maintain boundaries and not to let dangerous sex get in the way of good relations. It was more important that they got on with one another. Sex could wait until they arrived in Tampa, when the day before was spent washing and ironing their shore clothes, shaving off stubble, and in the first officer's case, removing his wedding ring. The girls were waiting on the quay as the ship docked, waving and laughing, and the men lined the rails, as they had when they fished, discussing which girl they were going into town with.

'When I am in Tampa, I am not married,' the first officer said with a broad bright white toothy grin when another passenger, Roz, asked what had happened to his wedding ring at lunch before we docked.

'And in Split, when you are in Tampa, is your wife also not married?' I asked.

He smiled happily. 'No. She is always married. She has two' – he extended his arms sideways as if they were being buoyed up – 'lifeboats . . . the two children to keep her good.'

After lunch, Roz and I agreed that he probably meant millstones.

Between the silence and delicately boundaried encounters with the crew, I read Conrad and concurred with him on the seafaring life. Magic monotony. Enticing. Enslaving. And disenchanting?

Travelling with no purpose is a purposeful business. I had put myself in the way of a long sea journey. The destination was of no concern to me. In fact, when I arranged the trip, the *MV Christiane* was scheduled to travel first to Rio de Janeiro and then up to Georgia. Only two days before I was due to leave, the plans were altered, the ship was leaving several days later and skipping the South American leg. Freight timetables are notoriously changeable, the profit margins are critical, companies will revise their schedules from one day to the next, sometimes in mid-journey. If you travel by freighter you'd better not have any definite plans or firmly fixed destination. I was sorry the South American stop had been cancelled, but only because it meant a shorter journey. I was prepared for a trip of six weeks or more before I arrived at Savannah, Georgia, after which I had made no firm plans except to purchase an open plane ticket back to the UK. A long sea voyage was the only point of the trip. Why? An exercise in sensory deprivation, I suppose. To find out what happened when one day followed another, one mile followed another and each was exactly the same as the last. What was a person left with, when there was no landscape except the curve of the horizon, and no anticipation in arriving somewhere you wish to be? How was it when the day by day went on, when only the routine demanded by the human needs of eating and sleeping distinguished you from your surroundings, whose single rhythm was the rising and setting of the sun? To be accurate, it wasn't so much that I wondered about how it was, as that those were the conditions I wanted to be in. But still, in all that silence and lack of interference, wouldn't there be something to listen to? I'm always supposing that if I can get things quiet enough I'll hear something to my advantage. Like the fish on the hooks, I wriggle away from activity, companionship, wanting to launch myself into nothingness where I will find . . . what? The fish find themselves gasping on deck, out of their element, suffocating in the poisonous inimical air. Somehow, I've developed a notion that I am more than a fish. Doubtless that's what the fish think, too. Get out of the water, get away from the circumstantial, and *then* we'll see.

There is never perfect solitude, a person is a fool to set out in search of it. A fool, at any rate, if they are disappointed by not finding it.

There were two couples apart from me travelling as passengers. Fogey and Roz were in their seventies, returning home after taking a holiday from a farm in Arizona. She was neat as a button, a large easy-care American matron; Fogey was silent most of the time, though he was known to ask for the peanut butter sometimes when it was out of reach at breakfast. Neither was talkative, but they weren't unfriendly. They were insular Americans, had taken a peek at Europe, but were uneasy at finding themselves in a strange world, in strange company. At breakfast, lunch and supper, we sat with the officers and after a decent interval of polite conversation – the weather, how they had slept, where we were – they slipped into silence.

The German couple, Stan and Dora, from Lake Constance, were also in their seventies, and they weren't silent. They were travelling with their brand-new, super-equipped, bells-and-whistles mobile home lashed to the top deck. They were planning to spend a year travelling around the States. They talked without stopping, without thinking, it came to seem. They were determined to speak as much English as possible before they disembarked for their New World adventure. What they talked about and how their audience responded appeared irrelevant. They lived in a bubble of their own perceived needs, like children. They were also a neat pair. Spruce, rather. Stan and Dora were several sizes down from the American couple, with well-nurtured bodies and immaculately cut, short white hair. They were turned out for a cruise: she wore silk scarves with naval emblems on them, he wore studiedly casual slacks, well-ironed polo shirts sporting an anchor or a knot on the breast pocket, and rope-soled deck shoes. These two had no idea of how to coexist with strangers. They buzzed like flies across all the careful boundaries. It seemed to me that they stalked me, so that no matter which secluded corner I discovered for myself, they found me there sooner or later.

'Ah, you are here.'

Dora babbled. She spoke entirely inconsequentially, staring at me as she talked with intensely blue, intensely vacant eyes. 'I brush my teeth after every meal. We must all brush our teeth after every meal.' 'I love all kinds of potatoes. Boiled, roasted, fried, chipped . . .' 'You were not at breakfast. Where were you? I said to Stan, "Where is she?"' 'You are reading a book. I like to read books.' 'Ah, you cannot change the past.' 'My mother always said that Hitler would be bad for us.' All of it was spoken in a monotone, with that staring look in her eyes, as if she were trying to recall and practise phrases she had worked up the evening before from her English book. Perhaps that's exactly what it was, but her eyes were uncanny. Behind her glasses they dragged downwards at the outside corners, as blue and dead as standing pools. Nothing lit them up. She watched Stan, who liked to think he spoke better English than Dora, make his declarations about the world – 'It is good', 'It is not good' – with her unchanging cold fishy eyes, while the rest of her face expressed devoted interest. Stan talked as much as she, mostly with reminiscences of his travels around Europe thirty years ago. He told the Croatians everything he knew (and they certainly did) about Dubrovnik, and me everything he knew about London, as if he remained familiar with these places he hadn't set foot in for a generation. At mealtimes he would complain about the state of Europe. Germany in particular. It was being overrun with 'Arabs. Not trust Arabs.' He rubbed his well-manicured fingers against each other. 'Money. Only money. And now they live in our cities with their minarets and their *wawawa*.'

I left the table at that point, but Roz told me that he had continued unperturbed and gone on to complain of Berlin being overrun by Russians, to which the usually uncommunicative Fogey had quietly murmured, 'Well, that makes a change.'

One morning Dora found me sitting on deck, reading, and after admonishing me for not eating fruit at breakfast ('You must have fruit. Fruit is good for you.') asked me my age.

'Ah, you are one year older than my daughter. I could be your mother,' she announced in a blue-eyed monotone. While this was chronologically possible, it was, aside from being inane, so historically and geographically inaccurate that I had to fight the gasp that rose in my throat. She then placed a firm hand on my right cheek, and bending down planted a brisk kiss on my other cheek. I froze through the maternal moment. Eventually, I managed a coldly polite and somewhat inappropriate 'Thank you'. But the panic stayed with me. The next afternoon I was in the wash room, wondering why the hell I was ironing a shirt in the blistering heat of the day. Dora found me again.

'Ah, you iron.'

I nodded my agreement, and sweat fell from my chin. She didn't rate my technique.

'No, no, you must open the buttons to iron correctly.'

She approached the ironing board with her hand outstretched ready to correct my sloppy ways. Reality began to slow down for me as she started to open the top button. I had to make a physical effort not to slap her hand out of the way.

'NO.' I actually bellowed at the harmless old woman as you might shout at a child to prevent yourself from lashing out. 'Leave it alone. Don't touch it. Do. Not. Touch. It.'

My face must have matched my warning tone. Dora started

and then backed away. She was alarmed and quite baffled by my excessive reaction to her helpfulness. I didn't care to discuss with her how much she couldn't have been my mother.

'Yes. It is your ironing. Yes,' she soothed, leaving the room without turning her back on me. But her surprise was no greater than mine at the rage I'd expressed. My admiration for the crew's capacity to live together increased greatly.

Dora and Stan's blandness and blank insensitivity were monumental. They spoke regardless of who was listening or what anyone else was feeling or thinking. It was a rare, infantile quality that I should have relished having the chance to observe. But the brutality of not observing other people was too stark in these cloistered surroundings, and as it turned out, *nothing* that happened to other people had any real impact on them.

I appreciated the distant good manners of Roz and Fogey all the more as the days with the German couple passed. Fogey turned out to be a radio ham and had set up an aerial outside his cabin, and without my asking fixed one for me outside my window so I could catch the World Service. He spent most of his time listening in and talking to strangers on his short-wave while Roz sat and did crosswords. Roz had been widowed, and after two or three years had married her brother-in-law, Fogey. They seemed content together. We were three days away from Tampa when for the first time the two of them arrived late for breakfast, clearly distressed, looking grim and drained, although Roz, who sat next to me, was, as usual, carefully and neatly dressed.

'Didn't you sleep? Was it the heat?' I asked, and then saw that it was more than that.

'We had some bad news last night. Very bad news.'

At ten the previous evening Fogey had got a call on his

radio from Arizona. Roz's 48-year-old son, Fogey's nephew
and stepson, had died suddenly that morning, probably of a
heart attack. Roz told me this in an undertone, her voice just
making it to the end of the sentence and her eyes welling but
managing to suppress the tears. There was nothing they could
do but wait for the ship to get to Tampa and then fly to her
son's home in California for the funeral. The luxury of distance became an agony of time. The vastness of the Atlantic,
the immutable sea-ness of the sea, the perpetual horizon that
promised more and more of nothing, all of which I was so rel-
ishing, transformed in an instant from the mile after mile to
the minute after minute that had to be lived through by a
woman stuck in the middle of nowhere, cut off from where
she urgently needed to be, suffering an unimaginable loss,
among strangers. Now the sea was just an intolerable inhuman
space to be covered before Roz could get back to her family for
the funeral of her eldest son.

'I'm sorry,' Roz said with agonising politeness. 'I'll try not
to be morbid for the rest of the journey.'

Fogey was silent as usual, slowly chewing his toast and
peanut butter, until Stan asked if anyone knew where we were.

'We're in the Doldrums,' Fogey said with geographical
accuracy, and fell quiet again.

Stan and Dora were exercised that morning about filling in
their US immigration forms, something about which
annoyed them. Throughout breakfast they complained
loudly about the US authorities and not being allowed to
depart in a year's time from any port that was convenient to
them. They went on and on about American bureaucracy
and how in Germany this sort of thing could never happen.
And on and on, inviting the whole table to share in their
exceptional troubles. Nothing about Roz's demeanour, or

my reaction to her news, silenced them. Later on deck I told Dora what had happened.

'Aha, I felt there was some sadness at breakfast. But how annoying is the immigration. Yes, it's a bad thing when a child is dead before the mother is dead. Well, that is life.' Her eyes as blank as ever. I had the impression that she was still quoting from her phrase book.

Roz told me before they left that while all the crew had offered their sympathy in words or with a silent handshake, Dora and Stan had said nothing to her about the death of her son. But Dora, about whom I felt so unreasonably angry, who, I have to say, I actually hated, was right about life. That was life. There had been another death during the journey.

Udi had been dying for several months before I left for Hamburg to join the *MV Christiane*. We were quite recent friends, although I'd known him for several years. I would see him at the table of mutual friends; once or twice I went to dinner parties at his house. But out of the blue, so it seemed to me, from time to time, he would phone to tell me he liked something I'd written and why. I received his compliments awkwardly. I was reserved. Udi was not. He had a flair, an insistence even, for friendship which made me nervous. Once or twice he called simply to say that he liked me. That excruciated me because I had no idea how to respond to such a statement. As when Dora kissed me, I could only manage a polite thank-you. Udi was fully married to and in love with his wife, but he was innately a seducer of people. His flirtation wasn't a demand for an actual sexual relationship, but part of a general campaign: a refusal to allow anyone he decided he wanted as a friend to escape into reticence. His forthright offers of friendship were, as I said, uncomfortable for me, but they were appealing too. He made liking someone and wanting them in his life seem easy, whereas it was what I found most uncannily difficult. I've rarely made relationships of any kind with anyone who didn't make more effort than I, who didn't in some way or other, insist. It's a safety feature of my psyche. I am paralysed by the idea of being said no to. If there are compulsive seducers in this world, there are also compulsive seductees. On the scale of things I wouldn't take an emotional risk for, friendship comes higher than a sexual relationship. It is more mysterious, more dangerous to me than a sexual affair, which I can easily relegate to a game and walk away from with a shrug. I am perhaps a child of the sixties. Or something. Sex can be serious, but it doesn't have to be. Friendship feels like a much weightier matter, but something I haven't ever quite got the knack of. Whenever I have most felt the dizzying deranging vertigo of betrayal (or of betraying), it has been in the context of friendship.

Ten months before my sea journey Udi and Judy came to my birthday party, all dressed up, bearing gifts and celebration smiles, and found me flopped in an ancient T-shirt and threadbare jeans on my sofa in front of the TV.

'Are we early?'

'By a week.'

We went to the local Indian, overdressed and underdressed; all of us delighted somehow by the discomfort of their mistake and the disruption of my idle solitude. The friendship started properly that evening. A week later, Judy came to the actual party alone. Udi wasn't feeling well. He was going to see the doctor in the morning. It was cancer. An investigative operation discovered a large tumour in his stomach. He checked with doctor friends and with anything he could find on the internet on his particular cancer and the stage it had reached, and concluded that he would certainly die of it, but had perhaps another three to five years. He was fifty-six. First thing back from hospital, he bought a Harley.

His wife took the emotional brunt of his death sentence. With his friends, Udi discussed the matter. We talked, he and I, about his absolute conviction that the end was the end. The terror of that, and the comfort, too. There was nothing to fear but nothingness; all the sadness was about the abrupt end of life, the interruption of his marriage, the awful fact of not being able to watch his youngest son grow up, the effect on his family. But the blankness of after the end came up often between us. He was unwavering about the reality of his dying and in refusing to fantasise about anything beyond it. Perhaps – almost certainly – his acceptance was not as complete as it seemed. It was as if he was trying on its reality for size, adjusting himself to its monumental dimensions. Our conversations were quiet testings of feelings of what was, or was not, to come, for him sooner, for me later to one degree or other. I found myself thinking a good deal about the condition of not yet having been born. Hardly a condition, but a state of non-existence which we had all already not-experienced. The nonsense of language reaching towards the void it was not equipped for, developed as it was by the living for the living, made us laugh.

'So you've already not been. How was it for you?' I asked.

'It didn't bother me at the time.'

Of course, there was time in that non-existence, or there would be. The beginning would come. The other non-existence abolished time for ever. But the more I thought about it, the more I tried to use the time before my birth as an idea to make death more tolerable, the angrier I became at having been excluded from the events that occurred in history, which is what we call the period before our personal arrival on the planet. I felt the same kind of panic and personal betrayal at having not been born for all that time, as I experienced at the idea of the world going on without me after I died. I hated the idea of those who would be part of my life getting on with their lives before I arrived, just as I didn't much care to think about people getting on with things, individuals, or great social and political forces, after I have died. I felt the rage of the not-yet-born along with the rage of the dying at being extinguished. We may try to console ourselves that death is not the end of the world, but it's the fact that it isn't the end of the world that is so blindingly difficult to cope with. I didn't do much more than mention these thoughts to Udi, whose perspective on the subject was at that moment more practical than mine.

Within a couple of months, Udi was back in hospital. This time things looked worse. He reduced his estimate of surviving three to five years down to maybe a couple of years. Udi's life expectation drained dramatically away over the next few weeks. His time grew less with each new medical intervention. Eventually, after an operation intended to give him some respite, he was told that there was nothing to be done except pain management, and that he had only a matter of weeks to live. He had never ridden the Harley. Now he had grown too weak to hold it upright. He sold it back to the dealer. The dealer was upset about Udi.

'I'm gutted,' he said.

'Me too,' Udi replied.

During the final weeks, Udi held court at home. A kind of permanent party began, as his hundreds of friends came to be with Udi before he died. Judy had to organise a timetable to accommodate them all, so that there wouldn't be too many people at once, and there was time also for his family to be with him alone. It was the most explicit dying I've ever come across, a wake with the subject the living host. In hospital they had to give him a side room because of the number of his visitors. At home, Udi received us on his sofa, manipulating his morphine machine to keep pain at bay, allowing us to provide a lap for his sore legs, demanding that we massage his feet, and continuing his life-enhancing seduction of the world. He was smoking again, having given it up when he got ill, and given up giving up when he was pronounced terminal. 'So shoot me,' he responded in hospital when a nurse in the day-room told him he was in a non-smoking ward.

I last saw him the day before I left on my freighter trip. He had left hospital. We sat at the kitchen table, drank coffee and smoked. I could see him tiring after an hour, but I found I couldn't make myself get up from the chair. I had never said goodbye to anyone before, never a goodbye that was so consciously, so absolutely final. I had no idea how it was to be done. My difficulties in ending a friendship were as great as in beginning one. I didn't know how to approach Udi's person and kiss him and then leave the room, the house, knowing that I would never see him again because he would die before I returned. It was outrageous, something that neither my mind, nor my muscles could take in. Monstrous. It was another half an hour of sitting as if we had all the time in the world before I managed to stand and walk to the end of the table. I bent down and kissed him.

'I know you're sure there's going to be nothing, and I expect you're right, but just in case it turns out that there is . . . feel free to haunt me if you find you can,' I said.

I meant it. I didn't want to lose this man, this friend who made it so easy to be a friend, to oblivion. He had made a place for himself in my memory, but I didn't want to lose my place in his. Death is always about the loss of self, even when it's someone else's death.

After three weeks we landed at the commercial dock in Tampa. It would take three days to offload the potash. Roz and Fogey left to fly to their son's funeral. The crew, spruced and eager, took off into town with the waiting girls on the dock to buy American bicycles for their children and cruise the bars. I walked unsteadily after so long at sea across the blank tarmac to a small wooden building on the other side of the dock where the stevedores drank coffee and played pool, and where there was a public phone. A small, salmon-pink cartoon cloud frothed by over my head. Flamingos, I realised, more astonished by that than by a salmon-pink cloud. Exotic, vividly coloured, weirdly ornate flowers grew in the bed in front of the unassuming building, and a US flag flapped lazily on a pole beside the door. Mack trucks, shiny leviathans, polished lovingly by their keepers, were parked, like horses tied up while their riders drank in the saloon, waiting to pick up goods. Telegraph wires sang high-pitched and tuneless in the bathwater-hot air. Behind the door of the building as I approached it, I heard Stan shouting, screaming actually, in German. Then the door flew open and he came storming out, followed by Dora. He was wiping his arms across the air in front of him in a repeated gesture of annihilation. Seeing me approach, he changed to English.

'They are no good. America is no good. In Germany the phones work. In America nothing works. No good. No good.'

He was an infant having a tantrum. The phone used cards which the waiting girls on the dock sold to the crew, so that they could phone home before their night on the town. Stan couldn't get his to work and so the phone system was

defective, the card a scam, America already a broken dream. I
offered to help with using the card, but he wasn't going to try
again. There was no point. It was all no good. Dora followed
behind, her eyes icily inexpressive, as he stamped back to the
ship.

My phone card worked fine. I called Edinburgh to speak to
my daughter at university, for the first time in the best part of
a month. She sounded pleased to hear from me, everything
was OK. That lurking anxiety fell away. Then I called Udi's
number. Judy answered. Where was I calling from? How had
the journey been? Was it what I'd hoped for? It's still an event
to phone someone from far away after a period of silence.
Then – how had we evaded it for so many moments? – how is
Udi?

'Oh, Jenny. Udi died a week ago.'

It was no surprise. I echoed her sigh with 'Oh, Judy'. I
probably said I was so sorry. Neither of us spoke as if something unexpected had happened. Judy told me how the end
had been. He had been in a hospice for ten days, holding court
as usual. Judy said it seemed impossible that he was going to
die. But he deteriorated over the final two days until he slipped
into a coma and died in the early hours with Judy and his two
older daughters sitting at his bedside. The funeral was in a
couple of days.

I left the stevedore's building and returned to the ship. I
spent the rest of the day out on deck, watching the bird life
through binoculars, and the men craning the potash out of
the holds on to moving belts that dumped it via a hopper into
the warehouse. If I thought at all, it was about how my nothing happening for weeks and weeks on an ocean-going
freighter had not been so uneventful after all. Not for others.
Not for me. Well, that is life. Around five, as evening was

setting in, I went in to the galley to make a cup of tea. I put on the water heater and stared out of the window waiting for the water to boil. Explosively, as if I'd received a blow in my lower spine, I doubled over and tears started to flow. Udi's death, the reality of his not being in the world any more, hit me, kicked in, quite literally it felt. By the time I got back to my cabin the tears were streaming down my face, and once the door was shut and I was private, I began to sob. Mostly I cried for myself, for the loss of Udi as a friend. I was wracked with sadness, bereft, quite unable to stop crying. It went on for an hour or so, and then there was a knock at the door. I wiped my eyes, though not very effectively, and opened the door. The third engineer, whose cabin was next to mine, stood in the hallway looking worried.

'Are you ill?'

I explained that I had just heard that a friend of mine had died. He looked sympathetic, and said he was sorry. I said that I'd known he was going to die, but still, hearing that it had actually happened . . .

'Yes. It is always terrible. Were you very close?'

'He was a friend.'

He nodded seriously. 'I am going in to the city for the evening. There is a cab coming. You come too. We will go to a bar and have a drink and see America.'

I thanked him, but said I thought I would stay on board and have a quiet evening, I wasn't feeling very much like socialising. My friend's smiling face took on dark, worried expression, and he shook his head.

'It is not good to be alone when you are sad. You must make an effort. Come out for a drink. Enjoy yourself.'

No, I said, thanking him for his concern, I was all right, but I wanted to be on my own and quiet this evening.

'It is bad to be alone. You must not be sad and cry. Yes, your friend is dead, that is a shame, but you are alive. You must live. Life goes on. You should come out and enjoy life.'

He spoke insistently, almost angrily, it was more now than just going into the city with me. I said as definitely and finally as I could manage without offending that I appreciated what he was saying, but that I would be staying on board. He shook his head one final time against mourning what was lost rather than grasping what still remained. I wanted to remember, he didn't. He had his reasons, I've no doubt.

'Well,' he said. 'I must get ready.'

The following day I called my friend John in Phoenix, Arizona, who I'd met on a previous trip to Antarctica. We'd kept in touch by email.

'Come and stay,' he said.

I had another couple of days aboard the *Christiane*, before I disembarked in Savannah, and no definite plans.

'Let us know what flight you're coming in on. We'll meet you at the airport.'

'No, I don't think I'll fly. I'll take a train.'

I hadn't thought about it before I said it, but it seemed I wasn't finished with watching the miles go by.

I returned to the *Christiane*, my cabin and my bunk, happy to feel again the gentle uncertainty of a watery existence. There was just a day or two left before I was permanently back on dry land. I idled the rest of the afternoon away recalling a message I once, long ago, left for myself and had only recently picked up.

I am nine years old, in bed, in the dark, in my bedroom. The detail of the room is perfectly clear. I am lying on my back. I have a greeny-gold quilted satin eiderdown covering me. I have just calculated that I will be fifty years old in the year 1997. Hard as I try, 'fifty' and '1997' don't mean a thing to me, aside from being the answer to an arithmetic question I set myself. I try it differently. '*I* will be fifty in 1997.' 1997 doesn't matter, it just complicates the thought I am trying to grasp. 'I *will* be fifty.' The statement is absurd. I am nine. 'I will be ten' makes sense. 'I will be thirteen' has a dreamlike maturity about it. 'I will be fifty' is simply a paraphrase for another senseless statement I make to myself at night: 'I will be dead one day.' Or, 'One day I won't be.' I have a great determination to feel the sentence as a reality, but it always escapes me. 'I will be dead' comes with a picture of a dead body on a bed. But it's mine, my bed, and a nine-year-old body. When I make a picture of the body as old, it becomes someone else. I can't imagine myself old, or dead. I can't imagine myself dying. Either the effort or the failure to do so makes me feel panicky.

Being fifty is not being dead, but it is being old, inconceivably old, for me at nine, that is. I know other people are fifty, and I will be fifty if I don't die beforehand. But the best I can do is to imagine someone who is not me, though not someone I know, being fifty. She looks like an old lady: the way old ladies currently looked. She looks like someone else. I can't connect me thinking about her with the fact that I will *be* her in forty-one years' time. She has lived through and known forty-one years to which I have no access. I can't believe I will become her, although I know, factually, that I must. I can't dress myself in her clothes or flesh and know what it feels like being her as I know what it feels like being me. This is immensely frustrating. I do the next best thing: I send a message out into the future, etching into my brain cells a memo to the other person, who will be me grown to be fifty, to remember this moment, this very moment, this actual second when I am nine, in bed, in the dark in my room, trying to imagine being fifty.

In my cabin moored at the dock in Tampa, Florida, I have been fifty for the past year, and I am recalling the nine-year-old who tried to imagine me. I mean that I am recalling her trying to imagine me, at that moment, in bed, in the dark in her room, some forty-one years ago. It is easier for me to acknowledge and know her than the other way around, for all that I have learned about the unreliability of memory, because I have lived the missing forty-one years that she could know nothing about. There is a track back for me. The vividness of her making a note to remember the moment in the future when she is fifty is startling. But it is not a simple, direct link. I have the moment, but the person I connect with is someone whose future I know. I do not know the nine-year-old as she was then, at all; the one who had not yet experienced the life I led between her and me. I can't imagine her as a reality, in her striving to understand what kind of fifty-year-old woman she would be, because she doesn't exist any more except as a pin-point in time. But she now has an indelible relation to me looking back through time, that I could not have for her aiming forward. There is a sense of vertigo, something quite dizzying about having arrived at the unimaginable point she reached out towards, at recalling her message and being in a position – but not able – to answer her question: here I am, it's like this.

It's not just the nine-year-old's illusive reality that prevents me from responding, it is also my own present inability, aged fifty, to imagine what it is like to be fifty. I know no better than she. I've heard a lot about it, read plenty, seen numbers of fifty-year-olds, both depicted and in real life, but that seems to be no help at all. This isn't surprising. The fifty I seek to understand in order to answer her question is the same fifty I wondered about as a child, and it turns out to have nothing much to do with having lived for fifty years or more. I don't know what it means to be fifty. I have no idea what to say to my nine-year-old self who thought that she would know what fifty was like once she had reached it. And I suppose the other question she asked herself, the one about the reality of death, will also remain a question, even though I etch into my brain cells a memo for the time of my dying to remember me now, this moment, as I lie in my cabin in the dock in Tampa, wondering how it will be.

Only the Lonely

'Imagine you're de Tocqueville. What do you think of us Americans?'

Imagine you're making a train reservation by phone in England. Imagine being asked such a question. I was back in the stevedore's building calling the 1-800 number for Amtrak reservations to find a train to take me from Savannah to Phoenix. Not impossible, but not quite straightforwardly possible either. I had to get a train for two hours from Savannah to Jacksonville, Florida, where I would pick up the *Sunset Limited* which ran only three days a week from Orlando, Florida to Los Angeles, California, passing through Jacksonville on the way. The Jacksonville connection was leisurely. I would arrive at Jacksonville at midday, and there would be a ten-hour lay-over before the *Sunset Limited* arrived at 10.06 p.m. It would reach Tucson, Arizona, as close as I could get to Phoenix by train, forty-eight hours later. I had to stay in Savannah for three days after I disembarked, until Saturday morning, and would get to Tucson at ten o'clock the following Monday night. There had once been a train connection between Tucson and Phoenix, but no longer, so Amtrak bussed passengers to Phoenix. I'd arrive there at just past midnight on Tuesday morning, the reservation clerk at the call centre in Chicago explained, and then he explained it all again so that this time I could pay proper attention and write down the labyrinthine arrangements instead of just letting my mind wander through the sound of the mythic places and suggested vastness of time and space of my proposed journey.

'So you're from England, by the sound of it. Have you got a minute? I guess you're travelling around. I'm curious. Imagine you're de Tocqueville. What do you think of us Americans?'

His name was Mike. He told people about the train schedules and took their credit card reservations. He also wondered what Europeans thought about Americans. He was well placed to find out. But I explained that I hadn't been travelling, and that I'd just come off a freighter and was in Tampa dock.

'Wow!'

Now he was really excited. He had a penchant for sea travel. In fact, he was currently reading Conrad: *Typhoon*. So had I on the ship. What did I think of Conrad? And Melville? How was the sea journey? And Americans? I must have been to the States before. We talked about the language differences between English and American. The formality I found in American speech that lived so strangely with the vivid slang. A magical combination of ease and discomfort. That, actually, was how I found Americans. We talked about the smallness of England, the oddness for me of being able to take a train that took three full days to get from one side of the country to the other. He said he hadn't realised.

'Really, less than a day to get from top to bottom? Jeez, that must really make a difference to how we think about the world.'

We talked about the sea again, and he said he'd just read *The Perfect Storm*. I'd seen a documentary based on the book just before I left England, and I'd videoed it. I promised to send it to him when I got home though he would have to get it transferred to the US standard. He gave me his address and we said our goodbyes. My train booking had taken half an hour or more and after three weeks of small talk, I'd conversed with some passion and thought about things that seemed quite important, to a stranger called Mike somewhere in a call centre in Chicago. Welcome to America.

I spent three days in the sweaty, mad heat of Savannah adjusting to living on solid ground. My hotel ('The Magnolia Place Inn, located in the heart of Savannah's historic district . . . Built in 1878 . . . each room is uniquely furnished with English antiques, period prints and porcelains from around the world . . . As featured in Southern Living') encapsulated the fabled gentility of the South. It was elegant, self-consciously beautiful and old world to a tiresome degree. Mint tea was served in the lounge ('parlour') at five every afternoon, the beds were four-posters, the owners distantly charming and the bedrooms and public spaces non-smoking.

Much of what I have to describe in this book is predicated on the fact that I smoke. Cigarettes and my desire to smoke them formed the humming rails of my train of thought as I travelled. What I did, who I spoke to, what I had to say, was very often directly related to my wish to smoke. Some travellers have a goal, a mystery they want to unravel, a place they want to reach, a mental task they want to perform, a world they want to describe, but I had none of these. For the most part, cigarettes dictated my actions. Where the difficulty of smoking is so prevalent, is, indeed, a moral force, nicotine addition and the pleasure of lighting up turned out to be as good a way as any other of finding a relation to a place and its people.

I have smoked since I was fourteen. When I wasn't travelling the Circle Line, I sat in front of a mirror in my bedroom illicitly practising my smoking skills, just as I worked at kohling and silvering my eyes and posing naked and enticing to my reflection in preparation for future public performances. Much of the time of the fourteen-year-old is spent in front of the mirror. Life must be rehearsed. At my boarding school, once I had got the social workers to send me back, there was a boiler house by the organic vegetable beds. Two or three people could stand in the space in front of the whooshing boiler, leaning against the brick walls, conversing idly. It was warm in winter and secluded in summer and the perfect venue for smoking breaks between lessons or if the weather precluded a trip to the neighbouring unmown field where sex as well as smoking could occur uninterrupted. I smoked Black Russian, black-papered, gold-tipped, and sometimes Abdullahs, Turkish and oval. A packet cost a week's pocket money but it was important, if one had to perform one's most sophisticated activity in the ignominy of a boiler house, to do so with style. At that time, style seemed to me mostly black and gold or oval and exotic-smelling. I toyed with the idea of a cigarette holder, but it was one more thing to hide in my knickers, and I decided that such extended glamour would have to wait. That year, a coffee bar opened in the town. It was, of course, off-limits. They served espresso and cappuccino in glass cups, which back then seemed to be very dangerous to the adult world and in fact announced the end, finally, of the fifties. There was also a juke box. It played Ray Charles's 'I Can't Stop Loving You'; Roy Orbison's 'Crying'; the Everly Brothers' 'Cathy's Clown'; Dave Brubeck's 'Take Five'. I sat there with my kohl eyes, my jeans and oversized black sweater, smoking (was there for a brief period a small pipe?) and idly stirring the froth on my cappuccino, wrote poems in a notebook, and waited for a kind word from the first love of my life, Tub (who wasn't, though he had crooked teeth which so moved me they made my heart stop), a junior reporter on the local paper. He called me Nej, reversing me, reasonably enough since I was in turmoil over him. He sort-of-let-me be his girlfriend, though he was careful to remain remote and dismissive. Most of the time I wasn't there for him, just a hovering shadow, who sat in silence while he discussed important matters of life and death with his friends. I existed for the brief moments of encouragement he allowed me occasionally, when he would smile suddenly directly at me, or turn at the door after he had got up without a word to leave and mutter, 'You coming?', not bothering to wait to see if I was or not. I could spend several hours at night lying in bed remembering and reliving the quality of that moment, of the bare acknowledgement that he wanted me, actually me, it had been only me he had been speaking to. Or at any rate, he didn't *not* want me. Hours would pass as I savoured his tone of voice, the fleeting warmth of inclusion, the inescapable fact (if I thought very hard about it) that he didn't want to leave without me that made up for being ignored entirely for the rest of the time we were together. All the disdain, the apparent absence of my existence while I was in his company, the endless periods of waiting in the coffee bar which often ended (after all) with him not showing up before I had to get back to school, the terrible moments when I couldn't get to the coffee bar at all and he might be there and waiting for me, thinking I had stood him up; all that, the majority of the time, anguish, agony, shrank to fleeting nothing beside the memory of his momentary encouragements. 'You coming?' *They* were real, the rest was reserve, resistance, a game of reticence that boys played for reasons that were not then obvious. And no moment was more treasured, unwrapped in the dark night of the dormitory to gleam hope at me, than the times when, after taking one for himself, he took a second cigarette from my pack of five and lit it before putting it between my lips. And Roy sang, 'Only The Lonely'.

So . . . smoking. Later, when I was twenty, I spent five months in St Pancras Hospital, North Wing, the psychiatric unit. Cigarettes were no longer an accessory, they were an addiction and a constant source of concern, since I had only the ten shillings a week that was doled out by the hospital to patients without income as pocket money. Not nearly enough to keep me in smokes in a world where smoking was a way of passing the time.

The Mystery Man had been admitted by the police after they arrested him, wandering and confused, at King's Cross. He had lost his memory. He didn't know his name, where he had come from, nothing whatever about his life. He was a blank sheet in his forties. I was twenty and became his first friend. We played poker for cigarettes. His inability to remember caused explosions of rage to erupt from time to time, but mostly he was extraordinarily gentle, a man who listened intently to whatever one had to say, whose interest in other people was as much a learning process for him who had had no life that he could recall. We talked a lot, he wondered who he might be, and we imagined a variety of lives for him.

It was a game in which he would accept or reject my suggestions according to whether he fancied the idea or not. In reality he was not at all eager to find out who he was, although having no access to his past made him bang his head against the walls sometimes. We considered the possibility, the likelihood, that he had a wife, certainly a family somewhere who knew him, and the idea was intolerable, like a narrowing of vision from a full panorama to a single ray of light that led only where it led. He preferred the more fantastical versions of himself: he was a spy, a master criminal, a private eye, a lost prince from far away. Probably these stories I told him about himself appealed to him because they were likely to be the furthest from the truth. Eventually the police discovered his name, and that he had been missing for a week or so before he had been picked up. He was a builder from somewhere up north. He had a wife and a daughter of nineteen. He had left his house one morning with the rent money and had disappeared. The police and his doctor thought he might have been mugged and the money stolen, or that he had spent the rent money – he played the horses, apparently – and then lost his memory in an attempt to deal with his guilt. John (we'd been calling him John, but it turned out to be his name) told me all this after he came back from seeing the doctor. None of it meant anything to him. The story was as strange as any that we had invented. His wife and daughter were coming to London in a day or two, and he would be meeting them, as far as he was concerned, for the first time. He was terrified, actually sweating at the prospect. I could quite see why.

'We've been married for twenty years. What if I don't like her?'

I understood the enormity of it. Much more shocking than being a spy or arch criminal. To be an everyday person, a family man with qualities and failings, a husband, a father, to have an intimate history with others, to be an ordinary person with a past was terrible. To have to find out that past, all in a rush, to come to terms with it, not over forty years, but in a matter of days, was frightening beyond belief. What was more, my friend John was going to turn out to be someone, to have a life of his own, and I, for a while the first and most important person in his life, the co-inventor of him, would become just a moment in his passing life, a part of an episode of forgetting that he would probably want to forget. He was scared and so was I. I felt as unconnected with my life, as unhinged from my past, as he was with his. We were outlaws together. Uncluttered and new. His 'Jenny' was just a few weeks old and without a history. The present in the safety of the hospital was far preferable to both of us than any ongoing truth.

At first he refused to meet his wife and daughter without me being present, but, of course, that had been vetoed by his doctor. 'What if I don't like them?' he said, haunted by the invisible past, threatened by the future.

How much I wished he wouldn't like them. But at the same time I could see the awfulness of that. Of discovering, say, that he had had a life of unhappiness to which he had to return, and of realising that the intensity of our friendship of a few weeks in a hospital with no past and no future was unsustainable. The doctor told him he was living a pipe dream, that not only did he have a past but so did I, and that real life would scupper us. Living in a brand-new present wasn't an option. I was difficult and needy; he wouldn't be able to cope. He refused to acknowledge this. We would manage. We had a special relation to each other. Old wounds wouldn't apply. The point was that we hadn't hurt each other, and without a past there was no reason why we should. If he didn't like his family, he told me, he wouldn't go back, and he and I would find a flat and live together, though in what relation we didn't specify. And what if he did like his family? That was simple, he would adopt me and I would go and live with them. I found it unbearable that he could even think it possible that he would like them. I knew our time was over. I stayed in my bed in the ward, refusing to see him, leaving him alone, the evening before his wife and daughter were due to arrive. My past, at least, had caught up with me.

When they left, he came to tell me about them. Nothing had come back to him during the meeting, but he liked both of them, an intelligent daughter of my age and a wife he found attractive and good company. He thought he might have had a good marriage. He couldn't imagine he had walked out. He must have been mugged. He was saying goodbye to me, although several meetings were planned, and he wouldn't be going home for a while. There was no more talk about adopting me, and though he spent most of his time with me when his new family weren't around, I could feel him separating. He talked about what they had told him of his life, as if trying to fit himself into it. It was an ordinary life, but clearly full of affection. He liked the idea of it more and more.

'But why did you run away from it?' I asked.

He shook his head. 'No, I'm sure I must have been mugged.'

I gave him up to his life. But we went on playing poker and smoking together until his wife came with a suitcase to take him home. John introduced me to her. She seemed very nice.

Smoking is a love that has never gone wrong, never seen sense. I trust cigarettes. Thirty-seven years after I first practised smoking in front of my bedroom mirror, I sat on the hotel veranda overlooking a lush garden in Savannah late into the singing, sweaty night, smoking and waiting for Saturday when I would start travelling again. I woke, washed and left my elegant bedroom to take breakfast on the front porch so that I could smoke while I drank my coffee and watch the joggers, alone, isolated behind earphones, alone but connected by mobiles, with dogs, with babies in buggies, with lovers or encouraging companions, young, old, fat, thin, black, white, running, puffing or effortlessly, round and round the outside of Forsthye Park across the road. Walking slowly, each step taking account of the saturating heat, I crossed the elegantly gardened public squares surrounded by gothic mansions, past live oak trees dripping with Spanish Moss to Shriner's bookshop to buy Faulkner to read while I lunched in Clary's Diner – 'Smoking section, please' – on gazpacho or a salt beef sandwich. Then I'd walk, to the river, or just through the squares. Never very far and always slowly. Watch people, take in place names and proud plaques on the older houses claiming not their inhabitants but their age as their fame, stop at a café (non-smoking) for mint tea, sit in a square on an unoccupied bench so I could have a cigarette and read or look at the squirrels – the city is overrun with them. One bench declares that it is in the place of the bench that Tom Hanks sat on in *Forrest Gump*. The actual bench has been taken away back to Hollywood by the studio. Still tourists come to stare and click their cameras at the substitute. It's a fake bench, but it's a fake bench in the right place. Back at the hotel I'd have a shower and then take my tea from the lounge out to the front porch again to smoke and watch the late afternoon joggers doing their programmed circuits round the sultry park whose one-mile-long periphery seemed to be its main civic purpose. I returned to the back veranda on the first floor to watch the light die and my cigarette begin to glow as I drew on it in the dark. One, two, three days. All stillness, all alone in a strange city, not lonely for a second. Never alone with a cigarette in my hand.

And if I thought about anything at all, I wondered with a heat-inspired lassitude what I was doing in this far-off southern city, waiting, pausing between a sea voyage and a train journey, neither of which I had any reason to do other than the theoretical wish to be moving through grand empty spaces.

A gangly young man queued behind me to have the conductor collect his ticket and board the train at Savannah station.

'Are you familiar with Jacksonville?' he asked me nervously as we sat next to each other in our allocated seats and he noticed from my ticket that I was connecting at Jacksonville to the *Sunset Limited*. 'It's a ten-hour layover. What will you do all that time?'

'Wait. There must be something to do in Jacksonville.'

He didn't look convinced. His name was Troy and he was making the two-hour journey to connect with the *Sunset Limited* at Jacksonville to get him to Sanderson, Texas from where he had a six-hour drive to the small town where he lived and worked as a teacher. He'd spent a long weekend in Savannah having read *Midnight in the Garden of Good and Evil*, a story of gay love and death in the mannered South. It was his first weekend away from home on his own. It was a real adventure, a breaking-away, an acknowledgement (though he didn't say so explicitly) of his own sexuality. He had wandered about the old city, and spent hours sitting in Madison Square looking at the house where the drama of the book took place. He had even knocked on the door, but no one had answered. He had cruised the gay bars and perhaps made contact with other gay men, but somehow it seemed unlikely. I got the feeling it was quite enough just for now that he had come to this sinful city alone. He was in his mid-twenties. Troy would come to Savannah again, he said, now that he knew he could. The town where he lived was where he had grown up. His father had been a teacher in the same infants school where Troy now taught, and still lived locally, widowed and retired. Troy had had to travel a long way to come out, and he was filled with surprise at himself. Even so, ten hours in Jacksonville on his own alarmed him.

'Well, we'll find something to do,' I comforted, half promising to stick with him.

'It's supposed to be a dangerous city.'

'Why?'

He shrugged, uneasy and awkward. 'Oh, you know . . .'

Jacksonville station was a utilitarian box, a few seats, a Coke machine and not much else, except a stationmaster who rather proudly told us there was nothing nearby. It was miles away from the city. So what did people with ten hours on their hands do? He shrugged. There was the Jacksonville Landing, a riverside shopping development, and a bus left for it every fifteen minutes. The answer to what to do in Jacksonville for ten hours, while the *Sunset Limited* chugged its way up to us from Orlando, was a mall.

'Hold on, I'm gonna hang out with you guys,' a husky woman's twang behind us said.

Bet stepped on the remains of her cigarette with the toe of her black cowboy boot and joined us at the bus stop. We had been adopted by a small, delicately thin woman in her early sixties, neatly packaged in tight denim jeans, a white poplin shirt with a black string tie at the collar, and a smart black jacket. Her face was scored with lines, well lived in but with a

recollected prettiness emphasised by big blue eyes starkly out-
lined with kohl and fringed with spiky mascara'd lashes. Her
thin lips were lipsticked pink and her cheeks rouged. Her
curly, reddish, light-brown dyed hair was caught in a small
ponytail at the nape of her neck. She had a swagger, a consciously boyish way about her that jostled with her physically
frail appearance.

The three of us sat on the bus with three or four other
people heading into town. During the twenty-minute trip the
bus stopped several times to pick up passengers, passing
through obviously black suburbs on the way into the centre of
Jacksonville. By the time we were nearing the mall, it was
almost full and we were the only white people on the bus. I
noticed this vaguely, but it seemed no odder than being on a
bus going through Brixton. Troy and Bet, however, had
become silent and I could feel their tension. Our travelling
companions were the usual range of passengers: old, middle-
aged, young, working people, noisy teenagers, the usual urban
busload, with us as tourists. When we arrived at the Landing,
Bet let out a deep sigh of relief. Troy nodded and said, 'Yeah.'
There were beads of sweat on his forehead from more than the
heat.

'Jeez,' Bet said, releasing her pent-up breath. She was
sweaty too.

'What?' I asked.

'That was pretty scary.'

'Why?'

'I don't care to be outnumbered like that. In a strange city.'

'Me too,' said Troy.

'But what was so scary? Outnumbered?' I insisted, as we
walked towards the entrance of the mall.

'We were the only whites on that bus. This is a black city.

People like us . . . white and strangers . . . it's not safe.' Bet
spoke in an undertone.

No one, as far as I could tell, had given us a second look on
the bus. But it wasn't what people did that represented the
threat, it was the idea of being a stranger, of being in a white
minority that made Bet and Troy deeply uneasy. Blackness
was dangerous. We didn't look substantially richer than most
of the people on the bus. So the danger from a black majority
would have had to come from our whiteness and their hatred.
It was a historical fear. And hysterical. Neither of them lived
in inner cities. Troy came from small-town Texas, and Bet
lived on and kept to the suburban outskirts of Albuquerque.
In their America a bus full of black people was a rumour, a
story they'd heard about an America in which they did not,
and were pleased not to, live. Nightmare in Jacksonville was a
bad dream come true. We might have been travelling on a bus
full of aliens, or retributive ghouls, those creatures from
movies that represent the fear of being overwhelmed by oth-
erness, so strangely dangerous, so dangerously strange was
the situation for them. It was probably the fact of the city
that frightened my companions as much as the racial ratio.
Neither had ever been to New York, neither would have con-
templated it. America might look vast on the map, but for
many people it's as small as their local town, beyond which is
an uncharted wilderness inhabited by monsters. Once we'd
left the street and entered the air-conditioned, security-policed
mall, Bet and Troy relaxed. The shops, restaurants and ambi-
ence were familiar or versions of the familiar, and peopled by
a much higher proportion of whites. Even so, the danger
lurked outside.

'We've got to make sure and catch the bus back to the station before dark. If we get separated, we'll meet at the entrance

at 5 p.m. OK?' Bet told Troy, who, delighted to find himself under the protection of this tough matron, nodded vigorously and checked his watch.

'I need a beer,' Bet announced.

There was a piazza outside by the river, with cobbles, a plashing fountain and half a dozen places to eat. We settled on the least crowded and found a smoking table. Troy didn't smoke, but he was happy to go along with the requirements of his two older women companions. Bet downed a bottle of beer fast and ordered a second. I sipped mine, more intent on nicotine. Troy ordered southern-fried chicken and fries and tucked in.

'So where you all going?' Bet asked.

Troy retold his story, wide-eyed in surprise at himself for his achievement. Bet concurred.

'Good for *you.*'

I explained that I was from London, had just been on a freighter and fancied taking the slow route across the continent to see my friends in Phoenix.

Troy was amazed. 'On your own?' He'd only just made it to Savannah, he couldn't begin to imagine crossing an ocean to another continent alone in the company of strangers. I wondered for the first time if it *was* a bit odd, remembering my sophisticated London friends asking, 'On your own?' in much the same tone of voice as Troy.

I said that I was writing about the freighter trip for a British newspaper, and that I liked travelling alone. He shook his head in disbelief. Bet approved.

'I'm a train freak. I travel the trains whenever I can. I write about them for local newspapers.'

We were bonded. Her parents were both children of Irish immigrants, and she had been a wages clerk in a local government office in Albuquerque for twenty-five years. Now she and her husband were retired on a small pension and living in the same house they had bought thirty-odd years ago. Before that he had been in the army, and she an army wife, travelling the world but living always in the America of the base.

'What was the boat journey like?' Bet asked.

I told them about how I'd set off with the idea of writing about nothing happening for three weeks while I crossed the Atlantic only to find tragedy caught up with people anywhere.

Bet nodded grimly. She took a long drag on her cigarette.

So was Bet writing about this train trip, I asked?

'No, this is a different kind of trip. I was in South Carolina for a funeral. I figured I'd take the train back to give myself time to recover.' Her mouth turned hard as she spoke. 'I guess one of the reasons I was so upset by that bus ride was because of what happened.'

Bet had a brother who lived in a small town in South Carolina. When he was young, he'd thought about becoming a monk, but Bet said that wouldn't have worked out. He was too keen on girls. Either in spite of or because of that, he had never married. He was in his late fifties and owned the town hardware store. He lived alone. 'Drank some,' Bet said. 'But he minded his own business and ran the store.' He sounded like a sad, ageing and lonely man. One night, a week or so before, he'd closed the shop, had a drink in a bar, and was walking home on his own, when he was shot several times in the back by three kids.

'*Black*,' she said in a stage whisper, after a quick glance at the nearby tables. 'The youngest was thirteen. When the police picked them up they said they had nothing special against him, they just wanted to know what it felt like to kill someone. They didn't even know him. He wasn't anyone to them. They wanted to kill someone and it happened to be my brother. They killed a perfect stranger for kicks. My brother. We weren't that close, but he was my baby brother. I buried him two days ago. Oh, it makes me so mad. What are kids like now? What the hell's going on in this country?'

The nightmare of America, although still somewhere else, was closer to Bet than I had imagined. Troy looked aghast.

'My god, you read about these things, but . . .' The house from *Midnight in the Garden of Good and Evil*, which he'd stared at with such fascination, was as close as he had come to the nightmare. Now he was right here, almost at the centre of the drama, he could reach out and touch it, and it wasn't just a story set in the past. 'Oh my god . . .'

He actually paled at the idea of his proximity to tragedy. Bet shrugged and drank down her beer. Her hand shook as she lit another cigarette.

'I want to forget it. But that bus ride . . . it got to me again . . .'

It didn't seem appropriate to point out that three black killers in a small town in South Carolina had nothing to do with a busload of people going about their business in Jacksonville. It didn't even seem decent.

'I'm going to look round the shops,' Troy said.

'You want to shop?' Bet asked me.

'Not really.'

We sat on while Troy went back into the mall.

'You think he's . . . you know?'

'Gay? Certainly. Sounds like it's difficult being gay where he comes from.'

'Jesus, small towns. I bet his father doesn't know. This'll be the first time he's been open about it even to himself. I don't have anything against them. So long as they keep it among themselves. Well, good for him for getting out. He's such a scared little kid. It must have been a real effort.'

Troy came back and reported on the shops. There wasn't much, but he'd got talking to a guy at the ice-cream stand. Adventure was coming thick and fast. He thought maybe he'd go back and talk some more. He checked his watch nervously.

'You won't leave till agreed. Without me?'

'Absolutely not.'

'We'll come and drag you away, kiddo.'

Troy beamed happily and returned to the mall.

'Ah,' crooned Bet. 'I feel just like his mother watching him go on his first date.'

There were hours still to kill. Bet and I walked down to the riverside.

'What's the river?' I asked.

'The Jacksonville,' she told me, as we watched the boats ply up and down. It was wide and flat, a busy river with new developments on both banks. The water was a weird rust-red.

'Let's go for a boat ride,' I suggested. There was a small ferry going back and forth, just a little boat with a sun shade and two benches on either side for about a dozen people. The heat, once we had left the air-conditioned restaurant, was exhausting. 'It'll be cooler.'

Bet and I stayed on the ferry for a couple of hours, going from one side to the other, paying the two-dollar fare on each turn. Every so often we got off so that Bet could get another beer.

'You don't drink?' she asked me as I got a diet Coke.

'Not much,' I apologised.

'Well, I *do*. I drink a lot.'

The afternoon on the river was quite blissful, catching the

breeze on the water, going backwards and forwards to
nowhere. Bet and I congratulated each other on having found
a perfect way to spend our layover.

'What's the river called?' I checked with the captain of our
ship on one of our crossings.

'This is the St John's.'

'The *Jacksonville*?' I turned to Bet.

'Hell, I don't know what the damn river's called. I was just
trying to be helpful.'

We giggled a lot, though we talked about nothing much.
Bet was catching the *Sunset Limited* as far as El Paso.

'My hero's picking me up and driving me home. There's no
connection to Albuquerque.'

'Your hero?'

'That's my husband, Jim. My hero. Because he is my hero.'
It sounded fine to me.

'He didn't go to the funeral with you?'

'He had to stay home with Mikey.'

'Mikey?'

'Our youngest. He can't be left alone. He's brain damaged.'
Mikey was in his late twenties and had just qualified as a
policeman when he was in a car wreck which left him in a
coma for eight weeks and damaged him enough to be completely dependent on Bet and her hero, who were just reaching
retirement age.

'He's a sweetie. Got the mental age of a kid. Can't remember anything from one day to the next. Hell, one moment to the
next. He's got to be watched all the time. He's always trying to
do things he can't do, and then he gets mad because he remem-
bers he can't do what he used to do. But he's so loving. And
funny. A real joker. He's a joy. Our other kids are all grown and
have families of their own, but we've still got our baby.'

Only the words were sentimental. She spoke sharply in the face of a permanent tragedy. She lived with Mikey as he was now. I liked Bet's toughness, though I wondered how deep it went.

Back at Jacksonville station we still had hours to kill. We sat on a bench in the open on the platform, where Bet and I could smoke, next to a huge young black woman, in her mid-twenties, with a voice so loud you felt it in your solar plexus. It was the only place to sit, and at first I felt Bet's uneasiness: she was on her guard at the excessiveness of the woman. She was sprawled lazily on the bench, her great thighs comfortably separated, monitoring the comings and goings of her two tiny children, a boy of six and a girl of three or four, who ran in and out of the station. When they had been out of sight for some internally judged time limit, she would call out their names, and although they were behind a glass wall and closed door at the other side of the station, they came running. She never turned to look at them, her antenna was so highly tuned she knew exactly when the kids needed to be recalled before they got on anyone's nerves. The children returned instantly and amiably to their mother and hung around her knees for a while, being groomed, hair raked, mouth wiped, while she smoked and warned them not to get themselves dirty, before they went off again, both they and their mother reassured.

'And don't you go bothering people, you hear?'

They were dressed smartly, quite formally, while she wore a voluminous red tracksuit and trainers ground down by the weight they carried. The two children were obedient but never frightened or cowed by her great voice and monumental presence.

Bet relaxed and she, Troy and I were entertained during our wait with watching the way the family worked together.

'Hey, they're great kids,' Bet said to the woman.

'They better had be,' the woman boomed in mock ferocity. 'Or they'll catch it.'

But her pride in the compliment and her smile suggested that they didn't need to catch it often, and whatever they caught wasn't anything compared to the love they received. Bet seemed quite at ease now with the woman, who though black, young, loud and outsized, and perhaps somewhat strange and potentially dangerous at first sight, exhibited what to Bet was a proper understanding of social control and correct public behaviour when it came to the children. They were never going to grow up to be disaffected, morally blank wanton killers. We introduced ourselves. Her name was Gail, she was on her way from Virginia Beach, where she lived with her husband, to stay with a girl friend in Los Angeles. She was exhausted, having had the same ten-hour layover as us, but with the added responsibility of keeping two small children entertained. She had spent the afternoon with them at the movies, window-shopping and buying food and drink for the train journey which was going to be the full three days. She got back to the station an hour or so before we had arrived hoping she had worn the kids out enough for them to fall asleep. She could have dropped off at the snap of a finger, but the kids had hours of energy left in them. Like Troy, they were travelling coach, which meant sitting all three nights in reclining seats which were comfortable by airline standards, but still seats in a public coach. Bet and I had sleeping compartments. Travelling by train is pretty cheap if you don't want a bed and a space to yourself for the night. If you do, the price rises steeply, well beyond the means of a working family with better things to spend their money on than the luxury of a bed on a train. My enjoyment of the day in Jacksonville with my new friends depended on the knowledge that when the train came, I'd have a bed and a door to close. But I was delighted by the way the layover had turned out. Bet and Troy were people I would never have come across travelling any other way, nor by spending time in one place in a hotel, not even staying with friends. I was intrigued by Bet's contradictions and her bearing, and moved by Troy and his lone efforts to be who he was.

A train passed through without stopping, hooting from a distance to warn anyone off the track which was flush with the platform. It slammed past us like a shiny tornado. Troy watched it come and go.

'When we were kids we used to hang out at the station. They put pennies on the rail when a train was due. Flattened them like pancakes. You ever done that?'

I hadn't. Trains had never been so accessible in the middle of London, and the tracks were always recessed. It was an all-American tradition.

'I never managed to do it,' Troy said. 'I always got too scared at the last minute.'

Bet and I gave each other a maternal glance at this confirmation of Troy's timidity.

'Well, there's another train due before ours comes,' I said. 'Do it now.'

Troy looked alarmed, and shook his head.

'It's OK, I was only kidding.'

Troy became silent. The loudspeaker announced the imminent arrival of the next train, which would be slowing but wasn't stopping, so we should keep clear of the track. Gail told us how she had missed the train this morning because her husband had overslept and she'd made him drive them hell for leather to the next station in time to catch it.

'Or he sure as hell would have caught *something*. But we got there, 'cos he was scared as a kitten,' she bellowed, laughing with every inch of her body so the bench and all of us shimmied in the failing light. It was quite dark by now. Abruptly, Troy got up and took a few steps forward. Then he stopped dead.

'You OK?' Bet called. Usually when he went off to the lavatory or to get a drink he would tell us where he was going. But he didn't answer, just kept standing with his back to us. In the distance we heard the incoming train whistle. It seemed to startle Troy into a decision, and he began to stride towards the track without looking back.

'My God, what's he doing?' I asked, quite alarmed at the intensity in his walk.

The train whistled again, it was much closer now. Troy put a hand in his pocket.

'You know what? He's going to flatten a penny . . .' Bet gasped.

The three of us watched in silent admiration as he bent down and put something directly on the nearest rail, stepping back just in time before the train arrived. Then, as the train slowed, he turned round to look at us with an expression of perfect satisfaction on his face. Bet, Gail and I cheered, whooped and clapped Troy's achievement. The other people on the platform and even in the station looked alarmed at the rowdiness. After the train had passed through, Troy collected his penny from the track and held it aloft as he came back to the bench. He held it out for me. It was now an elongated oval with distorted markings, and bright as a proverbial new penny from the buffing up it had received from the train's wheels. It was as thin as a sliver of ginger. I was as proud as anything of Troy.

'Wonderful. Well, done.'

'Isn't that great?'

'Yeah, you did it.'

He smiled hugely. 'Wow, I was really scared. It was just like being a kid again, my heart was in my mouth walking to the track. But this time, I was determined to do it. It's to celebrate my weekend. Here,' he said, holding the penny in the palm of his hand out towards me. 'It's for you.'

'Oh, you must keep it as a souvenir.'

'No, I want you to have it. It'll remind you of your day in Jacksonville with Bet and me.'

I was getting sucked in. America was rolling over on its back and waving its legs in the air, offering me its soft sentimental underbelly to rub. And of course, as with some stray cat that I was determined to resist, which I had not the slightest intention of taking in, I was overcome by its charms, won over quite, in spite of my objections to its shameless methods. The Jacksonville Penny rests proudly above the corkboard in my study, a monument to what a person can do when they make their moment come, and a reminder that, every now and then and in the right circumstances, I really do like people.

I had better come clean, and admit that the right circumstance, the essential circumstance, is strangeness. Strangerhood seems to be what I need in order to see people clearly and be touched by them. On the whole, I'd rather have been Jane Goodall. Well, not Jane Goodall exactly, but a Jane Goodall version of me who spent my life in a forest befriending and observing a troop of chimpanzees. In lieu of that I became a writer, which is not so very different, except that the forest and the chimps have to be imagined, and the discomforts are far fewer. I was once reprimanded at a dinner party for saying as much, by someone who said that she suspected people like that actually preferred animals to human beings. I said I could confirm her suspicions, which were certainly true in my case. At the very least, given a choice between a human family and a troop of chimps, I'd take the chimps. I quite understood her air of disapproval, I disapprove of me, myself, but it does seem to be an inescapable fact.

I have not, so far, given excessive rein to my delight in animals. I have three cats which were accumulated somewhat reluctantly at my daughter's entreaties rather than planned as the beginnings of a home menagerie. I try to keep control of my more questionable desires. Now the daughter has left home and the cats apparently are mine, because according to her, it was I who wanted them all along. She may well be right.

Sometimes, when one of the cats is sitting on my lap, I have one of those rare experiences of existing completely in the present moment, of apprehending the reality of now with a blinding clarity and of being part of something extraordinary. I find myself astonished that a creature of another species, utterly different to me, honours me with its presence and trust by sitting on me and allowing me to stroke it. This mundane domestic moment is as enormous, I feel at such moments, as making contact across a universe with another intelligence. This creature with its own and other consciousness and I with mine can sit in silence and enjoy each other's presence. It becomes remarkable. I smooth the cat's fur, feeling his muscles beneath the loose skin, and trace the structure of his skeleton, backbone, shoulder blade, and skull with my massaging fingers, while he sits and purrs with the pleasure of physical contact, encouraging my exploring hands by pressing his head and body against them, turning his face this way and that to receive extra attention here or there. This is a perfectly everyday scene but sometimes it takes my breath away that another living thing has allowed me into its life.

But then I wonder at my wondering. Not that it *isn't* marvellous and extraordinary that a cat chooses to keep company with me, but it occurs to me that I might be just as amazed by the company of other human beings who choose to make contact with me across the chasm of separate individual consciousness. Rationally, I know both cats and people have a built-in need for making contact, but that doesn't make the fact of connection less extraordinary. Yet when I try to transfer that state of awareness to contact with my own kind, I fail. I can't apply my sense of miraculous contact to people. It's a flaw, perhaps like being colour-blind, or my own spatial deficiency that prevents me from transferring the information on two-dimensional maps into actual geography. What I experience most with other people is my estrangement from them, the distance of a mutually unique separation that words or touch never quite bridge. Unlike cats, people interfere with my apprehension of reality, they muddy how I can know myself, confuse my understanding of how I am, which is centred around the notion that solitude is a state of perfection, and the simplicity of being alone a desired goal. Of course, I have not been entirely on my own. I have had, and have still, people in my life. People I love and whose company I enjoy. But people complexify things; they place their glass of beer on the table and break up my view of the horizon by including themselves in the landscape. A cat might walk across the table with impunity; a lover putting his beer glass in front of me at a beachside taverna announces his place in my existence and ruptures my uninterrupted vision of perfect nothing.

My problem, if that is how it should be termed, and it probably should, is that I am never lonely on my own, but I often feel estranged when in company. Alone, I might experience all kinds of discomfort, but hardly ever the kind of discomfort that I feel would be improved by company. The discomfort arrives when I'm with other people, and then the urge to find a remedy is strong. The best and most effective remedy I know for such discomfort is to get alone again. The problem is that being alone isn't a problem. The idea that someone I am with feels he or she knows me throws me into a fretful anxiety about what and who they think they know, and my sense of what I know of myself is threatened. To have one's knowledge of oneself questioned by connection to another is a perfectly proper human adventure but I have no internal drive to have such adventures. So for me familiarity is difficult, while strangeness is comparatively easy.

One day on the freighter, the reticent Roz commented on the ease with which I got on with the crew. 'You seem to be able to talk to everyone. And they want to talk to you. You have a way with people.'

I didn't say: only in the company of strangers who are guaranteed to disappear back into their own lives. There was no call for such an intimate admission.

When You're Strange

The *Sunset Limited* was late. The ten-o-six arrival time and the ten thirty-seven departure time passed, the night deepened, and no one was surprised. It was half past midnight before the gleaming aluminium double-decker, more than anything like a giant version of one of those trendy retro toasters, pulled in to Jacksonville station. It had started out at 6.50 p.m. from Orlando, Florida, so it had lost over two hours during the four-and-a-half-hour journey. This was so unremarkable that no one bothered to explain why.

The first thing you learn about rail travel in America is that the trains are late. Regulars vie with one another to win the competition for who has suffered the longest delay. People who travel by train do not have urgent deadlines. Once you purchase your ticket and set foot in a train station, you have given yourself up to Amtrak time, which has a delightfully eccentric relation to US time. The printed schedule that waits at your seat or sleeping compartment becomes a wormhole between the parallel worlds of America and Amtrak. With the schedule, a watch and a calculator you can trace the theoretical journey you will take, estimate where you would be when, and then, as Amtrak reality takes hold, compute and recompute the slippage as the train catches up and loses ground against the official timetabling. You can't ever be certain when you will arrive at your destination, but you can work out at each stop what your final arrival time would be if nothing further delayed your train. This bears no relation to reality, but it becomes a kind of hobby, a therapy, even, an exercise in holding on to the idea of a world beyond Amtrak. Of course, you have also to take account of the time zones and include in your estimations of arrival the fact that Eastern Time changes to Central Time between Tallahassee and Chipley, Florida, which becomes Mountain Time somewhere en route from Alpine to El Paso, Texas. Two stops later, between Lordsburg, New Mexico, and Benson, Mountain Standard Time, a zone particular to Arizona, comes into force before Pacific Time takes over as you leave Yuma and arrive at Indio, California. Take the officially scheduled time of arrival, remember that an hour has been added for each of these zones (apart from Mountain Standard Time which is a mystery all of its own), note the time of your arrival at the next station, calculate the difference between the time on your watch and the time the schedule claims you will arrive, and you are in a position to make a guess when you will get to your final destination.

This guess is, naturally, meaningless, because who knows what delays will occur in the meantime, but nonetheless the train traveller pores over the timetable and arithmetises away rather as a British traveller in foreign parts might tune in to the World Service to check that the realm she has left behind continues to exist, however improbable it might seem. Inside the time capsule of an Amtrak train, there is a choice of losing yourself entirely to a system outside your control, or trying to keep track of what was once, and will be again, what you call reality. The accomplished long-distance train traveller understands the futility of holding on to a time outside their temporary universe. In transit it doesn't matter. We are all going somewhere, eventually, but in the meantime, we are going nowhere, our lives confined to a narrow corridor, a long road that has no turning, which rocks and thrums along its predestined route, or sometimes just stops dead in the middle of any place. There is no way out, no taking command of the situation, so all that is left to people in transit with time on their hands is to be where they are for as long as it takes. To be a train passenger in America is to be in an altered state, the fifty-first and the only mobile state in the Union.

Whatever the quirks in the schedule, it would take me from last thing on Saturday night until at the earliest sometime late Monday night, or early Tuesday morning, to reach Tucson, and I would pass through seven states to get there: Florida, Alabama, Mississippi, Louisiana, Texas, New Mexico and Arizona. It was the Atlantic Ocean all over again, but with landscape. Almost the entire width of America was about to scroll past my window for two days and two nights like a real-time travelogue, and I would sit still in my space capsule and watch its passing.

Our friendly foursome parted company when we were directed by the conductors to our designated places. Troy, Gail and the kids disappeared along the platform to their seats in the regular coaches, while Bet and I were pointed in the other direction to the sleeper section, where we climbed aboard the train with the help of a portable yellow stool familiar from all train boardings in movies (which Judy Garland used to leap aboard the Atchison, Topeka and Santa Fe of *The Harvey Girls*, which Joseph Cotton climbed on in *Shadow of a Doubt* to visit his small-town sister and her family while the police were searching for the merry multiple widower), placed on the platform by each conductor to enable us to reach the elevated bottom step. The immense shiny tin can that was the outside of the train was thrilling, but as soon as you were on board, it vanished and you became exclusively an inhabitant of the interior, like a traveller inside the shape-shifting, time-travelling Tardis. Bet and I waved a temporary goodbye as she was sent up the spiral stairs to her compartment and I looked for mine on the lower deck. We planned to meet up again in the morning.

'Come and get me when you go to breakfast,' she called, telling me her compartment number. I said I would. 'Not too early,' she added from the top of the stairs.

After more than twelve hours in company, I was alone again in a space of my own with a door that closed and a curtain over it to keep curious eyes from invading my privacy. The compartment was the width of a single bed with a few inches to spare. The bed was already made up and ran beneath the length of the window. The bunk above the window was down so that I had somewhere to put my hand luggage while I found my washbag and something to sleep in. A 6-inch-wide cupboard between the bed and the sliding door had a rail and two hangers for the clothes I was wearing. It was as tight a squeeze as could be managed, and as I lay myself down to test the bed, I couldn't have been happier. I am very content in enclosed spaces, providing they enclose only me. I like cocoons. I also enjoy the fact that they require an order of their own. By the side of the bed, a ledge demanded I keep my washbag and travelling clock on it. My overnight bag had to go in the bottom of the narrow cupboard, with my shoes. My word processor slipped under the bed that would, in the morning when rearranged by the steward, become two facing seats with a fold-down table between. Light switches and the air-conditioning controls were above what would become the seat backs. The window had curtains that could be drawn and fixed against the distraction of stars and the roaming moon in the inky night or prying eyes at station stops in the early hours. Along the corridor there were several lavatories with basins for washing and tooth brushing, as well as two shower rooms for those truly committed to in-train hygiene. It was all perfectly self-evident and self-evidently perfect, that half past midnight in my sleeping compartment on a train in Florida, USA.

The steward knocked and introduced herself as Ashley. Fresh coffee and orange juice would be available from six the next morning at the top of the stairs. Did I want a morning paper? Breakfast was served in the dining car from six-thirty to nine-thirty. Was I comfortable, did I need anything? She was on duty all night, just let her know.

'Where can I smoke?'

There are various arrangements for smokers, depending on the route. On some routes smoking is entirely prohibited, on others there are designated 'smoking hours' in the bar, on most there is a small self-contained smoking compartment next to the bar. The *Sunset Limited* had the latter. To reach it, I had to go up the stairs to the upper deck, along the adjacent sleeping coach, through two seating coaches and then down-stairs in the middle of the third, where the bar was to the left and the door to smoking coach to the right.

'And there's nowhere else I can smoke?'

'No, ma'am.'

'Not in my room with the air-conditioning turned up full?'

'No, ma'am.'

'Not even by the outer door in the middle of the night when no one is around?'

'No, ma'am.'

'With the window open?'

Ashley was sympathetic but firm. I didn't fancy my chances if I crossed her.

'OK, I know when I'm licked.'

'Yes, ma'am,' smiled Ashley, acknowledging her absolute authority over sleeping coach M with grace. 'You have a real good night, now.'

And, reader, I had passed my fiftieth birthday. I was too old to smoke in the lavatory, or directly under the air-conditioner, or in the boiler house. It was not so much the perceived lack of dignity of the surreptitious act, as the sense of the ridiculous should I be found out. The humiliation of being caught is what has kept me relatively docile and law-abiding all these years, because although the desire to transgress rules simply because they exist no longer amounts to a compulsion, I still experience an innate and unresolved dislike of authority in any form. The gall rises automatically. I am always sorely tempted to transgress rules. I do have a problem with virtue. I have never liked virtue much in others or in myself. The idea that I might be being good, doing what I am told, what I am supposed to do, fulfilling expectations, living up to my promise, still has an actual physical effect on me that I have had as far back as I can remember. Rage is the word that covers it. Rage begins behind the sternum (a little above where depression lives), a small tightly wound coil which comes suddenly to life, unfurling, snakelike, extending itself upwards through the chest until it has you by the throat and then springing, striking like a cobra at the head, at the place between the eyes and spreading like a bloodstain over the entire brain, red and hot and blindingly furious. Blinding rage. This is not a rough approximation, a physicalisation of a mental experience, but as precise a description of the reality of rage as it develops as I can muster. Do not imagine the uncoiling spring or the snake's head strike as metaphor for a *feeling*. True, there is no organic internal spring or snake, but take their physical effects for the reality I experience. Always have experienced. And never more than in the area of goodness and badness.

My first vivid recollection of this kind of rage was recently confirmed when someone, recognising a description of myself and her in childhood in my book, *Skating to Antarctica*, called me and arranged a meeting. She had been my friend when we were both very small. We met at a café for the first time since we were ten. I at least was not convinced that it was a very good idea, but thinking about our friendship I recalled something terrible that I had done, and I wanted to apologise. A bit late, forty-five years on, but it was an opportunity to acknowledge one's misdeeds to another that we don't usually get.

'You were sitting in the bedroom of my flat when we were five or six,' I reminded S. 'I was ill, with measles I think – I remember there was a red bulb in the light socket because I wasn't allowed to be in brightness. I asked you to pass me something and when you refused, I flew at you, and bit you on the cheek. I can still picture the tooth marks I made. My mother came in and went berserk. She smacked me and made me apologise.'

My mother specialised in going berserk, but this time she had good cause.

'Yes,' my former friend said. 'I remember. I wasn't going to mention it.'

I said it was unforgivable and that I was very sorry. I'm not

sure how valid such an apology is. The more-than-fifty-year-
old woman is certainly ashamed that she behaved in such a
way, but I don't think the six-year-old who offered a sullen
tight-lipped apology after being smacked and punished was in
the slightest bit sorry, and as I recollect the strength of her
anger, I doubt she would be even now. What I remember most
vividly about my attack on my best friend was the sense that I
actually *flew* out of my bed and across the room to sink my
teeth in her flesh. I have a recollection of bridging the gap
between us yet remaining horizontal, without my feet touching the ground. I launched myself from my bed across the
admittedly not very large room, fuelled by an anger that was
more powerful than the force of gravity. I remember, with
astonishment at the thrust of its forward propulsion, the rush
of blinding rage and self-will. The two middle-aged women,
one apologetic and one forgiving, were, of course, in no position to do either on behalf of the enraged and wounded
children they once were, except perhaps in the sense that we
are all in loco parentis to our childhood selves. Aside from
that, it turned out, as I feared, that we had little in common
any longer from our past. In fact, it emerged that we had
always been somewhat at odds, even in our childhood.

S had read the account of my childhood in *Skating to
Antarctica* with amazement at the tale it told.

'I thought you had everything. You had everything – and
then you had nothing,' she kept saying, as if in wonder.

S's father had left her mother who, having S and her brother,
had to go to work while the children stayed with their grandmother. S had envied me both my temporarily present father
and my chronically underemployed mother. What I experienced as a family viciously at war in a very small flat, was for S
complete, present and attentive. She had *longed* to be me.

S had fine straight hair, which I'd always envied, mine being long and frizzy and prone to knotting.

'I remember watching your mum doing your hair every morning,' S recalled. 'Dipping the comb in water and combing it over and over until every tangle was out, then brushing it tightly back away from your face and tying it with satin ribbons she'd just ironed.'

I remember the daily hairbrushing sessions, too, but differently. The comb yanking at the tangles, pulling the hair out at the roots, my mother shouting, me crying, to say nothing of the bloody humiliation of having satin ribbons in my hair. I ached for a loose curtain of hair falling over my face as S had. She envied me my obsessive mother, I envied her her neglect. She knew nothing of the violence and fear in my life with my terrifyingly erratic mother and the fights between my parents; I knew nothing of the sense of deprivation, the lack of a father, the daily absence of her mother, in hers. Meeting up after all these years what we discovered was that as best friends we had been locked in jealousy and enmity, each pursuing our own misinterpretation of liberty and love. The everything S saw me as having was for me parents who hated each other and sometimes hated me. The everything I lost had not been the perfect family security that S perceived. But now, as an adult, it crossed my mind that perhaps S might have made a better job of being my parents' child than I had. I felt she thought something like that too as we perched on our stools in the café. My fury at S must have built up from all those moments I now remembered when my mother would shout, sometimes with S standing by, 'Why can't you be like S? She's a nice, loving child. She doesn't complain when I brush her hair. Why couldn't I have a daughter like her? What have I done to God that he should have punished me with you?'

It wasn't that I minded my mother thinking I was bad, it was that I hated the idea of S being good. I guess I wanted to consume her goodness, chew it up and spit it out. I discovered not just that I didn't want to be good, but that I did not want S (or others) to be good either. If I envied S her place in my mother's fantasies of a good daughter, I did not want to replace her with myself. I found that not being good was a characteristic I had to pursue, because the idea of my own goodness sent me into a delirium of rage.

Conforming to a non-smoking world belonged in the same emotional arena. It was not simply a matter of physical addiction – nicotine-replacement products work quite well in that respect – which prevented me from giving up (even on a pragmatically temporary basis) when confronted with the difficulties of smoking in the face of North American puritanism, it was the puritanism itself. I didn't want to do as I was told, I didn't want to be more comfortable by conforming, giving in, as I saw it, to the pressures of an anti-smoking policy that was reinforced by moral imperatives. Very childish. Yes, exactly. I also didn't want to become an ex-smoker, not if it meant that I became someone who tsked and sighed whenever I caught a whiff of smoke in the air. The tension in my solar plexus began to agitate as soon as I thought of it. It was almost organic, my desire not to be a virtuous, self-righteous non-smoker. I was deeply, fundamentally of the other party. And this, it turned out, was all to the good, because the other party was a three-day affair I wouldn't want to have missed.

The smoking carriage was an oasis of tawdriness. It was a slum at the centre of the train that was in every other part designed to please the paying customer. Even in coach the seats reclined and were upholstered, there were carpets, windows that had been cleaned at least at the start of the journey, air-conditioning that worked. The observation car and restaurant offered an approximation of old-fashioned comfort and hospitality, swivel armchairs, side tables, a bar, panoramic windows through which to see America slide past. The sleeping compartments added to these conveniences the details of flowers in vases and starchy antimacassars. The intention throughout the train was to attract the public back to an old form of travel by offering them a degree of physical pampering even if they weren't going to get where they were going on time. The smoking coach, however, was the sin bin, the punishment cell, a capsule of degradation where those who were incorrigible would suffer the consequences of their obduracy. And it was wonderful.

It was entirely correction-facility grey: the lino floor, the dull-putty coloured walls and the moulded polystyrene chairs that ran along the length of the short carriage, eight chairs on either side, bolted at their base to a shiny steel girder fixed to the floor. Between every two or three chairs was a small plastic table, also attached to the girder, on each of which was an individual-tart-sized disposable tinfoil ashtray. As grey as sin. As grey as smoke. These are the surroundings you deserve. An environment you can't spoil with your befouling habit. Something that won't be wasted by your obvious inability to appreciate decent conditions. It had only two smallish windows at each end on either side, the larger middle sections which in all other coaches were windows seeming to have been deliberately blanked out. At the far end, opposite the only door (the smoking coach was a dead end), a black bin-bag holder was fixed to the wall. Above it, a sign said, 'Do Not Bring Beverages Into The Smoking Coach'. Beside the door a handwritten notice instructed, 'Do not stay more than fifteen minutes at a time. Only cigarettes are permitted to be smoked.' The ashtrays were always overflowing, the tables dusted with ash, the bin bag between three-quarters full and overflowing, the floor scarred and scratched. The air was fogged grey with smoke, sometimes thick enough to choke someone coming in from outside. There was a small air-conditioning grille at the top of the far wall, but mysteriously it never seemed to work. The smoking coach was closed for one hour in each twenty-four, in order it was said for it to be cleaned, but there never was a time during the day or night when it was cleaner than any other, and the conductor responsible for the coach was seen only when he came through the door to enforce the rule about not bringing drinks in. Then he would peer through the grimy glass in the door before pulling it back with a look of disgust on his face as what remained of the air assaulted him. 'Jeez,' he would moan, and then bark at the offenders who had failed to hide their clear plastic glasses or bottles in time. He'd jerk his thumb towards the notice on the wall.

'See the sign? Get it outta here.'

Later he'd return and find things just as before.

'You want me to lock the coach? I want them drinks gone.'

'C'mon,' someone would call to him, inviting him to live and let live. 'Give us a break.'

He remained sullen. 'I didn't ask for this job. You keep the rules then I don't have to come into this hole and suck up a lungful of your cancer.'

Bet had her own way with the non-drinking rule. Wherever she went she carried in her bag a small, 300ml Coke bottle half-full of gin concealed by an insulating silver sleeve designed to keep cold drinks cold. Some became quite adept at keeping their drinks on the girder under their seat and bending down away from the door to take swift surreptitious sips. Others simply risked temporary expulsion and the wrath of the conductor with blatant cans of beer or liquor in clear plastic tumblers from the bar, right out in the open for any passing representative of authority to see. It probably depended, like so much else, on what kind of childhood the individual had been dealt. Concealment, sneakiness, risk-taking, defiance are learned characteristics instilled early in life. It was, in some way, thoughtful of the Amtrak authorities to retain an embargo that the tolerated, neutralised, exiled smokers could each in their own manner transgress. It left just a little edge in a smoothly rounded world.

The misfits and miscreants of the train, obviously in the real world a complete range of society, were equalised in their smoking-coach selves into a homogenous group with a fundamental set of values. Whatever our place out there, we were as Shakers or Albigensians in our train life: a despised community existing on sufferance in a world that no longer permitted itself the luxury of burning heretics. Between ourselves, and to outsiders, we stood for something, allied in our determination to persist in our desire in spite of all the effort of the moral majority and the do-gooders who would have saved us from ourselves and for their own satisfaction. It gave us a feeling of fellowship, a purpose even, that supplemented the mere journey that all of us, smokers or not, were taking. There was no sense here, as in many groups, of newcomers having to prove themselves or be superseded by newer newcomers before gaining acceptance. The simple act of entering the coach, laughing appreciatively at the smog and lighting up entitled you to full membership. The notion of the train being the longest main street in America was reduced in the smoking coach to a far more essential concept of an America where all kinds and conditions of humanity could coexist in spite of all their differences of status, race, religion, political creed, because of a recognised underlying common cause. This (*pace* the Native Americans) was what America had been for in the first place.

Bet and I headed for the smoking car directly after breakfast. To get there we passed Troy's seat. He waved and we said hello but didn't stop. Troy wasn't a smoker. Already we were in different camps. Gail was there when we arrived, wearing what she had been wearing the previous night, her bulky thighs splayed over the edge of the narrow plastic seat near the door.

'Hi,' Bet said brightly.

Gail groaned, and lifted her limp arm to take a drag, as if the half-smoked cigarette she held between her fingers weighed a ton or two. 'Is it breakfast time yet?'

She hadn't slept. The kids were asleep in their seats, and she'd been kept awake with their tossing and turning and the wondrous unconscious determination of children to take all the space they need. She spent the night in and out of the smoking coach. 'Where we at?' she rasped, as we sat down across from her and began to light our cigarettes.

Through the night I'd noted the stations on the way, as I was woken from my rocking sleep by the unfamiliar slowing and stopping of my bedroom. I'd open my eyes and see that we were in Lake City, Madison, Tallahassee, Chipley, Crestview, Pensacola: names on boards at half-lit middle-of-the-night stations where one or two people waited sleepily for the *Sunset Limited* to arrive, blowing its unearthly whistle at an unearthly hour. The travellers got on or off and the engine started up again, the wheels squeaked as they began to roll, and I lay back in my bunk beside the black-again window to watch the stars slip away at a gathering speed.

We were, of course, two hours behind schedule. We should have arrived at our first stop in Alabama – Atmore – at 7.05 a.m., but we had just left it at sometime past nine.

'We're an hour out of Mobile,' I told Gail. 'Though we should be in Mississippi by now. But we haven't lost any more time during the night.'

Gail shrugged. It was a long way still to LA and a comfortable bed. She heaved herself off the chair, stubbed out her cigarette and with a 'See ya' went off to wake the kids and get some breakfast.

It was a quiet time in the smoking coach. A woman in a knitted gold dress sat in the far corner, tap-tapping the end of her cigarette. A very young girl in floppy jeans and midriff-baring top sat huddled over in the opposite corner, drawing hard on her Marlboro. A couple of chairs down from her a very tall, thin young black man with a baseball cap on backwards read from a book resting on his crossed, outstretched legs. Gold Dress and Baseball Cap had looked up briefly and said hi as Bet and I came in. Marlboro Girl had remained hunched, head down, face hidden behind a fall of wispy blonde hair, in her corner. A few minutes after we arrived and were smoking contentedly, watching the bayous pass, a corpulent red-faced man wearing long shorts and a sporty open shirt slid the door open with his elbow so as not to disturb the contents of the plastic tumbler in his hand.

'For Christ's sake shut up,' he was muttering grimly. 'Sit down, stick a cigarette in your stupid face and shut up.'

He was talking to a woman behind him dressed formally in tailored pants and a neat blouse, a scarf wound around her throat and gold jewellery abounding on her wrists and fingers.

'Don't talk to me like that,' she said, but her face and tone had no hint of outrage in them. She spoke as dully as if he had told her the time and she hadn't wanted to know, as if he were always telling her the time and she always didn't want to know. Her 'don't talk to me like that' was automatic and weary, said with neither a thought nor an emotion behind it. That was noteworthy, but her voice was even more extraordinary. It sounded like a pneumatic drill on paving stone, a low rasping vibration that was only recognisable as a voice because it spoke words, so mannish it couldn't have come from a man.

'I'll talk to you how I want,' the man replied, though with as little interest in the conversation as she. 'Good morning, ladies,' he said in an altogether more jovial voice with a slight Irish lilt to his lazy American accent, lifting his tumbler to us in greeting.

'Hi,' growled the well-dressed woman like a fairground barker.

They sat down opposite us, him with his podgy naked calves ending in deck shoes planted wide apart, her with good court shoes, legs neatly crossed, lighting up with a gold Dunhill lighter.

'Light one for me,' he told her.

'Put your booze down for one second and light your own,' she monotoned at him.

'This delightful woman is my wife Virginia,' he leaned across to me. 'I am Conal. Glad to make your acquaintance.'

'Hello,' I said weakly, stunned at the performance.

'Oh, *hailo*,' he pantomimed in a posh English accent. 'Virginia, my dear, you must be on your best behaviour. We have a well-bred British lady among us. None of your filthy sailor's language if you please.'

'For God's sake, behave decently,' Virginia snarled. 'Please excuse my husband, he's a pig.' She got up and came to sit next to me. She was tall and quite stately, but beginning to stoop as if her height and stateliness were becoming burdensome to sustain. There was something unhealthily grey about her carefully made-up face. They were on their way home to Los Angeles, she told Bet and me, sucking hard on her cigarette and lighting another from it before it was half-way smoked. They had been on holiday in Florida and always took the train because she was frightened of flying. Anyway, it gave Conal more time to drink. The Florida trip was so that she could recuperate.

'I'm sorry about my voice,' she growled. 'I've just had an operation for cancer of the oesophagus.' She pointed at her scarf. 'I'm not supposed to talk at all. They took out what they could. They said I'll be all right. They think so.' She fell silent.

'Telling them all about your cancer, dear heart?' Conal called. 'That's it, don't keep it to yourself. I'm sure the nice English lady could care less.'

Virginia threw him a contemptuous look and turned back to me. She put one of her heavily beringed hands on mine in a gesture of intimacy and moved her head closer to my face. 'I don't want to die,' she whispered in her sandpapered voice, intense, yet hardly talking to me at all, shocked almost at the sound of her words, but at the same time almost pleading as if entrusting the thought to a stranger might function as some kind of prayer.

'Then you could try putting out your cigarette, not drinking like a fish in secret, and *shutting up*,' hissed Conal, pouring the remains of his whisky down his throat.

An expression of his love, perhaps. Two drunks locked together in life, panicking about the end. Their theatre of hatred sent me retreating into sentimental mode. It was enough for Bet, who whispered 'Jesus' under her breath and rose. 'I've got to leave,' she said. 'Knock on my door next time you go for a smoke.'

The tall young man with the backwards baseball cap finished his cigarette a moment after Bet had left and loped to the door, nodding a generalised, 'See ya later.' He was holding Heidegger's *Being and Time*.

'Hey, baggage,' called Conal, getting out of his chair and grabbing hold of Virginia's arm. 'You're going to frighten the refined English lady away. She's too good for the likes of us dirt Irish.'

She shook off his hand, but, growling goodbye to me, followed him out as if he were still holding her.

'Bye, Conal,' I said, waving a feeble hand at him as he disappeared through the door.

A moment after everyone had left, Marlboro Girl looked up and smiled shyly at me.

'Hello,' I said.

'God, wasn't he awful?'

I shook my head in wonderment at the degree of his awfulness. She got up and came to sit next to me. She looked so young, I asked if she was travelling alone. An expression of pure childlike terror crossed her face.

'I'm eighteen,' she reassured me. 'Maddy. I'm going home to LA. I had an accident.'

She was remarkably beautiful in a modern, huge-eyed, extremely wide mouth, gauchely tall and thin-as-a-reed sort of way, like an anorexic fawn. She was Julia Roberts as near as dammit. Her clothes were very expensive schmutters, pale ultra-baggy trousers just hanging on to her barely there hips, showing a waistband of boyish underpants and an expanse of exposed torso below a tight, skimpy T-shirt. She was as consciously and unconsciously waiflike as it was possible to be, but seemed quite at ease with her modish beauty.

'What happened?'

'I was in Florida for a fashion shoot,' she said, looking

pleased to start talking. 'I'm a model.' Of course she was. 'They think something's wrong with my brain.'

Eight days before, someone had opened a door too fast without looking and slammed it into her head. It bled a lot, and she passed out for a second or two. They took her to hospital and she was given a scan. She had a blood clot.

'A dark patch or something, the doctor said. They sent me back to my hotel to wait a few days to see if it would disappear. It can be nothing, apparently, something that just goes away. But it hasn't. When they did another scan this morning, they told me it hadn't improved. It's got bigger. They said I had to go home for surgery. I've spent eight days in my room sitting still, frightened that I'm going to drop dead. That's pretty crazy-making. It's better being on the train, with people around, and going home.'

'Your parents . . .?'

'I spoke to them on the phone every day. They're waiting for me. The doctors didn't tell me anything. Just that the clot had got bigger and I had to have surgery. They need a course in psychology, those doctors. I've been so frightened. They haven't really told me anything. I don't know what's going on, what could happen . . .'

'Why the train? It's a long journey on your own by train.'

'They said I couldn't fly. The pressure changes might make the clot, you know . . . And there wasn't a sleeping compartment available. It's slower but safer by train. They told me I mustn't do anything to raise my blood pressure.'

'Should you be smoking?'

'I've got to do something. And this has really messed up my trip. I've been modelling for six years. This was a really big job. *Vogue.*'

She shook her head slowly and then fell silent, perhaps at

how small the loss of the big opportunity seemed now she spoke of it, compared to the blood clot that had got bigger in her brain.

'If you want to sleep, you're welcome to use my compartment.'

She said no, she felt better being with people.

The door opened suddenly and a young man in his early twenties came in. He was black and hip, with even baggier trousers than Maddy's that concertinaed around his ankles, his head covered with a black beret. He saw Maddy and flung himself down in the seat beside her, offering her a cigarette which she took and he lit with a snap of his see-through Zippo before lighting and dragging hard on one of his own. Maddy perked up a little more at the cool new company.

'Man,' he wailed. 'I can't believe I gotta be on this train for two nights. But a lot can happen on a train.'

Maddy and I showed a polite interest.

'I'm a DJ. My man called from LA. He said come on out here, there's gigs and bitches and sunshine all the time. I think, fuck, I'll go. I can DJ in LA, NY, any place, you dig? Hey, you a fucking model or something? Wanna beer?'

Maddy looked quite perked up. Suddenly, just a couple of hours after I'd got up, I was limp with exhaustion. I decided I needed a nap.

'I'm going back to my compartment,' I said to Maddy and told her where it was if she needed to lie down later.

'Sure,' she said, distractedly.

I slept until we pulled in to Pascagoula, Mississippi at around 11 a.m. There was a tap on my door and Bet called out that she was going to the smoking coach. I said I would join her in a minute. DJ and Maddy were still there, smoking, sipping beers and deep in conversation. Gold Dress was back in the same place. Conal was sitting with a tumbler of bourbon and a cigarette, but no Virginia. As well as Bet, there were two or three men I hadn't seen before, a smiling Mexican, another tall, lanky black man with his baseball cap the right way round, and a middle-aged guy in a cowboy hat with a face that seemed carved out of stone, smoking solitary and quiet.

'Come over here, English Lady, and be friendly,' crooned Conal, his voice turning a corner into a sneer. I shrugged and sat next to him. He put an arm round me. I removed it.

'My people are from Kerry. You know Ireland?'

'Not really.'

'You don't say much, do you? A proper icy English lady with your grey hair and crossed legs. They teach you that at finishing school, did they? Do you ever uncross your legs?'

'Let it go, Conal.'

'I just want to know . . .'

'You never will.'

We were sitting at the far end of the coach by a window. Bet in the corner, then me and Conal. There was a slight lurch, barely noticeable, but enough to make Conal have to hold on to his tumbler to stop the bourbon from spilling. A second later, Bet, looking out of the window, made a low whistle.

'Well, I hope we didn't do that.'

I glanced out in time to see the wreck of an upturned car on the side of the track.

'Mmm,' I said, thinking like Bet how, though we hadn't done it, some train obviously had at one time. Then I saw that the cloud which for a second I thought was disturbed dust, rising from the wrecked car because of the turbulence of the passing train, was actually smoke. At the same time, the train was decelerating sharply.

'Oh my god, we did do it,' I gasped.

'Hell,' complained Conal, whose bourbon slopped over the side of his glass. 'They've no respect for good drink.'

Bet put her hand over her mouth, and whispered, 'We hit that car.'

'Shit,' said the stone-carved man, getting up to peer out of our window. 'Stupid bastards. They tried to beat the train. Happens all the time in these godforsaken places.'

The others gathered round the window, but we were too far past the wreck to see it. They headed out of the coach to the corridor and opened the door. Conal, Bet and I stayed where we were, Bet and I, at least, too stunned to move. The commentary came from the people by the door, and we saw our guard walking back along the track with another conductor, talking into a handset.

'Kids, probably,' one of the observers said. 'Playing chicken with a train. That only ends one way. The train's always gonna win.'

'Hit a truck last week out of Chicago. Same thing. Truck driver and his passenger were killed outright.'

Other people added their reminiscences of rail kills they'd experienced. Everyone seemed to have one, and the tones of voice were matter-of-fact. It was all part of train travel in America, apparently. But at least one life had been extinguished just seconds before by our train without us feeling anything more than a mild jolt. It turned out to be three lives.

'Hell,' someone said. 'This is going to make us even later. They have to test the wheel balances before we can move again. Every damn wheel. It can take hours. Jesus, we're going to be stuck in this hole half the day, and we're already over two hours late.'

Some voices mumbled agreement, the killing already forgotten in the inconvenience.

Our conductor came back.

'Sorry, folks. We hit a car. We going to be a while sorting
this out. Two kids were killed outright. One in the back's alive.
Pretty badly hurt. We're waiting for the ambulance and we
can't leave until they find the local coroner to pronounce
death. We're checking the train for damage while we're waiting.' He shook his head. 'It's a real mess. You all stay where
you are. The one in the back is screaming something awful.
But there's nothing anyone can do until they're cut out of the
wreck.'

So we waited in the dusty heat on the outskirts of some
nameless town between Pascagoula and Biloxi, Mississippi,
for a coroner to be found, for the wheels to be tapped, for our
journey to recommence. We were instructed over the loudspeaker system not to leave the train and asked if there was a
doctor or paramedic on board for one of the chefs who had
fallen hard when the train came to a halt and possibly broken
his arm. How much you felt the jolt of the car or of the emergency stop depended on where you were on the train. We were
towards the rear, so felt very little, because the first two carriages absorbed the force (and, of course, the car and its
passengers), but near to the engine, people knew immediately
that something had been hit. For us in the smoking carriage, it
had been little more than a few spilled drops of bourbon and
a flash of smoking metal, as the car was struck at nearly full
speed and somersaulted to the side of the track. It was hard to
take in. The upturned automobile I had seen might have been
there for weeks or months even – it was probably an ancient
vehicle already – so settled had it looked in its final resting
place. It was now already quite a way behind the train, so we

couldn't hear any sounds coming from it. The train had been speeding along on the flat, past one after another one-horse town with unprotected train tracks at their outer boundaries. To our right was the sweaty marshy landscape of the South and a bit of a dirt road that led perhaps to the next place; to our left, small groups of clapboard houses and unkempt rubbish-strewn backyards could be glimpsed between the trees. This was poor country. The train whistle had blown two or three times as it approached each residential area to warn of its coming. There were no level crossings, no traffic lights in these backwoods places. The single dirt road out of town ran across the tracks, an oncoming train blew its whistle, that was all. Although you could see it coming for a long way through the flat landscape, it is notoriously hard for someone watching it come to judge the speed and distance of a moving train, but who in a place like this would be in such a hurry that they would try to beat it? Someone suicidally, pointlessly impatient, someone whose judgement was hopelessly impaired by drink or drugs, or someone terminally bored. One thing everyone knew was that in a race between a car and a train, the train always won. At least everyone on the train knew that. Maybe the three people in the car didn't know. Or they were young enough to believe that nothing like death could ever happen to them, that taking risks always had the desired out-come. Perhaps they wanted to make the train and its passengers pay attention at whatever cost. But the one person left alive in the car was screaming. The worst thing in the world had happened and for no good reason.

The coroner came quickly. He was in the bar nearby, at the back end of town. The two people in the front were pro-nounced dead, the third cut out and driven off in the ambulance ('Nah, she's had it,' the conductor confided), and

the wheel balances were checked in record time, so that despite
the worst fears of my fellow travellers, we started to pull away
from the sight of the accident just three quarters of an hour
after we first struck the car. People expressed relief that the
delay wasn't as great as they had feared.

'What about the driver?' I asked my conductor, Ashley,
when I got back to my compartment.

She was very distressed, she had gone out to the car. 'It's so
terrible when that happens. If you're crew, you feel, I don't
know, sort of responsible. I know we couldn't do anything,
but . . . I heard that poor girl screaming.' She shook her head
hopelessly. The driver was back driving the train. There
wasn't anyone who could take over until we got to New
Orleans four hours or more away. Amtrak didn't carry relief
drivers.

'You mean he just got back in and started up?'

'He had to. He's real upset. It kills drivers when that happens, but he has to carry on until we get to New Orleans.
He'll be OK. But you notice we're going pretty slow.'

We were. There was no more hurtling through the bayous
that day. Not that he had been going too fast, not that, even at
our present speed, if we hit a car, anyone in it would survive.
But you could feel his distress and caution in the movement of
the train. And you could hear it. For the rest of the day, the
whistle blew, not just once or twice as we approached a road
crossing or a station, but from a mile or more away, long sad
wails that resonated back through the stifling air to my compartment – the train is coming, the train is coming, for god's
sake don't get in its way – the most mournful sound you could
imagine, much more than was necessary, as if the driver were
keening. Hear that lonesome whistle blow. And it blew and
blew for as long as the driver drove the train. It called out like

a banshee; while I lay in my bunk, watching the sky, it howled the miles away.

We got to New Orleans in the late afternoon where we stopped for an hour as scheduled to change crew and take on water. Bet and I walked through the chaotic station and stood outside smoking. We didn't talk about what had happened, but Bet was morose.

'Have you slept?' I asked her.

'No, I was just lying down. Couldn't sleep.'

I nodded. When she finished her cigarette she asked a porter where the nearest liquor store was and headed off in the direction he indicated.

'Supplies,' she said. 'Want anything?'

'Shall I come?'

'No, I'll just walk. See you back on the train. Kids, Jesus.'

She left, head down, marching towards a new bottle of gin.

Too Much to Ask

To travel any but the shortest distance by train is bizarre to most people in the States. Why take three days to cross the country when you can do it in three hours by plane? A glossy US fashion magazine thought it so quaint that they commissioned me to write an article describing the journey I was about to make. When I returned to the UK, I emailed the copy and then got a call from the features editor. It was fine, but could I cut some of the stuff about the train and my fellow travellers and put in more landscape and scenery? I did, of course, see a lot of landscape. I watched America go by inch by inch, just as I had obsessively examined the passing ocean on the freighter, staring for hours at a time out of the observation cars or the window of my sleeping compartments. My suitcase was weighted down with the books I had brought to read, but I didn't complete a single chapter while on the move because I couldn't keep my eyes on a page of print when every kind of the most extreme and extraordinary, changing and changeless landscape was rolling past my eyes. I often wished the train were slower so that I could examine the bayous, the rivers, the grasslands, the mountains and deserts in more detail. But it became clear to me that the *passage* of landscape before my eyes was in itself a particular way of viewing the country. At any rate, a particular way of being in the country. Everyone knows the pleasure, even on the shortest train journeys, of staring out at the world that goes by beyond the viewer's control, to the accompaniment of the rhythm of the wheels on the rails and the swaying of the carriage. Hypnotic, the landscape forever approaching and passing, skimming along, the eye snatching a detail, noticing a cloud, a bizarre building, a blasted tree, a startled creature, but not being able to hold on to it as the view rolls by. Our thought processes work more slowly than the speed of a train or the eye. There's as much relief as frustration in that. Thoughts can exist independently of what the eye is taking in, they can be allowed to take care of themselves. Alternatively, you can read a book or open your laptop and ignore the whole thing while you get from A to B. I, at any rate, couldn't tear myself away from the passing parade of America, and I let my thoughts do what they would. Passive watching is an intense and private activity. It leaves a residue. The eyes look and take in the fleeting images, absorb them into the processor inside the head which transforms them into a memory: the recollection of a split second gone by which will become a memory of something seen yesterday, a week ago, a decade past, somewhere back in the mists of time. The flashing pictures remain, but they settle in beside other related images. And most of the related images are in Technicolor and wide-screen. Was that image, that memory, from the train journey or a movie you once saw?

American landscape is *known*, like famous speeches in Shakespeare's plays or phrases in the King James Bible are known. They are already read, so that when you come across them in their proper context, they jar and falsify the moment. In the auditorium, Macbeth's nihilism and despair are weakened as you overtake the actor in his assessment of life as full of sound and fury, signifying nothing. On the page *In the beginning God created the heavens and the earth* slips by in a far too familiar rhythm, so you forget to wonder: what beginning? Created from what? Why? And as you actually pass through the boundless grasslands of Montana, or deserts of Arizona and New Mexico, a thousand Westerns complete with their wide-open background scores rush to clog the mind. *The Big Country, The Searchers, Stagecoach, The Man Who Shot Liberty Valence, Wagon Train, Red River* and, of course, *Blazing Saddles.* John Wayne, Henry Fonda, Ward Bond, James Stewart, Montgomery Clift stride or lope into view and people the empty vista outside the window, filling it with human endeavour. There's a stored image for every inch of the landscape passing by. Gunslingers on galloping horses kick up the dust getting out of town fast ahead of the posse, cowboys bed down by the campfire, guns at the ready beneath the saddle under their head, ranchers locked in sullen, greedy conflict with immigrant farmers plan violent evictions, wagon trains full of pilgrims in search of a new life and the odd run-out-of-town whore circle as the Indians charge down from the hills to attack the intruders, the lonely hero walks away westward from the danger of being included in the civil society he has helped to bring about. Each image comes complete with its own landscape. Every landscape comes with its own set of meaningful images, seen already in darkened cinemas and on TV. We know the landscape of America, even if we have never been there. We've inhabited it, even if we've never set foot outside London, Delhi or Helsinki. We've been a part of it, even if we've never been further west than the movie house at the local mall in a New England suburb, or if we spend our days shopping till we drop on Fifth Avenue.

But what do I do with all this *view*? I can attempt to describe what the eye catches, and try to nail down the strobing images in an approximation of words. So. The sky is vast and vacuously blue, the empty deserts at sunset threaten the spirit with their scrubby grey-green dying light, the rivers wind from bare trickles in parched earth to thunderous rushing torrents, the canyons dismay and dizzy you as you stare down into them and try to make out the bottom, the mountains loom in anthropomorphic shapes of things seen best in dreams, the grasslands and wheatfields wave like an endless syrupy ocean tickled into motion by the breeze. You know, you've seen it in the movies. What is remarkable, what is strange about passing through America, peering at it through the screen of the train window, is that everything is familiar. It is much more as if America is passing through you, what you are, what you've known. Sitting there looking out at the landscape is like having a dye injected so that the tendrils of memory in the brain light up and trace the private history of your mind. As I sit and watch the weird rock formations, sagebrush, cactus and Joshua trees of the desert land go by, the cinema in Tottenham Court Road where I saw my first shootouts jumps vividly into my present. The smell and plush of the carpet underfoot comes flooding back to me, the tense anticipation as the lights begin to fade, the solid dark presence of my father sitting beside me, the blue smoke from his cigarette curling up into the bright beam on its way to the screen which will light up with dreams and places and complexities of human joy and trouble that my striving six-year-old brain can barely imagine, let alone make sense of. That's what the landscape of America is like.

On sunny days in mid-fifties London, I went to Russell Square and played cowboys and Indians on a landscaped hill with a tarmacked path cut through it like a perfect canyon. When it rained, I went with my friend – S, I expect – to the Egyptian Gallery of the British Museum and we played my favourite game. Surrounded by monumental stone fragments – an icy-smooth foot bigger than a bathtub, a marbled sinewy arm extending to a closed fist as broad as the front of a bus – S and I would sit on a bench intended for weary or thoughtful culture seekers and pretend in loud voices and almost certainly execrable accents to be American children on holiday – no, *vacation*. With our voluminous knowledge based on the films and TV we had seen, we discussed the incredibly luxurious and automated homes we had left behind, what we thought of little England (cute, very cute), the contents of our wardrobes (bobby socks, real denim jeans) and the shimmering stars who dropped in regularly for tea. We could think of nothing more glamorous to be, nowhere more extraordinary and magical to persuade people we were from, while genuine American tourists – more crisp and matronly than glamorous – passed by smiling at our unconvincing twang and improbable fantasies. That is what the landscape of America is like: being a child in Fifties London.

But there is another way of looking at the journey. The fact is, I am not in any of the places the train passes through, I am on the train. That is my place, that is the real landscape. The extraordinary thing is not the difficulty of knowing what I am experiencing as I look through the window, but that my real landscape is filled with strangers who are thrown together

by the accident of travel and who, because of being human, or
American, or not English, or not me, are busily making themselves known to each other before they go their separate ways.
Just because we all happen to be going in the same direction,
an *us* has been formed. And I discover that however much I
wish to justify my private daydreaming and pleasurable alienation with thoughts of the difficulty of having the experience
of what has been already experienced, this random collection
of strangers has become a group to which I belong, here and
now and unavoidably. And I discover I don't want to avoid
participating in this group. Not that I could if I want to smoke
or eat or drink or see the landscape through the big picture
windows in the viewing car. But I am enjoying being a
stranger among strangers on a train making contact with other
strangers. Of course, that movie has been made, too. The
American dream or nightmare journey is as known as the
dream landscape. But the people on the train are undeniably of
my present as well as echoing my past. The bonding is fast.
We do begin to look suspiciously at newcomers entering the
smoking coach after the previous stop, feeling all the more
like an *us* as these new strangers arrive. But soon they are regulars, assimilated, and they look askance at the next strangers
to our group who enter our space. We are evidently a group to
the outside world. People who do not smoke look curiously
through the glass of the door as they pass by. Enviously even.
One woman braves the fug, opens the door, coughs, blinks and
says to us all, 'I wish I smoked. You all look as if you're having
so much fun.' We know we are a temporary agglomeration, a
group whose elements are always leaving, arriving, re-forming,
but I have the oddest, and rarest, sense of belonging in this
smoking coach and more generally on the train. A kind of
clarity of what kind of creature I might be that usually eludes

me. I see myself reflected in the company of these people who know nothing about me, and who will never think about me again once they have got back to their real lives. I sense I am seen. It may be true (it *feels* true to me) that only by being alone can I experience myself fully, but being a stranger on a train – at least for a little while – gives me a view of myself here and now, and of others, now and then, which, sitting solitary and staring, I rarely achieve.

But that too feels somehow familiar. Life on a train, in a circumscribed space with a group of others all with our lives on hold, has a correspondence to my past. The last time I experienced the enclosed life was in Ward 6 at the Maudsley Hospital in 1968. The way of the train is also the way of the boarding school, the convent, the prison and the psychiatric hospital. I was at a boarding school for a while, but my time on Ward 6 (nine months), the North Wing of St Pancras a year or so earlier (four months), the Lady Chichester Hospital in Hove when I was fourteen (five months), are my most marked experiences of life in a dedicated community, and what life on board the *MV Christiane* or the *Sunset Limited* immediately refers me back to are those intense and rare periods of camaraderie. A sense of belonging has always evaded me. For as long as I can remember I have felt myself to be not quite in the right spot, not exactly where I should be, in the wrong place, uneasy where I am, but uncertain where it is I ought to be. Even as a small child, I would prowl around looking for a spot that was mine. Usually, it was at the far end of somewhere, in a corner, behind something. A small, enclosed place with as many walls as possible to prevent surprises, and really no room for anyone else. People were more difficult. I hung around other people's families, or interrogated strangers to see if I felt all right with them. Occasionally I did, but the invitation to go home with and belong to them was never forthcoming. Finally, I concluded that the answer *on my own* was as near to being where I belong as I can muster. On a good day, it is still precisely the right location. I suppose I might trace the unease of place back to childhood and early adolescence when, for a period, I was sent to a variety of refuges, a children's home and to various families who took me in for periods to keep me out of the way of my mother. They were all kind and generous people, offering me asylum, but although it felt like ingratitude, the feeling of not belonging was perfectly reasonable. I was a stranger, even if I was glad enough not to be with my trying parents. And I have never quite shaken off the feeling that wherever it is I ought to be (as a child it should have been home, but I knew it wasn't, and therefore it was somewhere, but nowhere I knew), it isn't *here*. For a child the oddness of other homes or of other families' ways of doing things constitutes wrongness. The smells, the cooking, the patterns of daily life differ from home, and home, whether it's happy or not, is what you know, your only given place in the world. Later you may relinquish the pull towards the familiar, but the generalised desire for belonging remains, transferred in many people, I suppose, to a solid sense of themselves, so that they are not too threatened by other people and places. For me, other people and places induce what engineers call noise, and interfere with my ability to feel that I am myself, that, indeed, I have any self. But at home, in my own flat with my own mother and father, I still searched for the right spot, so the unease is internal. However, it turns out that there are places of hiatus where I can exist with other people for a while, places I can put myself in that provide me with a way of being me without having to be exclusively on my own.

Phyllis was officially catatonic. I knew nothing about her

life before she was admitted to Ward 6. What you saw was what you got with Phyllis. She was thin and somewhere in her late thirties. She was just there when I arrived at Ward 6, without a history that anyone bothered to tell me about. A fixture, with long, lank mousy-brown hair which the nurses sometimes drew into a limp hanging tail to keep it out of her eyes during the day when she sat slumped over, her back humped, her lean, expressionless face staring down at the hands in her lap. She spent all day in the chair beside the door between the television section of the dayroom and the dormitory where ten of us slept in open-fronted cubicles, five-a-side, head to head. Every morning Phyllis was pulled from under her blankets and sat on her bed, hunched like a rag doll, while the nurses manipulated her arms and legs out of a shapeless hospital nightie and into a shapeless cardigan, skirt, thick tights and carpet slippers, all dun-coloured. They washed her face and tied back her hair (though it always loosened and drooped into a semi-concealing swathe over her face) and, pronouncing her ready for the day, began to manoeuvre her towards the dayroom. A firm hand at the centre of her back once she was standing would get her to shuffle one or two reluctant steps forward to make a slow incurious progress from her bed at the far end of the dormitory to the chair beside the door.

'Morning, Phyllis,' her neighbours would say if they were feeling sociable as she came to a halt at the end of their bed, waiting for the next push. On a good day Phyllis might grunt without lifting her gaze from the lino floor. It was never clear whether it was a grunt of greeting or just a grunt. Those of us who were younger were differently angry and were likely still to be in bed, waiting to be turfed out by the ward sister after several warnings.

'Get up, get up. There's nothing wrong with you. You're

young, you're healthy. Nothing but bone-idle lazy, that's all that's the matter with you.'

The covers would be torn back, and we would hiss and curse and sit up just long enough to grab them back and bury ourselves underneath them. No different from being teenagers lying abed while our overworked parents despaired of us. Of course, we were on medication, had diagnoses, slashed ourselves, overdosed (as well as overdozed), cried inconsolably, hit out, acted out, over-ate, under-ate, withdrew, were injected, electroconvulsed, tranquillised, but essentially the three or four members of our dormitory in our early twenties were waging the same war against the grown-up world as any other right-thinking adolescent in 1968. Almost certainly, each of us had missed or muffed the opportunity to do so at a more appropriate time in regular circumstances. The game was played vigorously and to rules.

'All right, all right,' Sister Marshall would lilt at us, loud and West Indian, with a dismissive wave of the arms. 'Do what you want. You will anyway.' Her cry calls down the years. Every mother giving up, or wishing she could. 'Do what you want. You will anyway.' And Sister Winniki, an eastern European dynamo, frantically active, a haunting presence still, would tell us there was nothing wrong with us. We weren't ill like really sick people. 'Look at poor Phyllis. Every morning she gets up and dressed. She doesn't lie in bed all day. Why can't you be more like poor Phyllis? Up, up, up.'

Nobody really tried to make everyday sense of anything on Ward 6. Our everydays were different. The idea that it would be better to be like Phyllis was never challenged because its absurdity was evident, even to Sister Winniki. It was like a play we acted out, a necessary, even enjoyable pantomime that had its own rules and satisfactions, as well probably for the nursing staff as us. Their job was to make us get up and confront the day, the real world; our job was to huddle and hide from it in various combinations of fear, resentment and disgust. Phyllis just kept still. But sometimes, when one of us had a particularly noisy, riotous run-in with the staff, if you looked carefully, sidelong so she couldn't see you were looking, you might catch the catatonic, immobilised Phyllis enjoying life. For an instant, a smile would flit over her face, a wicked irrepressible grin that came and went in a second. This happened particularly when we claimed Phyllis as our commander-in-chief.

'Phyllis says I shouldn't go to occupational therapy. She says it's a waste of fucking time . . . Phyllis wants to watch this programme and she insists on it being this loud; she likes satire. Well, of course that's what she wants to listen to, she's a big fan of Hendrix, who do you think put the record on in the first place . . . Phyllis doesn't think my skirt is too short . . . Phyllis thinks knickers are a waste of the earth's resources . . . Phyllis says I shouldn't take my medication, I should smoke, refuse to go to ECT, spit out my lunch because it tastes like shit, chuck this vase of flowers just past your ear . . . Oh yeah? Just try and make me, Phyllis'll have something to say about it. Watch out or I'll set Phyllis on you . . . You don't want to mess with Phyllis, when she gets angry, anything can happen . . .'

And if you were lucky, as well as exasperating the nursing staff, you might get one of those covert grins from Phyllis, just a flash from behind the fallen curtain of hair. We firmly believed that Phyllis enjoyed playing her subversive part in the war between order and chaos. She was, after all, one of us. And so to my surprise was I.

Us were the people in our dormitory. Some willing and vigorous, some, like Phyllis, co-opted. There was another dormitory, our mirror image at the far end of the dayroom. They were not-us. They listened to John Denver and wore knee-length pleated skirts and believed in God, and that passive obedience would overcome their emotional difficulties; we listened to Hendrix and Jefferson Airplane, took drugs and demonstrated whenever possible against authority in the belief that our rage was righteous and that if we were disturbed it was only to be expected, having been born into a deeply disturbing world. I can only imagine that the staff must deliberately have organised this bipolar arrangement, it seemed so satisfyingly clear-cut. Bad girls to the left, good to the right. Most virtuous of all was Velda, in her twenties, and as smugly good as good can get. She went to church every Sunday, battled for the use of the solitary record player to clean the blasphemous air with Cliff Richard, wore her hair and clothes neat and tidy and expressed her god-sent disapproval of me and my fellow bad girls at every opportunity. In return for all this virtue she had been visited with a strange and terrible affliction. Just the sort of thing that God is known to gift to his chosen ones. She had woken up one morning ready to brush her teeth and rush off to the office only to discover she could no longer walk in the way that most people walked. Velda now lurched wildly through the world, flinging one leg out sideways and then roughly righting herself to move forward by flinging the other out at the opposite extreme angle. It was a strangely circular motion that generally got her to where she wanted to go, but very slowly and often by endangering anyone in her path. If you didn't see Velda coming in time, you were liable to get violently kicked in the shins or take a nasty poke in the ribs. In spite of months of medical investigation, no physical cause had been found for her ailment, and so, to her respectable distress, she was a patient along with the depraved and depressed in the Maudsley. On the whole, our end of the dormitory was unsympathetic. We decided it was just a way of taking up more space in the world and of threatening the rest of us, who walked in straight lines, with being knocked off our course. We didn't do sympathy much. Whether we took our tone from Sisters Winniki and Marshall or they from us, I can't say. Then the American evangelist Billy Graham came to town to save Swinging London from the wrath of God. He held mass meetings at Earl's Court where true believers, after being harangued on the horrors of hell, could queue up for the touch of Billy's wonder-working hands to absolve and cure them of whatever ailed them. To hoots of derision from the bad side of Ward 6, Velda went one evening in her Sunday finery, and after the sermon got in the queue. The next morning when she got out of bed she was cured, and with tears of joy and hallelujahs, she walked as straight a path into the dayroom as her God might wish. The devil was silenced, Cliff sang out in triumph and the shrinks discharged her as, if not cured, then symptom-free – though some of us murmured that miraculous interventions were as good a reason as any we could think of for incarceration in a mental institution. But Velda packed her bags with a superior smile on her face, in the sure and certain knowledge that the Lord was on her side. I dare say these days she tells her grandchildren about the miracle cure. I wonder if Phyllis has any grandchildren.

Also *not-us* was anyone from outside the world of the hospital. Visitors, our relatives and friends and concerned, baffled boyfriends, were not welcome. They intruded our other lives into our retreat. They dropped in on the ward from having got on with it, worked, worried, coped with all the things we couldn't or wouldn't cope with. We felt the pressure of the real world arrive with them through the ward door like a cold blow. We were vaguely aware that this life apart couldn't go on for ever. Indeed, the hospital had a two-year time limit for in-patients. Either we had to go back to the world eventually, or become permanently hospitalised in one of those places they used to frighten us with. 'If you don't make more effort, we'll send you to St Bernard's . . .' The temptation to become a basket case in a vast uncaring mental institution was very great when faced with leaving and dealing with the world in which our friends and relatives lived. Or there were the revolvers. People who left and returned, had done for years, were greeted as old friends when they came into the ward and settled back into its routine and safety with sighs of relief. Somehow, this seemed even more terrible than permanent incarceration, more terrible even than freedom. In any case, our visitors presented us with too much reality, and they did not know our codes. Sometimes it seemed they were speaking another language, in careful, patronising words about things which we had no concern for. Indeed, we had no real concern for them. We cared passionately about each other, the members of our dormitory were our family, the people we knew from outside were strangers, crude and devoid of understanding, too fearful for our psyches to speak as brutally as we spoke to each other or to know how to deal with our panic or depression or what to do when we cut our wrists. When one of us had a crisis, the staff would ask another patient to help out, because we knew the language, what the deal was. For those who didn't, who were nervous with us or took the wrong tone (too soft and gentle, too harsh and condemnatory), we had nothing but contempt. We sighed with relief when the visitors, ours or others', left us to get on with our proper existence. And for me, an only child taught by my mother that our troubles had at any cost to be kept from others, this was a most uncommon experience.

On the *Sunset Limited*, thirty years later, as evening closed in, we set off from New Orleans, Louisiana, towards Texas, and on my next visit to the smoking coach after the hour's stopover, I discovered that we had acquired some new members. A heated conversation on the relative merits of pixies and leprechauns was in full flood as I entered. A man of about fifty but looking older, the ghost of good-looking on his wrecked features, in open sandals, slacks and a short-sleeved shirt that had seen cleaner days, was sitting with his upper body propped against the end wall, a roll-up drooping dangerously from his fingers, a can of beer aslant in his other hand. His head seemed too heavy to be held quite up; his body was slumped as if at any moment it might lose its muscle tone entirely and slide to the floor like an empty bundle of clothes. Still, there was something about him, a bid for dignity perhaps, that lifted him out of the category of a regular drunken bum, and he was holding the attention of the entire coach as he spoke with slow alcohol-sodden care, waving his beer can airily about in order to emphasise the absolute reliability of what he was saying.

'Don't you talk to me about pixies, sir. Everyone knows the pixies don't exist. They are just for children and the simple-minded. Leprechauns, however, very much exist. There is one here right now. Just there in front of my right foot. Do you see? I have known many of them. I am perfectly familiar with leprechauns. The leprechauns are my friends. And if you think that they dress in green and wear ridiculous caps, then you're a fool who has never really seen the little people. They are quite normally dressed, but a lot smaller than we are. And they are Irish. As I am. Which is why they choose to accompany me and tell me things I need to know. You may claim to be Irish, but only the true Irishman can see the leprechaun. Can you see him?'

His accent veered towards English, overlaid with a slight American twang. As pure comedy he was W.C. Fields, in the current genre he was that drunken doctor who always sits in the corner seat of the stagecoach. He was explaining the reality of the invisible world with exaggerated patience to Conal, who was sitting next to Virginia several places down the carriage. I sat down in a vacant seat opposite the troubling couple. Conal sipped his whisky and smiled scornfully.

'Yah – you don't know what you're talking about, you drunken old fool. I'm an Irishman through and through. I know my leprechauns, by God I do, and they're very good friends with the pixies. And there are no pixies or leprechauns on this train because pixies and leprechauns don't travel by train. They teleport. You're completely drunk, you are drunk as a horse's arse and you know sweet fanny adams about the little people. You are a fraud. Where do you claim to be from in Ireland, my man?'

'I do not respond to abusive attacks from the coarse and ill-educated,' the other man said very grandly and with an even stronger English accent. 'I was born in Ireland but educated at Cambridge University although I was unable, because of financial constraints beyond my control, to complete my degree. I have been used to a better quality of debate and a far better class of person. The sort of person and debate, sir, that you could not even imagine. You merely show up your own ignorance and rough origins by such poorly phrased linguistic attacks. You would be regarded as very uncouth in decent society. I shall speak to you no more. And the leprechaun doesn't think highly of you, either. He's just said so, in so many words.'

He closed his eyes to show that the conversation was over. There were whoops and calls of 'Right on, man', 'Yeah, you tell him', 'Bravo', and 'Let's hear it for the leprechauns' from others in the carriage, who were convulsed with laughter at the intensity of our new man's conviction on the subject of pixies and leprechauns, as well as delighted by Conal's evident annoyance at being dismissed as a social inferior. He was cross, though he had obviously been baiting the drunken leprechaun man for some time. He muttered to Virginia about penniless drunks not knowing their place, and then having received a look of disgust from his wife, he lurched from his seat to nudge his semi-conscious rival with his elbow.

'Here, my boy, us Irish mustn't hold grudges. Have a drink.'

He held the bourbon towards the new man who wrenched his eyes slightly open at the disturbance. Seeing the glass, he lifted his head to squint a clearer view and reached for it with the hand that was still holding the smouldering stub of a cigarette.

'That's very decent of you. Let bygones be bygones. I'll drink to that.'

A man who was also new to me, sitting across the aisle, leaned forward and spoke quietly to Conal. 'Don't give him any more to drink. He's had enough. Bourbon'll finish him off.'

'None of your business. This is between me and my new friend. Man to man. Have a good drink . . . what's your name?'

'Raymond. Thank you, perhaps I misjudged you.' He took the beaker and had a long swig, then coughed convulsively for a moment. 'My word that was good. You know your liquor. Very kind. Very kind indeed.'

He coughed a little more and then sank back into semi-consciousness. The man opposite, middle-aged but smoothly handsome and gleaming like a second-string actor in a US television series, wearing neatly hemmed and pressed denims and white socks with his loafers, reached towards Raymond and took the dead cigarette stub from his fingers. Beside him were two boys in their early teens playing with a computerised fishing game, both with lank, long blond hair and blue eyes, dressed in ripped jeans and T-shirts. They had to be brothers, if not twins, and since they were too young to be legal smokers were presumably there because their father, who they called Chuck, was keeping an eye on them. They were snorting with laughter to each other at the old drunk.

'It's not funny, guys,' Chuck said, and then spoke to Conal. 'Hey man, don't give him any more to drink. The conductor only let him on the train if I promised to keep an eye on him. He's going to turn him off the train if he sees him drinking.'

'What are you, his father?' sneered Conal.

The man shrugged. 'Why get him kicked off the train? Let him sleep it off.'

The discussion was interrupted by the entrance of a boy who, having slid back the door, stood for a moment and looked carefully at everyone in the carriage. He was about fifteen, short and stocky with high, tight shoulders, a mop of thick, jet-black hair and the broad features of a Mexican Indian. But something wasn't right with him. He breathed in shallow pants as if catching the air was difficult. He was immaculately neat and clean in a checked shirt, ironed jeans and new-looking trainers, his longish hair carefully brushed back off his face, but his eyes, too wide, overtly staring at people, and with something bland and unknowing in them, suggested a young child trying to take in the world, not an adolescent in full possession of it.

'Hi,' he said in a deep, slow voice.

People in the smoking coach acknowledged him.

'Bit young to smoke, aren't you?' Conal asked.

The boy took a couple of steps into the carriage, and stopped.

'Hi,' he said again. 'I'm John.'

The voice was too slow, the speech slightly slurred, the general invitation to greet him too open. There was something wrong with John. Born wrong or an accident. He walked up to a young woman in her mid-twenties with blonde hair and stood squarely in front of her.

'Hi, I'm John.' He waited.

'Hi John,' she said with a smile that showed she understood John had difficulty.

John grinned hugely and stuck out his hand. He shook hands with the girl vigorously.

'John, I'm John. Hi.'

He went around the coach, stood in front of each of us, introduced himself, waited for each of us to say 'Hi, John', and then chuckled happily as he shook our hands. He returned to the first girl.

'Hi, I'm John.'

'I *know*,' she said with a jokey impatience, but his eyes widened and his nodding face urged her to play her part. 'OK. Hi, John.' She held out her hand again to have it shaken.

John took the hand and held on to it.

'Can I hear you breathe?'

'What?'

'Can I listen to you breathe? Can I? Please.'

The girl looked mystified. John moved up close to her so that their knees touched, and bent down to rest the side of his face and one ear against her chest between her left breast and shoulder. She stiffened.

'Breathe. Please breathe. Like this,' John pleaded, and panted exaggeratedly to show her what to do. 'Like that. Do it. Please. Do it.'

The girl threw a look of helpless what-the-hell around the coach and panted a little, while we smiled at the comedy and at her willingness to do something for the unfortunate John. What the hell?

'Don't stop. More. Breathe harder,' said John hunched over.

She panted a little more and then stopped, taking John gently by the shoulders and lifting his face off her chest.

'That's enough.'

John stood up and grinned hugely.

'Thank you. Thank you.'

Then it was my turn. John rested his head against my chest and I did a bit of panting. Virginia and a couple of other women declined to perform, but gently, with smiles. Bet agreed and did a quick pant. Then one of the men, all of whom had been looking on amazed, as much by our letting John put his head on our breast and panting for him as by the oddness of John's wishes, said, 'OK, that's enough, John. I expect your parents are wondering where you are.' The children's hour was up.

John grinned his understanding that his period with the grown-ups was over. All children know they are on borrowed time when adults indulge them. 'OK. Bye,' he called amiably and waved to everyone at the door.

'Bye, John,' we called.

We laughed a little nervously when he left and speculated about what was the matter with him. The men were uncertain.

'Do you think it's all right, him going around like that? Doing that stuff? Where are his parents?'

'Having a well-earned break, probably,' I said. 'He's

harmless. It must feel good and safe having his ear against someone's heart and hearing their breath.' One of my cats does much the same thing.

'Yeah,' said Conal. 'I bet. Can I have a go, Miss British?'

'Shut your mouth,' Virginia rasped. 'You're the wrong kind of retard.'

A small spark of hatred lit up between them and then died.

The women in the coach, even those who had refused to join in John's game, conceded the weirdness of John's public behaviour but recognised his infantile condition and his unconcealed needs. The men were disturbed and suspicious. Poor John, stopped in his emotional and intellectual tracks by something, was getting away with behaviour that they were forbidden. He was somehow cheating, and like older brothers no longer permitted the breast, they were battling with and failing to conceal their jealousy. Maybe, even, he was perfectly all right, but putting it on to get what he wanted: a cunning perve. Men knew about these things. And if he was a genuine retard, then who knew what he would do if he lost control. Desire without control was a terrifying prospect. Men knew about these things.

'Well,' Raymond's defender, Chuck, said. 'He ought to be supervised. You never know with these people.'

There were masculine murmurs of agreement, even from the younger men. The women glanced at each other knowingly, I thought, and let it go. I assumed that what the women knew was not just about male anxiety, but also what I had noticed when John had his head on my chest and I looked down into the well between us: that he accompanied the pleasurable smile at the sound and vibration of another's breath and heartbeat with rapid light movements of his hand on his penis under his jeans. It was more like vague flapping at himself than considered stroking. If it was masturbation, it was half-hearted, not designed to achieve an orgasm, almost an absent-minded accompaniment to his delight. He hadn't touched any part of anyone's body apart from with his cheek and ear. I presumed the other women had seen this, as I had, and concluded that it would be better if the men didn't know.

Raymond slept through most of this, but the next time I looked at him, he was staring hard at me.

'You're an English lady,' he told me. 'Speak to me in your lovely English accent. Come over here and talk to me.'

I sat next to him and told him where I came from in London.

'Yes, yes, I know Hampstead. The Heath. Ah, you remind me of my past. I had a happy childhood. Now . . .'

There was a rambling story of a privileged childhood in Ireland and England, of ex-wives, of money made and lost through carelessness and alimony, of a daughter who would have nothing to do with him, who had refused to take his call when he had phoned. He couldn't remember what he had been doing in New Orleans. He lived in Los Angeles. Chuck, sitting opposite with the two boys, had found him (he himself had no recollection of anything until he was on the train) unconscious on the floor of the station concourse. People had stepped around him fastidiously, taking him for a drunken sleeping bum. In fact, although he was paralytic with drink, he had actually been knocked unconscious and mugged by some kids who had taken all his cash but who, in their hurry to get away in the busy station, had left his gold chain bracelet, expensive watch, credit cards and a return ticket for the *Sunset Limited* to LA. Thus he was penniless but his credit was good so he could buy drinks and cigarettes from the guy in the bar.

Chuck had poured some coffee down him, taken him to the train after Raymond had refused to go to hospital or have anything to do with the cops, and battled with the conductor to allow Raymond to make the journey. Eventually, the conductor agreed on condition that Chuck remained responsible for him and with the proviso that if he caught Raymond drinking he would be thrown off the train at the next station. Chuck, who was listening to Raymond's slurred and halting story, raised his eyebrows in a what-are-you-going-to-do gesture when I looked at him.

'It's the booze, you see,' Raymond sighed, explaining everything. 'But when you've lost everything because of the booze, you only have the booze left to comfort you.'

We were in a different genre now. Raymond was one of those remorseful, hopeless, sentimental drunks that Hollywood did so well. James Mason in *A Star is Born*, Ray Milland in *The Lost Weekend*. A bit of a gent who had had something to lose and who had lost it, all except the ghost of a bit of class, real or imagined. I have a soft spot for remorseful, hopeless, sentimental drunks. Raymond had trailed off and was asleep. I took the can of beer from his hand and put it on the table.

'I can't make him eat anything,' Chuck said. 'I got the bartender to refuse to sell him any more drink, but people keep buying him beer.'

The two boys had left the carriage to get sandwiches.

'It's good of you to look out for him. And you've got your sons.'

He shook his head and laughed a bit. 'They're not mine. They latched on to me at the station. Going to LA, back to their mother. They were in trouble with the police, just petty theft, kids' stuff. I got the police to put them in my care until we get to LA. They're good kids. Just a bit messed up.'

Chuck was an all-purpose Samaritan. Maybe he travelled the rails doing good wherever it was needed. Perhaps the boys were the ones who had rolled Raymond, and Chuck had scooped the whole damn lot of them into his care. Or maybe Chuck was a railroad Fagin who still had his eyes on Raymond's bracelet and watch. Or the Pied Piper. Anything was possible. Everything was a raw component in a story that had not been finalised. We were on a train, out of the way of our lives, any of us could tell any story we liked. We were, for the time being, just the story we told.

'Do you live in LA?'

'No. Just making a visit.' He had no more to say about himself. The two boys came back carrying cans. 'Hey, guys, I said no beer. You're underage.'

They moaned a little but handed the cans over. It seemed they wanted to be in someone's charge.

Raymond snorted awake. He turned to look at me, and sighed. More like Alice's White Knight than James Mason. He sloped towards me, partly leaning against my shoulder for support, partly speaking confidentially close to my ear. He stroked my upper arm gently with his fingertips.

'You've got such silky skin. And the way you speak. If only I had met you a few years ago. I could have offered you . . . You could have loved me and I'd never have got into this mess . . .'

'Oh, I don't think so, Raymond. I'm not very good at relationships.'

I wasn't keen on the notion that it was only an accident of timing that had kept us apart; not for either of us. I didn't think it would help him much to have something else to mourn, and I didn't like his appropriation of my alternative past. That story was mine to play with. I resented the twinge of guilt I had to suppress at not having turned up in time to prevent Raymond sliding into alcoholism. Still, I spoke gently, because what else do hopeless drunks have but their recollection of pasts that never happened? He wasn't listening. He'd shifted to a present which suddenly had become to him as tractable as his own history.

'Come and live with me in North Beach. I've got enough money to take care of you. You wouldn't want for anything, I swear. I'd stop drinking if I had you, I know I would. I wouldn't need to drink, I'd have everything I wanted. I'd cherish you. We'd be so good together. There's culture in LA. We'd go to the theatre and read books, and walk by the sea. What do you say? I mean it. We could be happy.'

I didn't answer. I didn't think it was my place. He wasn't really talking to me. He was merely musing on how life was supposed to have turned out. It was all very simple, how could it have gone so complicatedly wrong? He gazed into the how-it-might-have-been.

'All I want . . . all I want is to wake up in the morning next to you still asleep with your leg flung over my thigh. Is that too much to ask?' he murmured, and then turned to me directly. 'To feel the weight of your sweet silken leg stretched out across my thigh when I wake in the morning. Is that too much to ask?'

Well, yes, it was. I was quite sorry that it was, because as wishes go it didn't seem unreasonable, but it was, in fact, too much to ask, or at any rate more than was going to happen. My leg had other places to be. My own plans and daydreams didn't reside in Long Beach with a recovering alcoholic. But for a fleeting second it didn't seem too much to ask as I caught the image of our two bodies, entangled from the exertions of love, drifted into sleep . . . The morning sun glows through the bedroom curtains and Raymond wakes, filled with a new life and a love that cleared away the mess to reveal quiet joy and contentment. I wake, we smile, sip coffee. Beneath his sloughed off self-destructive shell I've discovered layers of knowledge and being that astonish me with their understanding and grace. His drunken intuition was right. We are matched: companions and lovers, settled into a gentle, long-term alliance, two halves come together, at last easy. We kiss good morning and there are no more battles to be fought. Is it really too much to ask? Couldn't an act of will, a leap of faith, make it possible? Why not an accident of timing *not* missed and regretted, but presented and taken right now in the present? Why shouldn't people make good things happen? Just ordinary good things, love, contentment. Is that too much to ask? Why not take a random encounter and a sentimental fantasy and make them into a fact? Say yes to Raymond. Follow the fleeting whim. Take a risk, turn life upside-down and head for North Beach. What's to stop this story from being the one where she gets on a train, takes an unnecessary journey, meets a drunk and turns it deliberately into a happily-ever-after? Make it happen. Why shouldn't happiness (whatever that is) be made to happen; we make unhappiness happen all the time? It's true I'm not unhappy in my real life, that it is very close to precisely how I want it to be. And it's true that the rescue fantasies of drunks are invariably built on sand. I also know that the chances of my being content with anyone who wears a gold bracelet are very slim. But to what extent is what someone else needs more important than what I want? What if I could be just plain useful to Raymond's life? What do I ever do for other people? Isn't my life good because I please myself? Why should I have it so easy? Why not make the effort to be with someone who is light years from my heart and mind? Who the hell do I think I am?

Here's the thing about sentimentality and fatally flawed wishful thinking: it's virulently contagious. And that capacity we have for making unhappiness happen is powerful enough to take the apparent form of its own opposite. For just a moment it's as if I've never lived, never had any experience of anything. The fantasy solution of living together with my memoryless friend from St Pancras Hospital was not even the first. The first was a daydream of living alone with my father – it would all be all right if only my mother wasn't around, if only my stepmother could be got rid of. It came disastrously true when he left my stepmother and got a flat for just him and me when I was thirteen. Hopeless. Domestic battles, his romances and/or financial plans (often one and the same thing, it turned out) ruined by my presence, my jealousy, my disappointment, his insensitivity, his disappointment. He was back with my stepmother in just weeks, and I was a defeated prisoner living sullenly in the attic until I got my social worker to send me back to boarding school. I know what happens when dreams come true. Then the memoryless man. And then there was Ralph: me twenty, him mid-fifties and far gone in alcoholism, also at St Pancras after John had gone back to his life. Hours and hours in a side room persuading him not to go out and get a drink. So much talking. Then he'd disappear and come back days later shaking and frail, full of determination not to let me down. In love with me, his young angel of sobriety. Eventually, they threw him out. Too many lapses. His liver was shot. His case was medical. A few weeks later I got a suicide note, apologetic, lyrical with love and loss. What might have been. But the actual suicide was several months later when he was found dead in bed with a case of empty whisky bottles beneath. That was Ralph. He used to come with me to Biba's and watch me buy feather boas and minidresses. His father had been a Georgian poet. And there was H from the French Pub – wistful but very married with kids. And Michael, wildly, enchantingly drunk while he was young, always forgiven, so unreliable that if he said he would meet you at the cinema, you could be sure it was OK to stay in and wash your hair. Then older, still charming, but with the shakes, all the opportunities that his talent and charm had brought long gone in his conscious preference for alcohol. Then Michael was dead and we had a rousing funeral with hundreds of old friends and fellow drinkers, singing the Internationale and 'The Wild Colonial Boy', and celebrating the story that in his final moments he had raised a ghostly glass and said, 'Fuck the begrudgers.' A veritable Don Giovanni of the Gin. Somehow a string of hopeless drunks and wishful thinkers who conceived of me as a route back to life or included me in passing on their journey in the other direction. And I was moved by their intentions, their hopelessness, their existential necessity, their self-destructiveness. Each time, I forgot for a moment what I already knew. Maybe this could work, I'd think, as I never thought about sober, reliable lovers. Though the fact that none of them could ever work must have been the real attraction. Eventually, I stopped doing that, because, perhaps, I no longer needed other people's desperate daydreams to animate my life. Or finally, experience had told.

But there I was on the train in America, and for just a second, as if I'd been born yesterday, Raymond's unrealisable fantasies sounded plausible. Or the rhythm of the metal wheels on the track made them sound so. Or my immersion in the sentimental narrative of an American train journey had given cliché credibility. And why not? Redemption stories and romance are woven into the fabric of the human mind, just

like the other apparently tougher tales of solitude and loss, disappointment and hardship never recompensed. The fiction of
dirty realism is no less sentimental and clichéd than the
romantic fantasy of dreams come true. In America every story
has happily-ever-after either as an ending or a howling oppo-
sition. The template story is known, how it should be, and all
the stories told on the journey are exemplars of closeness or
distance from the true tale. Is that solely American? Probably
not, but the dream of meeting the stranger who is the com-
pleting half, the compensating force, takes a decidedly
dystopian, misanthropic turn in the hands of the Englishman
who made *Strangers on a Train*. Hitchcock's stranger is the
devil, a nightmare, a punishment for not keeping oneself
safely contained while in transit between realities. In England
we don't talk to strangers, we sit solitary and silent on our
journeys. In the movie, Bruno Anthony is Guy Haines's retri-
bution for allowing his island self to be breached. Hitchcock,
the archetypal Englishman, knows through and through that
you must never talk to strangers. He issued a gleeful warning
to America about the terrible repercussions of openness and
optimism. But still they talk to strangers on the train and hope
that they will transform their lives into all the good things a
life should be. And still the strangers listen, lulled into imag-
inative compliance by their temporary rootlessness and the
dreamy syncopation of the rails.

'So, what do you think?' Raymond asked me, determined to
be taken seriously. He didn't even know my name.

'Get sober, and we can think about it,' I said, knowing I was
asking too much, at least, hoping so.

'I'll stop drinking and get everything straight in North
Beach. Then I'll call you, and you can come out for a visit.
How's that?'

'OK. When you've been sober for two or three months, I'll come and see you.'

What the fuck am I talking about? What if, unlike all the other drunks I've known, he actually goes and stays on the wagon? Well, then, I'll visit him in LA. Why not? In any case, as soon as I leave the train, he'll forget he ever met me, or I'll slip into all the other misty opportunities that were not taken. Still, I'm sorry I said it. But Raymond is asleep or unconscious.

When I looked up, Chuck was watching me.

'Appealing, kind of, isn't it?' he said, looking steadily at me as if he were underlining the thoughts and unease that had been going through my mind. I was beginning to get the feeling that Chuck might turn out to be the authorial voice of our journey. I nodded, guilty and embarrassed that I had been so obvious, at any rate, that I had been so observed.

'You get sucked into daydreams.'

'Yeah. Best not though, it won't help him.'

Three meals a day came as part of the fare if you had a sleeping compartment. People in seats had to pay to eat in the restaurant car, bought snacks at the bar, or came equipped with food for the journey. Bet and I usually ate together in the restaurant car, on the lower floor just before the smoking coach. We had breakfast, lunch and dinner, seated by the dining steward opposite paired strangers or married couples. You don't get to choose where you sit in the confines of a train dining car. It was a realm of its own, where the maître d' was both host and not so very benevolent dictator. Waiters zipped up and down the narrow corridor between the tables, more or less immune to the swaying of the car. Speed, efficiency and an indefinable mix of banter and contempt was what you got with the restaurant car staff. Throughput was the thing. You booked a time to eat and waited until your party's name was called, then you'd better get there quick if you didn't want to feel the honed edge of the dining steward's tongue. The food – 'regional specialities freshly prepared by on-board chefs' – was awful: beef or chicken in a variety of glutinous sauces (Cajun around New Orleans, spicy chilli in New Mexico, but all generally brownish), microwave reheated to within an inch of its miserable life; salad as an automatic starter – shards of flagging iceberg lettuce and a choice of distressing dressings in plastic pouches. Breakfast was the best, at least bringing to mind the wonders of sausage and hash browns at a diner, though currently as we were in the South it was necessary to avoid at all costs the 'grits' option. Some claimed that quality had nothing to do with avoiding the grits (something dangerously like wallpaper paste mixed with, well, grit) served on the train, that one should avoid them at all times and anywhere. But the quantities were vast and those of us who had sleeping accommodation had paid for it, so we chomped through our portions. In any case, the mealtime calls served the same function as they do in hospital, breaking up, pacing out the day. It was part of our institutionalised behaviour.

Dinner over, in the dark of Sunday night, we slipped through the South, past invisible bayous and alligators, and into Texas. I put out my final cigarette around midnight somewhere between Lafayette and Lake Charles and said goodnight to my fellow smokers, only the younger of whom were still up. Chuck had persuaded Raymond to return to his seat in front of him and the boys. Bet had gone to bed straight after dinner. She had been subdued all day, ever since the accident, about which people spoke only in undertones to newcomers to indicate what kind of a journey it had been so far. Maddy and her DJ friend had popped in and out of the smoking coach all day, but apart from a generalised greeting, were locked onto each other, talking close and urgently. Conal wandered in now and then with his bourbon for a quick cigarette and a sneer while Virginia slept in their extra first-class double sleeping compartment. George with his baseball cap on backwards had finished with Heidegger and was now on to Viktor Frankl, but it was face down on his lap as he listened to (and I eavesdropped on) another young black guy, Chris, no more than twenty-five, I guessed, who sat next to him. He was telling George that he was travelling with his wife and two young kids from New York to California to see his family who had never met his children. 'I got unpaid leave from work. My folks haven't seen my kids, and who knows when I'll be able to visit them again?' He couldn't stay talking long, because he had to get back to his wife. He'd tried to persuade her to come and sit in the smoking coach, but she couldn't take the fumes.

'I told her there were some real interesting people in here. But she hates the smell of smoke, and anyway, she's shy.'

Chris had a worried look about him. When he'd booked the train, he told George, he hadn't realised how expensive food was on board. He'd run out of money and there were two more days and a night to go before they arrived. Last night he'd got the dining-room steward to let him do some washing-up in return for a meal for himself, his wife and the kids. This evening he was helping the sleeping-car stewards clean up. But he was anxious about the following night. Still, he figured he could persuade someone on board to let him work for food.

'Maybe, if I get lucky, they'll let me drive the train,' he laughed.

George listened sympathetically. Two young women came

in who I'd never seen before, and I would have remembered.
They weren't more than teenagers, very young black women,
and they were dressed to kill, standing out as madly, idioti-
cally glamorous among the other, comfortably dressed
travellers. They wore skin-tight jeans, high heels, midriff-
revealing tops with extra holes cut out to expose as much
flesh as possible, glossy make-up and gold jewellery wherever
there was space. They spoke to each other intensely, as if they
had urgent information to convey, though clearly it was a
strategy for appearing not to notice that they were being
noticed, which was their main objective. They chattered and
chirruped their way into the smoking coach without acknowledging anyone else but found seats for themselves next to a
young white man who had come in not long before and sat on
the other side of George. He went on high alert as they
arrived, sitting to attention as the girls settled themselves,
wriggling and giggling, down. He tried to stay cool for a
second and a half before he gave up all appearances of resistance and nervously offered them each a cigarette. Soon they
were all deep in conversation and getting on like a house on
fire. George looked across at me and nudged Chris. He raised
his hand to his throat, stroking it once or twice. Their cigarettes finished, the girls teetered noisily to the door, followed
sheepishly by the young man.

'Hey man, later. We're heading for the bar,' he said to
George, a mixture of pride and wonderment on his face.
George gave him a warning look, but the trio were gone. He
shook his head in amused pity.

'Did you see?' he said to me, and then turned to Chris.

'See what?' I said. Chris looked baffled.

George put his hand up to his throat again. 'He's going to
get a shock. Did you catch their Adam's apples?'

I had been too entertained by their self-excited manner-
isms and gaudy seduction technique, and Chris was absorbed
in his own problems.

'They were really good, but there's nothing you can do
about the Adam's apple. They were guys. Take a look next
time they come in.'

And, of course, it would have explained everything. I waited
for a while, but they didn't return to the smoking coach.

It was my last full night on the train. I spent a long time
lying awake in my bunk, not wanting to miss the stars passing
and the rhythm of train rocking me. Bet, Raymond, Chris,
Conal, Virginia, Maddy, the TVs and John rolled around in
my mind, a handful of human stories, only a tiny sample of
the available lives that the train happened to be transporting
along with me. As I lay there, all the separate stories, all those
minds and hearts took on volume and mass, occupying the
empty space in my compartment, squeezing out the very air
before spreading to the corridor outside and the entire train. I
breathed in the stories, known and unknown, and felt their
weight bearing down on me. When I checked on the inky sky
outside there was all the empty space of the universe, black
and endless, stars and vacancy, on and on in silence for ever,
while on the speeding train the crush of human consciousness,
of existence, all of it, crammed in, congealed into a sticky
writhing narrative, telling itself repeatedly, and saying everything and nothing. I tried to make it feel normal – the longest
main street in the USA – but it remained overwhelming, cat-
astrophic. Finally I slept to avoid the panic that was rising.

After breakfast, the smoking coach was almost full with all our
regulars deep in urgent conversation and a few newcomers. Bet
was already there, she had skipped eating.

'Jesus, Jenny, you'll never guess . . .'

I was barely through the door. She was scandalised.

'That John. He's just been in—'

'Yeah,' said Conal. 'Your sweet little innocent kid.'

'He was tricking us . . .'

'You women . . .' Conal snorted in disgust.

'He was, you know, touching himself . . . down there, you know . . . all the time . . . while we let him put his head on our—'

'Masturbating?' I said. 'Yes, I know. Well, sort of masturbating.'

'You knew?' the blonde girl said, astonished.

'You knew, you mean, you knew what he was up to?' Bet said.

'He wasn't up to anything. He was just getting his pleasure confused, or not confused.'

'He was being sexually abusive,' Chuck said, with a look of grave anger on his face.

'Yeah,' Gail bellowed. 'Getting off on it.'

'Well, yes. Didn't you know?'

Everyone was horrified, though there was a degree of amazement rather than wrath in the women's outrage. The men were solemn and vengeful. Their worst fears had been confirmed. Poor retarded John had been getting sexual pleasure right there in front of our eyes, and getting away with it. Had he been laughing at them all along?

'He's a pervert. We ought to tell the conductor to get the police at the next stop.'

'What kind of parents are they, letting him wander round on his own?'

'He could be dangerous. What if he molests kids on the train? We've got to report him.'

'He should be restrained.'

'He ought to be thrown off the train.'

'But he's not dangerous,' I said. 'He's just not sophisticated enough to keep things separate. He makes associations that we don't allow ourselves to make.'

'He's got no control. There are little kids, Gail's kids, on the train. How do you know he's going to stop at touching himself?'

Of course, I didn't. Bet was intrigued by my lack of alarm, she was half convinced I was right, but it occurred to me now that I might be wrong. Maybe he could spiral out of control. What about kids? What made me so sure John was a harmless innocent? Yet I was sure, and I was more disturbed by the growing anger in the smoking coach which threatened to turn nasty. A mob was in the making.

'Why don't we ask the conductor to check with his parents or whoever he's with, and see what they say? He's very well cared for, they don't seem to neglect him. They must think he's safe if they let him wander about on his own.'

'Or they don't know, and don't want to know.'

Maybe they were right. Who knew what people were capable of? Who knew how much people chose not to know? Anyway, John had been expelled from the smoking coach. Chuck had sent him out and told him not to come back, that he was too young to be there (his blond charges notwithstanding) and that he had to stay with his folks. John had taken fright, according to Bet, who wasn't sure whether this was a good thing or not. No one mentioned him to the conductor as he scowled in on us during his regular inspection. He walked through the coach and examined the contents of the garbage bin on the end wall, wrinkling his nose in disgust at the butt ends but not letting that stop him checking for empty beer cans. I looked around at the irate passengers, but no one seemed inclined to say anything to the conductor about John.

Later that morning the train came to a halt in the middle of nowhere, between San Antonio and Del Rio. Nothing happened for half an hour and then a message came over the tannoy that we were held up on the single track by a goods train that had broken down in front of us. It had been decided that we would shunt the train ahead to the nearest branch line. It would be quicker, we were told, than waiting for it to be repaired. This way only another hour or so would be added to the three we had already lost. Groans of disbelief went up in the smoking coach, and doubtless throughout the train. Mostly we were laughing and wondering what else this journey would have to offer.

The moment of connection between our engine and the goods train turned out to be more than the slight bump we were warned of over the tannoy. We lurched hard as we made contact with the train in front. People were thrown back, in some cases off their chairs. Raymond, in a drunken haze all morning, slid almost gracefully to the floor and seemed comfortable enough where he landed. But Bet, being tiny and tense, was thrown hard against the wall. She yelled in pain, and when we had got straight again, she held her shoulder and winced.

'I think I've dislocated my goddammed shoulder. Jesus, what else is going to happen? How bad can a journey get? It's not enough why I had to take this trip at all, but we ran over three people and now we're shunting trains. I can't take any more of this.'

After a moment's silence, there was a message on the tannoy again.

'Is there a doctor on the train? Would anyone with any medical training please see the conductor.'

'Jesus. Jesus Christ,' Bet moaned.

Eventually we got going again, at a snail's pace, and pushed the train in front for about an hour before a somewhat gentler lurch indicated that we had disconnected from it and could get back on course. By this time, the drinks were flowing and a party was in full swing. We were quite fearless about the conductor now. Just let him try to chuck us off this sorry apology for a train journey. There was a mood of reckless abandon, of lost souls trapped on a drifting ship, of simply waiting for the next disaster to occur. I went down to the bar to get Bet and me a couple of cans of Manhattans (yes, really, *cans*). Chris was sitting at one of the tables with his wife and kids having Cokes. Without thinking about it much, I fished in my bag and went up to their table, saying hello to his wife and the little ones. Then I squatted down beside Chris. I hadn't rehearsed anything.

'Hi. Will you do me a favour?'

Chris looked alarmed, glanced at his wife, but didn't look at me. 'What?'

'For dinner this evening,' I said, sliding the scrunched up fifty-dollar bill I'd taken out of my bag across the table and under his hand. I've rarely felt so inept. It wasn't a big deal. I had intended not to make it a big deal, but I hadn't the faintest idea how to give someone money. He hadn't asked for any, I had enough not to make it painful. I just wanted to shift some of my surplus to Chris, who could use it. I didn't want to offend him. I didn't see it as a handout, more as a redistribution, and not particularly princely at that. But I had been so awkward. *Will you do me a favour?* Apologetic, surreptitious and alarming. I had somehow embarrassed all of us. Chris's wife signalled him to take the money. He looked at me coldly.

'OK,' he said. 'And?'

I didn't understand. 'Nothing.'

He continued to look at me as if waiting for something.

'Sorry . . .' I tailed off, and fled back to the smoking coach, minus the Manhattans. It didn't matter. Conal had arrived and was freely distributing his bourbon. It had got quite rowdy. People were telling tales of their worst train journeys and great historical Amtrak disasters. Even Maddy and her DJ dragged themselves apart from each other to contribute.

'There was that train wreck a few years back on this route. Back South. You remember reading about it? This paddle-boat had hit the rail bridge but they didn't report it. The bridge must have been weakened or something, because part of it collapsed when the train crossed. All the coaches went down into the swamp. But it was a pretty low bridge – I guess that's why the paddleboat went into it. Amazingly, not many people were hurt. They got out of the coaches and were swimming in the water. Some people drowned, I guess, but most were OK. But it was an alligator swamp. The train wreck didn't kill them, the alligators did. Came from every direction, and you know they can't chew. They get hold of a bit of you and just twist themselves round and round until the victim's drowned. Anyway, most of them survived the train wreck but were killed by alligators.'

There was a wide-eyed silence for a moment. Then Bet wailed.

'Oh Jesus . . .'

'Yeah,' DJ said. 'And they don't just eat them there and then. Alligators don't like fresh meat, I heard. They keep them until they're well—'

'Shut up,' Maddy squealed. And the coach collapsed into gales of ghoulish, whooping laughter. Even Raymond had peeked out of his semi-coma and grinned hugely at being part of the fun.

Chris came into the smoking coach and sat down next to me. 'I'm sorry about earlier.'

'Why?'

'I'm sorry I was suspicious. When you said do me a favour, I thought you were giving me money . . . to do something. I thought there was something you wanted.'

'Oh Christ. I'm sorry, that was my fault. It was a stupid thing to say.'

'No, it was me. I didn't believe people did that kind of thing without wanting something.'

'It isn't anything. It wasn't much. I had it. When you've got a spare fifty, you can give it back to someone who needs it. I just didn't want it to be anything special.'

Chris nodded. 'Yeah, I've given stuff to people. But no one's given me anything until now. Thanks.'

It was all out of hand. A very small donation. I had handled it so badly. Why is it so difficult? Only my embarrassment had made it difficult and allowed a misunderstanding. The whole episode made me ashamed. Chris and I shrugged a smile at each other and he went back to his family.

By now the party slipped easily into community singing (Johnny Ray, Sonny and Cher, Tammy Wynette and Patsy Kline were deemed suitable) until, about eight-thirty, over four hours late, we arrived for a twenty-minute stop at El Paso. This was the end of the line for Bet, who had been free with her covered Coke bottle, and was quite jolly in spite of evidently having a bad pain in her shoulder. There were fond farewells from her fellow travellers, who were losing one of the old-timers. She invited me on to the platform to meet her hero. He was there, a middling-height, stocky man with a broad moustache, cowboy boots, jeans and jeans jacket. He ducked his head in acknowledgement of me as Bet started to introduce us, but he was busy. He had a small child in one arm and a large suitcase in the other. A massively pregnant young woman was walking just ahead of him.

'Hi, hon, be with you in just a moment.'

'It's this coach,' the pregnant woman called back at him, and she and the hero disappeared on to the train. Bet and I stood watching him.

'Ain't he wonderful? Always helping people.'

I had a moment of alarm, but Hero returned.

'Hero, this is my new friend Jenny. Jenny, my hero.'

We shook hands. I said I was happy to meet him, that any hero of Bet's was a hero of mine. He grinned modestly.

'Ready, hon?'

'Sure thing. Jenny's gonna come and visit with us real soon.'

'Great.'

We hugged goodbye, and Bet winced as I crushed her sore shoulder. As they headed off for the hero's four by four I could hear Bet's rasping voice.

'How's Mikey been? Jesus, you won't believe what kind of a journey I've had . . .'

By the Time I Got to Phoenix

Suburban Phoenix is a perfect place to take refuge from an excess of commerce with the world. I sat in the shade of a banana tree by the swimming pool fringed with towering date palms: a garden oasis, the silence of the late morning heat buzzing, nothing moving under the blazing sun except an occasional butterfly lurching between shrubs, the cat raising its head from time to time to see if anything had changed and dropping back into its torpor. Now and then I slipped into the water to cool off before returning to my chair and a recuperating torpor of my own. I felt as if I had been ill. With that sense of consciously getting yourself back, of relearning the normal you after the body has been haywire, I was hyper-alert to my own processes: aware of every movement I made, of the precise physical requirements for each activity, of microscopic muscular changes as my eyes followed the passing butterfly, as my chest raised and lowered to breathe, as I reached for my

glass of orange juice or stretched out my leg to stroke the cat
with my foot. I didn't even blink without knowing I was doing
it. The heat (it was around 108 degrees) had something to do
with making every slight effort noticeable, but it was also a
mental state of watchfulness that came with the sudden release
from the company of others, a stark focusing on who that
person had been who had watched, listened, talked, and inter-
acted and been seen by others. The impression of my fellow
travellers remained with me, I felt, almost physically, like the
pale marks left on the flesh after it has been squeezed.

Every two weeks in rotation, each subdivision of suburban
Phoenix is flooded. The water authority dammed the Salt
River into a series of lakes in the mountains east of Phoenix
and then created two canals to deliver the water to residents so
that their gardens might thrive in the desert. Every fortnight,
at a given time, each householder turns on the taps connected
to buried pipes linked to the canal, and the water authority's
man, the *zanjero* (Spanish for ditch-rider and pronounced
sahn-hair'-oh, the website explains helpfully), opens the company valve so that hundreds of gallons of precious water seeps
up over the ground. The flood inundates each property, and
the water sits on the surface three or more inches deep for
hours until it is absorbed into the soil to keep the front lawns
the most garish green imaginable, to make the palms so tall
and so heavy with dates that they have to be collected profes-
sionally, to make the banana trees fruit, and the oranges and
lemons hang heavy from their branches in this reclaimed patch
of Arizona desert land. Arizona: named I suppose by the
Spanish for the aridity of the area. (Maria, my hostess, is orig-
inally from Ecuador. Sometimes she goes to New York, or
back home to Ecuador purely to find some rain. She longs for
clouds, dull days and downpours.) The water from the

dammed Salt River sinks into the naturally bone-dry cultivated gardens so that suburban America can live in a high
degree of aesthetic and physical comfort in an environment
inimical to all life except the cactus. The date palms, called
Sphinx, are known only in Phoenix and possibly Saudi Arabia.
Word is, the Phoenix trees were first obtained in Saudi Arabia
in 1917. Another story tells of a single Sphinx date tree being
'discovered' in a backyard near Phoenix in 1919, and its twelve
offshoots providing the stock for all the rest, no other examples of the species being found anywhere in the world.
Whatever the truth of the origin of the Sphinx date palm, it is
strange to find oneself sitting in this modern high-tech water-
hole. Except for the furnace-like heat, which human ingenuity
has yet to find a way to control economically, I might have
been lounging in a glassed-in bubble, a cultivated Eden in a
surrounding wilderness. My kindly hosts had left me to myself
for the afternoon. At least some of the time I wept.

In 1962 I left the Lady Chichester Hospital in Hove for
London, rescued by an act of charity, taken in by someone I
had never met who had heard of my trouble from her son,
from whose school I had been expelled. She offered a place to
live, more education, a kind of normal life. After the ups and
downs of being with my parents and spending several months
being kept apart from them in this psychiatric hospital by
doctors who had no more idea of what was going to happen
next in my life than I did, the arbitrary rescue came and it
seemed I was all set for everything turning out well, quite
against the odds. It was, I was, going to be OK after all. A
lucky escape from chaos and distress. Some dark doomed alley
it was generally agreed I would have been forced to go down
by previous circumstances beyond my control had miraculously been avoided. I'd been offered the chance to subvert the

poor prognosis assumed by everyone, including me, for someone of fifteen already expelled from school, alienated from
her parents and in the loony bin. So there I was, in London,
saved – and I was consumed with guilt. Survivor guilt, they
would call it now. I had lived, at the Lady Chichester, with
others whose chaos and distress at least matched mine. Now,
for no reason that I could fathom, accidentally, arbitrarily, I
had been rescued. I had left my fearful, desperate friends
behind. But who was going to rescue them? My fellow
inmates – friends – had waved me off generously, quite
pleased, I suppose, to discover that rescue from out of the
blue was at least possible. I left them in hospital with either a
little more hope, or, suspecting that good luck from out of the
blue was a limited commodity, a little less. I was of the latter
sort, and felt I carried away with me a large chunk of the good
luck generally available to the inmates of the Lady Chichester
Hospital. Bolts from the blue, I and they knew quite well,
could be bad as well as good news. The blue, we like to
believe, is a place apart from life, a separate realm where the
discontinuities exist, queuing, or more likely jostling, for their
moment to drop on an unsuspecting world. The bolts from the
blue manifest themselves in unscheduled knocks on the front
door, the phone ringing late at night, a follow-up visit to a
doctor's surgery, a lost footing on the stairs, someone else's
heart attack or the snapped brake cable in a car passing you on
the street, the notification that you are not the only one who
knows the pin number of your credit card, a sudden gust of
wind uprooting *that* tree, the erupting of a nearby volcano
that has been inert for decades before you arrived for your
holiday, the parting of the earth along a quiescent fault line
that runs along your route to work, the absence of a scheduled
knock on the front door or ringing of the phone. Or a letter

saying, you don't know me, but I've heard about you from my son, come and live with me and I'll sort things out. Out of the blue. Who could have expected . . . ? How could you guess . . . ? Why would you imagine . . . ? How could you know . . . ? And whether the bolt is good or bad there are two equally valid, equally felt responses: *why me?*, and *yes, of course, what else could have happened?* So we wait, when we are stuck, anticipating, with hope and fear, the bolt that will come out of the blue. And sometimes, like a bolt from the blue, it doesn't come.

Saved from whatever unimaginable but obviously dreadful fate would have been mine, in a comfortable house in London, waiting to find a school that would risk accepting me to let me take O levels, I became remarkably unhappy at having been chosen to survive. And then guilty too about my ingratitude to my rescuer for being so miserable about it. I spiralled down into a depression just as things had started to look up. In retrospect, it's not at all surprising – what is more frightening than having been saved (for what?) and by someone who has taken you on trust, sight unseen, quality untested? What is more terrifying than having to make something of an opportunity that the people you left behind have not been given? But at the time I was baffled by my new, unjustifiable distress. And now, in the spectacular heat and singing silence of my Phoenix oasis, I was shot through with similar feelings of remorse at the relief I felt on having left my travelling companions behind, at getting solitary and self-absorbed again.

The train had pulled in – four and a half hours late – to Tucson station at two-thirty in the morning. Once there had been a direct link by train to Phoenix, where my friends John and Maria lived, but that had been let go to ruin in the name of profit. Now there was a two-hour bus journey to get to where I wanted to be, or the kindness of my friends who had followed the train's whimsical journey on the internet and knew that the ten o'clock arrival time was going to be more like two or three in the morning, but were still not put off coming to pick me up. Compared to the people on the train they were old friends, but actually I had never met Maria, and knew John only from a previous trip I had taken to Antarctica.

I had said goodbye to my fellow smokers around midnight. Raymond was asleep. I asked Chuck to say goodbye to him for me.

'Aren't you going to give him your phone number in England?' he asked.

'No.' It hadn't occurred to me.

'I think you should. You told him you'd go see him if he stopped drinking. What if he does?'

I scribbled my phone number on a piece of paper, in the certain knowledge that it wouldn't survive Raymond's journey home. But then, there was also that soft spot in the back of my head.

Chuck nodded that I was doing the right thing. Maybe he was employed by psychologists at Amtrak headquarters as a peripatetic super-ego of the rails. Morality lurks everywhere in America. Not surprising, really, that I couldn't tell if Chuck was saint or sinner, Samaritan or hypocrite: I feel much the same about morality when I come across it. I should have liked Chuck more. I should at least have admired him. But what I mostly did was not trust him. My problem, I suspect, rather than his.

The go-go girls who may have been boys got off at Tucson, though even with my last long look I couldn't decide about their Adam's apples. The only other people who got off the train were John and a middle-aged woman who was met by a man who enfolded them both in his arms, delighted to be reunited. There was not the slightest hint of Mexican or Indian about either of them, so I supposed they were John's adoptive parents. They were a bourgeois smiling couple, who turned their amiability towards me as I waved goodbye to John and he gesticulated at me and told them who I was. They looked pleased that John had made friends on the train. So was I. The man put an arm around John's shoulder and they walked off towards the car park.

My friend John, who was in his late sixties, waited while my suitcase arrived from the baggage train and then drove us for two hours through the desert blackness of Phoenix. At five in the morning, before we said goodnight, he lit up the swimming pool and the date palms in the back garden to show me that they were there for the next day's recuperation. He thought my three-day trip from Jacksonville to Tucson by train the kind of heroic journey that had taken valiant Englishwomen to the heart of African darkness in the nineteenth century. On the Antarctica trip, he had already revealed a profound and romantic attachment to English eccentricity, and he shared the more general American attitude that the US rail system was as good as defunct, useless for getting from A to B, dangerous, dirty and full of dreadful people, because who else would travel in such a way when there were cars and planes? Only those travelling by the once renowned Greyhound buses were more suspect. The lateness of the train and my tales of death and drunkenness as we drove through the desert in the dark only confirmed the foolhardiness or quaintness of my choice of transport to Phoenix. Being English I could not be a fool, so I must be one of those faintly mad, innocent and intrepid Englishwomen who pick up their skirts, caring nothing about revealing ankles, bloomers, God-knows-what to God-knows-who, and voluntarily stamp around in the murky undergrowth of the nastier parts of the world. At any rate, he was sure that I must be exhausted and shaken to my very core at the conclusion of such an experience and that I would certainly want to spend the following day quietly in his backyard oasis. Even though intrepidity is something no one can accuse me of, and since, not knowing the general opinion of the rail system, taking a train to get from one place to another had not struck me as heroic so much as sensible, I was nonetheless inclined to agree with him about my core, which, being made of far flimsier material than he supposed, was indeed exhausted and shaken.

My unintentional confrontation of other people had been surprisingly distressing. I sat in the Phoenix garden having escaped their company, their explanations, their trajectories, and I was both relieved and guilty at having done so. I was also overwhelmed by the weight of stories, by the unrelenting fact of the existence of so many stories, which in my mind now branched and multiplied to include every individual on the planet. Think of all the people in the world and then think that each has a story to tell. Think of them telling it over and over again to each other, to their children, to their parents, to officials, to strangers who pass by, to their livestock, their pets, to themselves if no one else is there to listen. Think of the noise, the weight of stories bearing down on the earth, the burden of incident and consequence, and then think how each of those stories connects to other stories and changes them, and is changed itself so that even the already unimaginable number of stories of each individual multiplies exponentially to an utterly terrifying and panic-making figure that is beyond the unimaginable. So my heart thumped and my head reeled with the life that was seething on the planet. And that, I knew beneath the panic, didn't matter, was just a neurotic twitch of mine, an aspect of my own story, a tendency I have to frighten myself with the world I would keep at a certain distance, like someone with a loose tooth who cannot help but play with it with their tongue. I could breathe my way through that panic. But then something else occurred to me. A new thought, sort of. Part of what alarmed me about the mass of individual stories was that they so conformed to stereotype. It was as if each story illustrated the old cliché that there are no more than ten set pieces about how lives are lived. What discouraged was the similarity of the stories, the repetition of the basic forms. Here's this one, now that one. Only a handful, really, with rather fewer variations than you would expect. You listen to them and think, is there nothing new, why doesn't anything change, what has been learned over the centuries of the same stories being told over and over? It's true that some are magnificently styled as literature or art or music, others staccato statements of one thing following the next, stoical, heroic even, yet others are whines of self-pity, blind lack of insight. There exists a whole range of possible tellings, but just a small range of individual narratives. But as I tried to deal with the panic of quantity qualified by duplication while I sat in my silent oasis, I remembered in Raymond, Maddy, Bet, Chris and all the others the urgency with which each of their stories was told, and, for a change, I understood that whatever repetition I experienced as the distant and weary witness I wished myself to be, every single one of them experienced their own story as extraordinary, unique and worth the telling because it has happened to them and not to someone else. It was their personal existence that made their story remarkable and worth the telling. The same story told by another person was not the same story. It did not matter how many times people had carelessly opened doors and caused an untroubled life to have to confront death, how many times the goodness in life had been squeezed dry by an addiction to alcohol, how often a damaged brain had caused an innocent to be sent away from society, to each person it happened to, it was the first time it had happened to them, their one and only story and each of them told it, to themselves and others, with a sense of wonder that they had such a story, that they had a story at all.

And that thought – no, not remotely a unique thought; obvious, indeed, but suddenly urgent – pressed so hard on my unaccustomed core that I was heavy with grief. Though for what and for whom exactly, I couldn't, and still cannot, say.

Journey Two

Live Tracks

A year later, I was sitting in Starbucks on Seventh Avenue opposite Penn Station waiting for the train to Chicago that would begin my railway circumnavigation of America. Back in London after the last trip and poring over the Amtrak brochures, I had discovered that it was possible to travel by train in a circle around the edge of the United States. The Circle Line to end all Circle Lines. The irresistible circle. I couldn't resist it, and nor could I resist the deliberate repetition of an accidental experience that had stayed with me when I got home. I wanted more, a substantial journey without going anywhere exactly, meetings and conversations which also would go nowhere. Even better than the Atlantic crossing, I could sit still, listen to people talk, travel many miles and end up back where I started, and all for the effort of changing a few trains.

So I made my plans for a second, deliberate journey, tracing a route delineated by a series of romantically named trains. I would start in New York, take the *Lake Shore Limited* to Chicago, and connect to the *Empire Builder* for the rest of the journey west to Portland, Oregon. From Portland I'd pick up the *Coast Starlight* down the West Coast as far as Sacramento, California, where I decided that I would take a wedge out of the circle and make an inland detour so that I could visit Bet and her hero in Albuquerque. To do this I had to take the *California Zephyr* from Sacramento across the Rockies to Denver, Colorado. At that point Amtrak failed me, as it fails most US citizens who want to go anywhere off the main routes: branch lines have been severely pruned in the name of profit. There was no rail connection to Albuquerque either directly from the *Coast Starlight*, or from the *California Zephyr*. I would have to take a three-hour bus trip laid on by Amtrak at six o'clock on the morning following my arrival in Denver the previous night, which would take me, via Colorado Springs and Pueblo, to Raton, New Mexico, where I would catch the *Southwest Chief* to Albuquerque. Since this was America, the land of vast spaces, it was only a hop and a skip to the oasis in Phoenix (four hours, say) by the *Southwest Chief*, so I could go and visit John and Maria again, before catching my old friend the *Sunset Limited* in the other direction this time (the 'Sunrise Limited', I suppose it should have been) from Tucson as far as New Orleans and then connecting to the *Crescent*, which would take me from New Orleans back to Penn Station, New York where I first started.

Sitting at my desk in London with the Amtrak timetable and a highlighter pen I whispered aloud the names of the trains as you would a poem or a psalm. It wasn't enough to read them and think them. Amused, but also beguiled by America's romance with itself, I wanted to hear the words out in the world, bouncing back at me in the silence: *Lake Shore Limited, Empire Builder, Coast Starlight, California Zephyr, Sunset Limited, Crescent, Southwest Chief*. I regretted that I would have to miss the chance to travel on the *Adirondack*, the *Ethan Allen Express*, the *Silver Service*, the *Cardinal*, the *Capitol Limited*, the *City of New Orleans*, the *Texas Eagle* and the *Cascades*, but I didn't miss the opportunity to utter their names along with the trains I would be taking.

My route was planned, my Phoenix friends checked with to make sure it was all right to visit, a month-long Amtrak rail pass purchased, a flight to New York reserved for October, a book contract signed. Everything was sorted. But why? What was I doing? The book? Well no, the book was going to pay for what I wanted to do, and it was a useful cover.

'Why are you spending a month going around the States on a train?'

'To write a book.'

'Ah.'

Once you've written other books, people don't usually question why you want to write any particular one. And most of the time I could tell myself that the book was the reason I was going and leave it at that. But it wouldn't quite do. I'd done the long train trip already, got the essence of the thing. Why do it again? Why not, if I wanted to do some travelling, go somewhere and do something I hadn't done before? Because what interests me is repetition, intensification, moreness. I say interests me, but that is too cerebral; I mean what alarms me, frightens me, disturbs me, because at a visceral level what I want is singularity, reduction, lessness, but like that ever-troubling tooth that I cannot resist testing with my tongue, there's the need to make certain. I never quite believe that I really want what I seem to want. Only by doing the opposite can I check to see if I'm not just making it all up. In any case, forgetting for a moment the degree of socialising involved, what was more beguiling than the idea of playing out the singularity of the straight line, the enclosing reduction of the circle over the whole geography of America?

But once I had set off, only got as far as New York City, I remembered also how much I like *being a stranger*, alone and unidentified in a place I don't belong. I feel bold and free, journeying alone in another country. Uncluttered by connection. A planet watcher. Unfathomable myself because of my alienation. Sitting alone in a busy coffee shop on Seventh Avenue was exhilarating enough. I could sit in a coffee shop in London and get a little of that feeling, but it's stronger being geographically elsewhere, being sure that no one you know is going to pass by and greet you as yourself. I thrill at being a stranger. I thought of the other travellers I would be with on the train as vignettes, moments or summaries of lives, flashing and vivid as they passed me by, then gone back to their regular existence. I can see other people so much better in my strangerhood. Strangerness brings people into sharp focus, so that like a firework display, vibrant patterns can be seen in sudden blazing light before the overall blackness of the sky returns and prepares us for the next revelation. Everyday busyness and regular social contact is more like a firework display in broad daylight. Of course, the other thing about a firework display is that you look at it, but it doesn't look at you. The opportunity to see myself was another central motive. Being looked at, being known, even just being acquainted, fogs the glass between me and myself. I can't see what I am. The narcissism of this is inescapable, but the 'What am I' question still beats in my head even after all this time, the adolescent question that should have been finished with but which remains, decade after decade, an incessant query. Better to admit it – that's as far as maturity will take me. I spend my life trying to find the right circumstances to circle myself, to catch myself unawares and finally see what it is I am. Then what? I've no idea. I imagine, when the question is at last satisfied (no, of course it won't be, but I imagine), a shrug, an 'OK', and then with infinite relief just getting on with it. In the meantime I take occasional wanders, using my separation from others as a mirror, or looking into the dark centre of strangers' eyes to catch my reflection. The eyes of those who know me reflect a story, my story or their story about me – and tell me more about them than about me. I suspect that the desert fathers, those crazed hermits, suffered from a similar self-obsession. That my narcissism is insatiable is not a pretty truth, but there it is. It was the condition of being always in transit, of never arriving, of being a travelling stranger for as long as possible that I was after. I thought of the train as the twin centres of my sleeping accommodation and the smoking coach – the rest just a corridor I passed through in order to get to one or the other. I thought of America as the ground plan for this fractured but contained investigation of myself and others. Travel had nothing to do with it.

What of the folly in trying to repeat the unplanned and unexpected by instituting the planned and expected? I knew perfectly well that it couldn't work. But supposing it did? And if it didn't, wouldn't that be interesting too? I had quite forgotten my shaken condition in Phoenix, and how badly I had needed to get home after experiencing the human interaction of a simple three-day journey. Or if I hadn't forgotten, I thought at least that I could deal with it. I always think I can deal with things. And I never completely believe, when I am securely on my own, that my discomfort in the company of others and away from base is really more than a conceit. I find I need to test it.

So I was waiting for a month of strangerhood to begin. I wasn't expecting anything to occur to me, just a series of events that I happen to be in the same place as. But how did I explain to myself the visits I had arranged which punctuated my journey? To Bet and her hero, for all that they were unknown quantities and therefore a continuation of strangeness, and to my friends John and Maria in Phoenix. A fear of the consequences of cutting myself off for so long without any familiarity? A failure of courage, perhaps. Probably. Or, less excusable, a thoughtless acceptance of convention? An unquestioned idea that a journey must have some points of reference, you can't just go round in a circle without any destination. Why not? There have to be stations on the way. Do there? Wanting to be *not* in America, not travelling to places in America, but travelling on an American train, I had nonetheless arranged for myself to spend time with Americans, in the places of their homes. A contradiction. So what isn't contradictory? Why not include contradiction in the contradiction of someone who wants most of all to keep still setting off to keep on the move for a month?

The smoking coach on the *Lake Shore Limited* was very different from the one on the *Sunset Limited*. As we pulled out of Penn Station and started our journey to Chicago, I was quite put out not to find grey lino scarred with burn marks, moulded plastic chairs bolted into serried ranks, overflowing ashtrays: all the hallmarks of a waiting room for reprobates who deserved nothing better, the ambiance of a punishment and isolation cell. This smoking compartment was a smart, square glass booth beside the bar. It was half the size, but designed by someone who had respect for smoking as a cultural marker. There was a carpet on the floor and the benches on two sides of the box were upholstered. By the windows were two small tables, like coffee tables with a couple of fixed chairs on either side. We were no longer isolated. The plate-glass wall looked on to the corridor, where people passed to and from the bar. They saw us, we saw them. To the passing non-smokers we may have been a warning in our glass case, an exhibition of an endangered species which owed its forth-coming extinction to its own foolish behaviour, but to us inside it felt like more a clubhouse than a sin bin. The back partition even had a mural: a man's silhouette leaning lazily against the edge of the wall, full size, wearing a snap-brim hat at a jaunty angle and broad trousers that placed him in the Forties, the smoker's finest hour, the great period of the ciga-rette: *Now Voyager*, 'Why ask for the moon, Gerry, when we already have the stars?' *To Have and Have Not*, 'You know how to whistle, don't you? You just put your lips together and blow.' *Casablanca*, 'Of all the gin joints in all the . . .' When a cylinder of tobacco meant something. Curling up from the cigarette between the man's fingers, held to his silhouetted lips, a black wisp of smoke, delicate, genie-like, spiralling up and up, from his mouth to God's ear. Smokers had the ear of God, back then. The painting must have been designed by someone who once smoked and who still understood the cul-tural imperative of smoking, the value-added glamour, the addition of addiction to a ruminative soul, to say nothing of the sheer all-encompassing pleasure. If this smoking area was a cell, it knew the true nature of the crime it contained. But still, I missed the stripped-bare dinginess of the *Sunset Limited*'s mealy mouthed concession to nicotine junkies.

Sleeping compartments get booked early and Amtrak never take demand into account by adding extra sleeping coaches. I was too late to get one for this leg of the journey. So from New York to Chicago I was travelling coach, huddling with the huddled masses. It was just the one night. I boarded at 4.35 p.m. on Friday at Penn Station, and was due to arrive (although I knew better now) at Chicago at 11.15 the following morning. Sitting up, sleeping in a seat, would be no bad thing, I told myself. If I was going to experience train travel, I should spend one night un-feather-bedded. I made a point, however, of booking sleeping compartments for the rest of the journey, which made the trip much less flexible, of course. I had thought I'd be keeping timetabling to a minimum, just in case, you never know, to keep me free for spontaneity. There was still that lurking sense of how one ought to be a travel writer, free to make detours, when detours were the last thing I wanted. But the prospect of a month sleeping upright, of having no door to shut myself behind, made me decide to dispense with any fantasy of spontaneity.

The journey away from New York is most marked by what appears to be an entire suburb for the dead. A graveyard so extensive and ramshackled that it seemed as urban and frantic as Manhattan itself. Or perhaps it was New York's statement on what exists beyond the city: nothing, just chaos and the dead. The seat in which I would spend the night was spacious and comfortable in maroon leatherette and it reclined. There was a footrest that could be raised so that the legs could be completely extended, and wide armrests. It would have been first class on a plane. There were worse places to spend the night. In the two seats beside me were a Filipino woman in her sixties, dressed smartly, and a small boy I supposed was her grandson. She didn't speak, beyond nodding hello as she sat down beside me. The child fell asleep almost immediately. I watched New York State go by for a little while, and then made my way to the smoking compartment. It was empty. No Bet, no Raymond, no Good Samaritan, no camaraderie. I didn't mind. So far, apart from ordering a caramel macchiato at Starbucks, I hadn't spoken to anyone. Supposing it went on like that? What if the Savannah to Tucson trip had been an aberration and the entire present journey was to be spent in silence, in contact with no one? Another kind of trip altogether. In fact at that point I had so little desire to talk or make contact with strangers that when the door slid open and two round, smiley middle-aged men came in and nodded amiably at me, I had to make an effort to respond with a civil smile. It had begun, and oddly, I was reluctant to get started. Inertia probably, a built-in resistance to moving from a present state into a new one, whatever it may be. Which is why doing nothing seems such a plausible life choice. The men were a couple, taking a holiday, they told me. Travelling to and from New York.

'Where are you from?'

The essential first question of all train-travel conversations.

'He's from the Philippines, and I'm from Bermuda, but we live in Las Vegas.'

'I thought people went on holiday to Las Vegas, not from it.'

'Oh no,' the man who had been silent began, as if he had explained it many times before but never tired of giving the news out. 'People think Las Vegas is just casinos. But that's just the Strip, like Broadway's got theatres. No, there are people living real lives beyond the Strip. Do you realise that a million people live full-time in Las Vegas? Things have changed. It's a real city, and growing. We have families, suburbs, everything, just like a regular town.'

'We love Las Vegas,' the other man said. 'Can't wait to get home.'

We slipped into silence, as I, a little disappointed, came to terms with Las Vegas turning into just another regular place instead of a theme park of American toomuchness. A dowdy woman in her thirties arrived and sat silently in the corner smoking concentratedly. And soon a young black man with short dreadlocks arrived and sat down at the unoccupied table beside her. He lit up and inhaled hard, all the better to sigh deeply as he expelled the air from his lungs.

'Whoa,' he shook his ringlets slowly. 'Man, I am coming from a cold situation.'

'Yeah,' the woman next to him said, nodding, but keeping her eyes down towards the carpet and smoking on. 'My seat's up at the front of the coach with people coming through all the time. The door opens and closes, opens and closes. It's real cold.'

The young man stared at her for a moment. 'No, no. I'm coming from a real cold place. From my baby-momma. We had a fight, a bad one so I packed my things and said I'm gone. She said go. Yeah, right, I'm gone. Man, it was a cold situation. You see? So I figured I'd head out west and visit with some brothers who left New York. I reserved a sleeper. I had a sleeper, man, but then I cancelled it because we got back, my momma – we made it up, my baby-momma and me. Next couple of days we fought again, and this time I was really gone. I was outta there in the middle of the fucking night. So I ain't got no sleeping compartment because now they're all gone and I gotta spend three nights sitting straight up in those goddamed seats. Three nights. Jesus. If I'd have gone the first time, I'd have had that fucking sleeper. Three fucking nights on a fucking train and no bed. But I tell you what, I'm feeling better with every mile that passes, the further away I get, the better it gets.'

'Yeah,' the woman next to him said. 'But it's real cold where I'm sitting. And they don't let you change seats.'

The gay couple threw each other a glance, confirming their good fortune in their own contentment and their warm situation in the world.

At dinner I was seated in the spare place left by a party of three. Two very elderly men and the middle-aged son of one of them. Only one of the old men spoke throughout the meal. His friend remained silent, occasionally nodding agreements, but mostly concentrating glumly on the apology of a steak he was eating. The man who did speak was garrulous and cheerful and informed me, once he heard my accent, that he had been in the US navy and stationed in Falmouth during World War Two. I regretted that I didn't know the area, though knowing of it pleased him enough. He had joined up to fight in the war aged fifteen, pretending he was old enough. His son, he told me, had been stationed in Guam during the Vietnam War. The son smiled his agreement. His friend continued to say nothing. They were holidaying, the two friends and the son, as they regularly did, by travelling the trains to fishing spots, and 'to get away from the women', he cackled. His son laughed tolerantly (one of the women being his mother) and his friend snorted his agreement.

'You know, it's so good, getting away, I might send your mother to live permanently with you,' he teased his son.

'Yeah, you'd be coming to get her soon enough. Once the dishes were piled high.'

They told me what I needed to know about travelling the trains, what every experienced train traveller or enthusiast would tell me as soon as they asked and I told them why I was on the train. The old men had travelled the US by train to all but five states.

'We're working on getting the other five under our belts before we die.'

What they wanted me to know was how terrible the service was, how run down the system had become and what a criminal neglect (or even deliberate destruction) of American heritage that was. The trains were invariably late, and it was because Amtrak's profit only came from freight; passenger trains were required by law but ran at a loss. Freight, therefore, had priority at all times over passenger trains.

'Course, they're obliged by the federal government to provide passenger services, but they hell of a don't care much for it. No money in us. Passengers are just another kind of freight, but not nearly so valuable. It's all cargo – people, containers, pig iron – but there ain't no profit in people. Any real business would adapt; supply and demand. Not Amtrak. If more people want to travel than there are seats, that's just too damn bad. They wouldn't even think of putting on extra carriages. Some of them freight trains are a mile or more long. You can wait half an hour for them to pass by. The passenger trains have got a set number of coaches and that's that. So folk can't rely on getting places on time, and they have to reserve a seat months in advance. Who's going to use the trains? Just old guys like us with no particular place to go and all the time in the world to go to it, and a few holiday-makers. It's a crying shame when you think of the history of the railroads. Hell, railroads made this country. Railroads forged a way east and west. Opened up the whole damn landmass. Now they just let the weeds grow if a route isn't profitable. People died in their hundreds, in their thousands, making the railroads and blasting their way through the mountains. They don't care. These new people. All they care about is making profits.'

The other man became quite animated in his nods of agreement, and the son, though he clearly agreed, had the look of someone who had heard this all before and too many times. But the old guy was right. It was extraordinary that the passion and drama that had gone into creating a comprehensive rail network in a country so large that you had to be slightly crazy to dream of it in the first place, had just died away. The achievement was so grand, so saturated in heroics and corruption, and so central to the development of the States, it was hard to believe that people would let it deteriorate into a remnant. But they had.

So far I had more or less avoided sitting at my seat. Either I was in the observation car while it was daylight watching New York State pass through Pennsylvania into Ohio via Schenectady, Utica, Syracuse, Rochester, Buffalo, Erie, Cleveland, Elyria and Sandusky; or I was in my stateless condition in the smoking compartment. Whenever I went to pick up something from my seat – a new pack of cigarettes, money for the bar – the woman and her grandson were asleep. En route from my seat to the smoking coach I passed a group of Amish, a whole bunch of them, taking up several rows at the back of my carriage. Somehow I was surprised to see them out and about, though I shouldn't have been, because Hollywood has included the Amish in its shadow story of America, and, in *Witness*, precisely travelling by train. Still, the point of Amish in a movie, even if they are in Grand Central Station and observing a murder, is that they are Amish and their being out of their usual context was the axis of the plot. But here their unreality was startling. There were, I guess, about fifteen or so, and they spanned the generations,

tiny children to old men and women. Young families and elderly couples. They spanned the centuries, too. The men wore
pudding-basin haircuts under their pudding-crowned flat-
brimmed hats, under-chin whiskers, blue workshirts, baggy
trousers held up with braces but, because I supposed of their
high-tech nature, no flies or even buttons, and heavy black
coats. They reminded me of the seven dwarves in *Snow
White*. The women's faces were scrubbed pink with health
and lack of make-up, as if they were permanently blushing,
and they wore crisp blue dresses with dirndl skirts, flat black
shoes and pleated white starched bonnets over their heavily
controlled straight fair hair. The children were exact minia-
ture versions of their parents, even the smallest; little adults
bright-eyed and ready to go to a nineteenth-century fancy
dress party. They were charming to look at, and as a group
utterly oblivious of their own odd appearance or, if you like,
everyone else's odd appearance. Even the children appeared to
show no curiosity about the people around them. They
played quietly together or concentratedly alone as if there
were nothing interesting to see in the world: all too neat, quiet
and well-behaved to be entirely comfortable to observe. They,
their parents and grandparents reflected only each other, as if
the whole group was a single entity, an inwardly curved one-
way mirror. They were perfectly self-contained, the women
entertaining and fussing the clothes of the youngest children,
the men reading or chatting to each other in a language of
immigrants, though not recent immigrants since the language
they spoke was Low German from two hundred years back,
non-existent now in Europe. They made the interest I had in
them, my urge to question them, seem crude and intrusive,
although, in all reason, their dress and manner courted attention. But everyone on the train sitting nearby or passing to

and fro made a point of ignoring them, as if their quaint
clothes and manners were a form of disability that was not to
be remarked upon or stared at. How strange it is during childhood that we are told it is rude to point, that is, to point out
what is pointedly different, to remark on the remarkable, to
notice the noticeable. Don't look, my mother used to say,
whenever there was anything worth looking at. So we all grow
up and the fact that there were fifteen throwbacks to another
century and another continent sitting among us as if either we
or they had made a massive cultural slip was to be treated as
nothing out of the ordinary. The young women smoothed
the starched aprons of their tiny children playing with puzzle
books, whose obedient eyes remained undrawn to the kids in
jeans and sweatshirts who passed up and down the aisle with
hand-held computer games or zizzing Walkmans, who themselves were oblivious of, or politely tolerant of, the alien
presence among them. Me, I wanted to sit down next to them
and say, What are you doing? Why? How can you imagine
that locking yourselves into the imagination of a people dead
for hundreds of years can be godly or whatever it's supposed
to be? Can I come and stay with you and see how it works?
But then I find it just as difficult to pass by Hassidic Jews in
London without a desire to ask them the same questions and
why they think dressing and living in the past will keep them
safe from the present. I knew the answer both Amish and
Hassidics would give, so that wasn't really my question. It
was really a question about their fear, exclusion, their terror of
individuality and modernity, and perhaps also a question
about my fascination with such a structured form of rejection
of the world. Like monks or junkies. A kind of group-
identity that permits abandonment of the world. Why not do
it in company and create a firm way of life around the

rejection of all other ways of life? There were all kinds of ways to do it. I was once tempted to become a permanent resident in a mental hospital for much the same reasons. A fear of some kind of crucial loss – of individuality, probably – kept me from putting it into action, though individuality and independent thought are troublesome burdens much of the time. In any case, did I know for sure that individuality was suppressed in an Amish community? I made the assumption from the similarity of dress and the religious fervour, but perhaps that's a crass assumption. Still, when I wanted to hole up in the bin, it was because I wanted to be shrived of the task of being an individual.

When I returned to the smoking box after dinner there was a strikingly beautiful black man wearing a white collarless shirt and soft cream trousers, and a young Chinese boy sitting next to him, concentrating hard. The beautiful man was explaining to the boy about languages, how he spoke a great many, and the Chinese boy, who evidently did not, or at least English wasn't yet one of them, was nodding hard with perfect incomprehension in his eyes.

'Welcome. *Wilkommen. Bienvenue* . . . You see? It's easy. And Russian: *Dobro pojalovat.* I can communicate with people from all over the world. Hello, goodbye, my friend, *mon ami, mi amore, muchacho, camarade* . . . Now, you teach me Chinese. You . . . teach . . . me . . . Chinese.' He pointed at the boy, back at himself and then at his mouth. 'Speak Chinese. Chink, chink, chink. Hoi sin. Szechwan noodles.'

The boy nodded, remained baffled and smiled. 'No good English,' he said, confessing.

The linguist lost interest and leaned forward to me across the compartment, forcefully extending a hand. I took it and he enclosed it with his other one.

'You touch an ethnic hand. These are black ethnic pinkies that you are clasping.'

'And very nice, too,' I smiled.

'English. You're English. I speak English, too.' He nudged the ever-amiable Chinese boy. 'She's from England. Where we all once came from. Well, not you, or me, but America. She comes from the source of language.' He turned back to me, still clasping my hand between his and shaking it heartily up and down. 'I am overwhelmed to meet you. I am known to all my friends as Chef. You are now one of them. Do you ever have tea with the Queen? You can call me Chef.'

'Thanks, Chef. You can call me Jenny. Are you?'

'Am I what?'

'A chef.'

'*Ah oui.* I am. *Ja. Si. Da.* I am a multilingual chef of the *haute cuisine.*'

The chef was tall and beautiful and either naturally manic or stoned. He had that ebullience and breathless need to talk that could have been either bipolar illness or cocaine. Or he was just a natural comedian. But although he was delightful, I felt a kind of anxious tension in my head and neck that I recognised from being with people close to exploding with manic energy. A scrawny woman in the corner was laughing as the chef babbled on.

'You're a chef, huh? You make cakes? You make pound cake? I make great pound cake. In my book no one's a chef unless they make a great pound cake.'

The chef rattled off his recipe for pound cake.

'Well yeah,' the woman acknowledged. 'You know how to make a good pound cake.'

'Did you doubt me? You, *chère madame*, recognise a great

pound cake recipe when you hear one. I salute you. Wait. Wait here.' He rushed out.

'Crazy guy, eh?' the woman said. 'But he might really be a chef.'

The chef came back, triumphant, and ceremonially placed a pleated, tall paper chef's hat on the woman. 'I declare you now an honorary chef, *madame.*'

The woman kept the chef's hat on. 'Marie's the name. Can I keep it?'

'Sure, I got a dozen in my bag. I'm on my way to Chicago to cook a lunch for Willie May.'

An elderly black man in the corner who until now had been silent suddenly became animated. 'Willie May? Willie May's dead, ain't he?'

'That's his father. The great Willie May. This is Willie May, the son. Also great. The father died not so long ago.'

'That's sad.'

'Yup. But this Willie May called me from Chicago, and said, "Chef, I'm having some guys round for a barbeque in the garden. You wanna come and make it?"'

'So what are you gonna make?' Marie asked.

'Aha.' Finger touched to his lips, hands expressing the exquisite nature of the food he was going to prepare. 'I plan to begin with a sweet potato soup. Then Beef Wellington. You know what Beef Wellington is?' He described in detailed how he made Beef Wellington. 'You just gotta taste mine one day. And we'll finish with a fresh fruit sorbet, lime and lemon. Good. Oh, very, very good.'

Marie nodded, impressed, making her chef hat tip forward over her eyes. The old guy in the corner nodded appreciatively.

'Who's Willie May?' I asked.

There was a stunned silence.

'Come *on*,' the old man said.

'You're *kidding*,' Marie gasped.

'No, man, she ain't kidding. She's from England,' the chef explained, racing to my defence.

'You mean they don't know Willie May in England?'

I tried to look apologetic.

'He was the greatest, I mean the greatest baseball player this world has ever seen.'

'We don't play baseball in England,' I said by way of an explanation.

'Yeah, but Willie May was something else. He was . . . he was great. What's his boy like?'

'A chip off the block,' the chef said.

The old man nodded his satisfaction at the way of the world.

'Hell, all this talk of cooking makes me homesick,' Marie said. 'I miss my farm. I didn't want to leave my husband and my grandbabies. He and my son sent me on a visit to my sister for a birthday gift, so I had to go. But all I really want is to stay on the farm, cook up a storm in the kitchen, and bounce my grandbabies on my knee.' She laughed. 'That must seem pretty unadventurous to you, coming all the way from England and all.'

Actually, it seemed quite exotic to me: the grandbabies, the farm, the pound cake, the contentment. I realised I'd forgotten about the musicals. Here was *Oklahoma* and *Seven Brides for Seven Brothers*, and never mind that beneath the corn as high as an elephant's eye and in spite of the joys of spring, spring, spring, the plots are as dark as death, and thick with murder, rape and criminal ignorance. I was back on a sentimental, celluloid journey.

Maybe the chef hadn't just gone to get Marie a hat, because since his return he'd been more ebullient than ever, jumping up from his seat, taking everyone's hands and shaking them vigorously, his eyes glowing with something more than happiness, I thought.

'You want to dance?' he asked Marie.

'I don't dance.'

'You want to sing?'

She shook her head, making her chef's hat wobble. 'I don't sing. Sister Mary Ellen said it was bad to sing. So I never sing.'

'No, no, it's good to sing. Forget Sister Mary Ellen. Sing out, Marie. Sing your heart out.'

'You'll be sorry . . .'

'Sing,' we all urged. 'Sing.'

Marie stood up in her chef's hat and good travelling clothes and wailed an entirely tuneless but passionate hymn to life being grand. There was a brief stunned silence as we began to see that Sister Mary Ellen may have had reasons other than religious for preventing Marie from singing. But the chef wasn't daunted.

'That's it, she outta the convent now,' he crowed and we all joined in with Marie to celebrate her liberation.

It was around midnight by now. The young man and the woman who were both cold for different reasons had dropped in a few times for a smoke; a couple of men in their early twenties, in jeans and T-shirts and with longish hair, each solitary travellers, were settled on the corner bench chatting to each other about guitars but both aware of a straggly-haired girl probably not out of her teens sitting next to them. She had got on at Syracuse. She was following their conversation, or trying to, at any rate, attaching herself to them as roughly her age and peer group. One of them clearly was going to become her lover (or whatever kind of fumbling was possible at their seats or in the lavatory), but neither the boys nor the girl had yet decided which. They were drinking beer and the girl, who was a lot younger and more displaced than she wanted to seem, was making a show of getting drunker, of being one of the guys. She was quite plain and rather grubby but sweetly wide-eyed and lost, almost certainly always lost, used to wandering and coming together briefly but not for long with new human beings. I doubted that Syracuse was where she had started her journey, I even wondered if she entirely remembered the start of her journey, and I was sure she had no idea where or when it would end. Suddenly she became animated as she recalled something she had seen while waiting for the train, something she'd been dying to tell someone about.

'There was this sign, you know, like a warning sign, in red. It said "Live Tracks".'

She waited for the boys to show proper astonishment. When they didn't, she helped them out.

'I mean, like, *live* tracks. What's that supposed to mean? The sign was to stop people from crossing the rails to get to the other platform, you know, to scare them, so they wouldn't do it, but, I mean, do they think people would really believe the tracks were alive? Like, how stupid do they think people are? You know, like rails are made of metal, how can they be alive? Only people and animals are actually living. Everyone knows that. *Live* tracks. Isn't that incredible?'

She shook her head in disbelief at the contempt with which the authorities held people. The boys darted a glance at her (as I did) to check if she was making a joke, but she was genuinely outraged. The boys didn't look at each other, but down at their knees. Eventually, after she continued to complain about the sign, one of them, very hesitantly, spoke.

'Uh, I think it's a sort of way of saying that they're electrified. Like, electricity is running through them. They use live to describe something that's electrified.'

He seemed to be waiting for the girl to laugh at him for taking her literally. She didn't. She didn't laugh at all, ever, probably. Her mode was intense and puzzled earnestness.

'Really? So, like, this table is dead, right?'

The boy opened his mouth to explain that it was a special use of the . . . but he shut it again, deciding there was no point.

'Jesus, I wish people would say what they mean. I mean especially official people. They ought to be clearer. Why confuse us? It's like that door.' She pointed to the door of the smoking box. 'See, it says *Out*. Lots of doors say *Out*, one side *Out*, the other side *In*. What's that? I'm always going in somewhere, whenever I go through a door I'm going *in*. I was in this place, then I go through a door *into* another place. That's how I see it. I don't go out, I go in. It's just not truthful to say *Live Tracks* and *Out*. It's like lying.'

And although this was possibly the most profound comment on language and perception that was made during my entire journey around the States – or even maybe in the history of linguistics – we remained excruciatedly silent, because we were all wrapped up with wondering, though hardly able to bear to imagine, what the inside of this waif's mind could possibly be like and how she had made her way even this far in the world with only the capacity for absolute literalism to help her along. I felt we were in the presence of something extraordinary, a kind of idiot savant, whose absence of irony, whose complete inability to grasp the plasticity of language, might easily be mistaken for transcendental wisdom. The boys looked confused, as the question of which of them was going to sleep with her was superseded by what it might be like and whether it would be advisable to sleep with someone so innocent or of such a potentially dangerous cast of mind.

The chef, linguist that he was, who might have been expected to be interested in the problem but was too far gone in mania or drug high to concentrate on anything other than the frantic energy zipping around his body, simply maintained his own relation with the world and went on, never silent, restlessly talking, no longer listening or waiting for a response, jumping up, touching, leaving, coming back. I thought the time right to give sleep a go, and saying I'd see everyone later, in that American way I like, meaning in an hour or a year, I headed back from the smoking box to my coach.

The Filipino woman was slumped sideways in her seat, her grandson sprawled across his. I climbed over their hand luggage and her legs to get to my designated place by the window, and managed not to wake them up. The main lights were off in the carriage, just a couple of overhead lamps of those who couldn't sleep causing a dim glow. I reclined the back of the seat, hoisted the footrest and covered myself with the blanket Amtrak provided. It wasn't uncomfortable for taking a nap on a train but I've never got to sleep in a sitting position, even a half-sitting position; not in front of the TV, not on a plane, on a train, or in a car. Never, not once. Still, I lounged and listened to the rattling of the rails and the rocking of the carriages, the two women whispering a couple of rows behind me, the snoring from around the coach. I shut my eyes. Two hours later I was still awake and getting stiff. I turned and sort of curled up on my side. An hour later I was still awake. Maybe I had dozed occasionally, but if so, it was the kind of dim half-sleep where you drift off for a second and then jerk awake, as if your body has not given you permission to lose consciousness. I thought I'd read, but I was worried about waking my neighbour by putting the overhead light on. I gave up and tiptoed over legs and bags out into the aisle where I was free to make an inspection of my coach and its mostly unconscious inhabitants.

In the 9 February 1878 issue of *The Illustrated Newspaper*, Frank Leslie, travelling by railroad for much the same reason I was, noted:

From our Pullman hotel-car, the last in the long train, to the way-car which follows closely on the engine, there is a vast discount in the scale of comfort, embracing as many steps as there are conveyances. It is worth one's while to make a tour of the train for the sake of observing these differences and noting the manners and customs of travelling humanity when tired bodies and annoyed brains have agreed to cast aside ceremony and the social amenities and appear in uneasy undress. The old assertion that man is at bottom a savage animal finds confirmation strong in a sleeping-car; and for the women – even under dear little five-and-three-quarter kids, the claws will out upon these occasions. For here, at 9 P.M., in the drawing-room sleeper, we find a cheerful musical party howling, 'Hold the Fort!' around the parlour organ, which forms its central decoration; three strong, healthy children running races up and down the aisle, and scourging each other with their parents' shawl-straps; a consumptive invalid, bent double in a paroxysm of coughing; four parties, invisible, but palpable to the touch, wrestling in the agonies of the toilet behind the closely buttoned curtains of their sections, and trampling on the toes of passers-by as they struggle with opposing draperies; a mother engaged in personal combat (also behind the curtains) with her child in the upper berth, and two young lovers, dead to the world, exchanging public endearments in a remote corner. Who could bear these things with perfect equanimity? Who could accept with smiles the company of six adults at the combing and washing stages of one's toilet? Who could rise in the society, and under the close personal scrutiny, of twenty-nine fellow-beings, jostle them in their seats all day, eat in their presence, take naps under their very eyes, lie down among them, and sleep – or try to sleep – within acute and agonized hearing of their faintest snores, without being ready to charge one's soul with twenty-nine distinct homicides?

But if the 'drawing-room sleeper' be a place of trial to fastidious nerves, what is left to say of the ordinary passenger-car, wherein the working-men and working-women – the miners, the gold-seekers, the trappers and hunters travelling from one station to another, and the queer backwoods folk who have left their log homesteads in Wisconsin and Michigan and Illinois to cross the train of the sunset – do congregate, and are all packed like sardines in a box? It is a pathetic thing to see their nightly contrivances and poor shifts at comfort; the vain attempts to improvise out of their two or three feet of space a comfortable sleeping-place for some sick girl or feeble old person, and the weary, endless labour of the others to pacify or amuse their fretted children. Here and there some fortunate party of two or three will have full sway over a whole section – two seats, that is to say – and there will be space for one of them to stretch his or her limbs in the horizontal posture and rest luxuriously;

but for the most part, every seat has its occupant, by night as well as by day, a congregation of aching spines and cramped limbs. The overland journey is no fairy tale to those who read it from a way-car!

Certainly, it was the antithesis of waking in the middle of the night in a hospital ward. No night nurses maintained a dimly lit vigil, overlooking the helpless sleepers. And the sleepers themselves were not contained tidily in rows of beds, but in a free-for-all quest for unconscious comfort. It was true that the Amish group were as neat and disciplined in their sleeping as they were in their waking. They sat in their seats (only the children were fully reclined) with their legs straight and their arms folded. Some of the younger men had allowed their heads to loll on their wives' shoulders. Some of the women slept with an arm around a small child as if to contain it, and train it in propriety even in the uncertain world of sleep. The men's legs were spread out, feet planted comfortably apart or crossed at the ankles; the women's were together and parallel with the vertical drop of their seat, their skirts straight as if they had smoothed them before setting off for sleep and hadn't moved since. A few snored, probably in Low German. Who knows what they dreamed?

The sleeping habits of the rest of the coach told a different story altogether. Repose, like hunger or sexual need, is a powerful human drive which, when the need is strong, overcomes training in social niceties and our public pretensions. Mostly people do it in private, with at most one other who is licensed to share the ultimate intimacy of sleep. What you discover, when you first spend the night with someone else, is that, whatever the quality of togetherness the sex might bring you, the quality of separation and of utter aloneness when the one

of you that isn't you is asleep is unlike anything else in the
world. People sleep alone, no matter that you are in their arms
or they in yours. They go away when they sleep to a private
place surrounded by overgrown briars and walls of unconsciousness as impenetrable as stone. They leave behind
nothing but a careless, even an uncaring effigy, an empty shell
that might toss and turn, snort and snore, but is no more the
container of the mind and heart you communed with than an
empty tin of baked beans. Sleep is a haven. Every man is an
island when asleep. And this truth being disturbing, distressing even, we keep it for those we love, or those we have grown
used to, and only then probably because we have to, if we do
not want to make the choice between experiencing the comfort
of others and the bliss of solitary unconsciousness. It's a private truth. There are some between people. The solipsism of
sleep is one of them.

So public sleeping is a kind of revelation, and the observer
of strangers asleep is as much a voyeur as someone peeping
through a gap in the bedroom curtains. If you are not a dedicated voyeur, there is a degree of discomfort in witnessing the
sleep of strangers, though it is a fascinated kind of discomfort:
you look before you look away. Most of us wish to peep on the
privacy of others, to see what people are really like when they
are alone. Even those you live with are alone sometimes and
retain momentary secrets. You can't watch all the time. And
even if you can make a guess that other people alone are pretty
much like you are, you can't ever be sure. Worse still, you
can't ever be sure that you alone are pretty much like other
people alone. Some things we never find out by asking or being
with other people, so when we get the opportunity to cheat, to
look through a crack in the door, watch a silhouetted figure
through the window across the street, gaze at candid

photographs taken with a high-powered lens, we do so, and the instinctive guilt is usually about equal to the thrill. What are we hoping to see? If they are like us; if we are weird; if they are weirder than us; but we also want to see what we are like, not just the individual peeping eye, but the general, collective *we*.

Everyone slept as best they could, as comfortably as possible, shoes off, belts and zips undone, clothes loosened or rucked up, revealing bellies, bosoms and thighs. Each person slept under a spell that allowed them to fight for another inch of personal space, an extra ounce of ease regardless of what their waking self might think of how they appeared. Heads back, mouths agape, snoring freely, slapping their lips together, scratching, snorting, legs wide, torso flopped: with the perfect self-centred innocence of a child asleep. For all the world as if humanity had decided to forgo entirely all the social skills it had acquired in order to live peaceably in a group. Not the original savage animal, as Frank Leslie saw it back in the 1870s under the influence of evolutionary theories that threatened us with simian ancestors, but a tangle of individual post-Freudian omnipotent egos, each separately grasping for physical gratification, each engrossed in private dreams and desires.

By 8.30 the next morning the train had arrived at Toledo, Ohio. People had gradually started waking from six o'clock on, and tried to make themselves respectable again, straightening up their clothes, combing their hair, heading for the coffee in the restaurant car that would make them social human beings again. The chef was nowhere to be seen, but Marie, who was bright and perky and puffing up a morning storm in the smoking compartment, said that he had finally collapsed on the floor in the centre of an aisle and just lay there sleeping for the rest of the night while people carefully stepped over him.

I was nauseous with lack of sleep, but smoked and drank coffee through the morning, as we passed through flat anonymous country shrouded in morning mist. All I could think of was arriving in Chicago and connecting with the *Empire Builder*, where I had a bed. We were running an hour late, but when we reached the outskirts of Chicago and the tracks multiplied, merging from all directions into the frantic hub that was the dead centre of the American railroad system, we slowed to that alarming speed where you know that nothing but a complete halt can come of it. Surrounded by goods trains and containers, overhead cables screeching and singing, iron and steel, clinker, smoke, rust, dust, grime and the bone-juddering noise of metal wheels on metal rail jangling and grinding, shuddering to a stop, lurching into movement, the *Lake Shore Limited* finally came to a dead standstill about five hundred yards outside Union Station, Chicago. We waited in an expectant silence, and then waited some more. The child in the seat next to me began to sing tunelessly: 'One hour we've been waiting . . . two hours we've been waiting . . . three hours we've been waiting . . .' He got to ten hours and then started again. And then again. I don't know how many times he started again, but a real-life hour and a half later we were still waiting in the goods yard as the freight trains took priority. No one murmured any complaint, we just sat, our bags packed, ready after our nineteen-hour journey to disembark and go home or make the next connection. Apart from the child next to me, who was beginning to sound like our psyches singing in our ears, and who, like my psyche, I thought needed suppressing, there was the grim silence of a captive, helpless audience with nowhere else to go staring through the grime of the windows into the noise and shunting chaos of the filthy, smoky air just yards from, but utterly beyond the reach of, our destination.

Two hours later we were allowed into the station, and I arrived at the check-in desk in Chicago with just fifteen minutes to spare before the *Empire Builder* left for Portland, Oregon. Given my anxiety level, you would be forgiven for thinking that I had to be somewhere at a given time. But missing a train is missing a train, a thing in itself, a source of compulsion that needs nothing more than a timetable. There would have been a very long wait until the next train to Portland, but waiting was what I was doing – what difference if it was on the train waiting for the next station, or in the station waiting for the next train? But I was nevertheless hugely relieved to get to the check-in desk before it closed.

'That was nothing,' a woman behind me said as we were bustled along by the porters as if being late was our fault. 'I once waited in the Chicago yards for eight hours.'

I understood the silence of the others on the train. It was sheer terror of what could be.

Expending Nerve Force

The *Empire Builder* left on time at 2.10 p.m., picking up speed through the yards and beyond, through the steel and smoke of the factories, past the suburbs, heading west, its engine pulling energetically out of the industrial north-east, tracing the dreams of the nineteenth-century railroad entrepreneurs of constructing a mechanised way to deliver civil society and all its subsequent unquenchable and profitable needs further and further into the westward wilderness. Did I care? Not then. Not one bit. I hadn't had more than twenty minutes' sleep and now I was shown to my *deluxe* sleeper. I had got the last late-booked possibility of a bed – *deluxe*: a double-sleeper with its own shower and lavatory at a hefty premium – or it was up and sleepless for the next two nights. I would have paid anything for horizontality. The conductor introduced himself as Chris and before he had a chance to tell me about the complimentary coffee and morning paper, I asked him to make up my bed so I could sleep, which I did until 5.45 p.m. When I woke and examined my deluxe accommodation, I found that not only was my bed twice as wide as the regular sleeper, but I had an armchair and a decent-sized table as well as my own mini, modular bathroom. The single sleeping compartment was essentially a lofty coffin, an enclosure almost exactly the width of the narrow bed with head room but no standing room. Even the slightest degree of claustrophobia would make an overnight trip impossible, quite without Edgar Allan Poe-ish horrors of feeling buried alive. I, however, have no degree of claustrophobia. On the contrary, I particularly like the small, just-so fit of confined spaces, so I was perfectly happy in spite of the contortions and wrigglings required to change clothes while sitting cross-legged on the bed, or the inevitable spillages of essential creams and lotions that I had managed only with difficulty to find while hanging upside down to reach the overnight bag wedged in the slim space under the made-up bed. To me, it all added up to cosiness and was, in any case, infinitely preferable to a night of insomnia in a public coach. This double compartment, though, was spacious enough to swing a cat in – not a large cat: I had a mental image of a small kitten swirling around at the end of my arm – but it was extraordinarily roomy as sleeping compartments went. Pity I had to leave it immediately for a cigarette.

On the way to the smoking coach I stopped at the bar to get a coffee and found myself queuing in front of an Amish woman and her son of perhaps eight or nine years old. They were everywhere on the rail system it seemed, the Amish. Was anyone back on the farm leading the horse-driven ploughs and hand-churning the butter? The boy stepped back as the train jerked and trod firmly on my foot. I responded with a

yelp of complaint – he wasn't a small child. When he turned
round and saw me I pointed down to my foot and made a car-
icature grimace of pain. He was delighted by my mock
anguish and his plump, owlish face, topped with the regulation
pudding-basin haircut, creased into a great grin, hugely but
shyly amused at his achievement. I raised my eyes in cartoon
hopelessness, and he started chuckling. His mother turned
round and looked at him, smiling benignly down at the boy,
and then nodding politely at me. They got their order and sat
at one of the tables, and the boy glanced up at me now and
then, still amused as he sank his teeth and most of his face into
one of the most evil-smelling microwaved hotdogs it was ever
my misfortune to have waft my way. Even so, feeling we had
been introduced, or at least that I was owed one, I sat down
with my coffee on the opposite side of the table.

'Is that all right for you?' the woman asked the boy in a
hushed, concerned voice that had a foreign but indefinable
lilt to it. 'It is good?' She was like one of those mothers you
only see in old Hollywood films; a little old lady well before
her years, utterly beyond womanhood, beyond sexuality, a
matron who had done her reproductive duty and had no further need for allure, even of whatever minimal kind the Amish
permit. She was unadorned, with a skin almost silvery with
cleanliness. Wisps of grey hair strayed from under her
starched white bonnet. Her wholemeal dress was light grey,
rather than the blue the Amish women on the last train wore,
but just as smooth and neat. There was something almost
wizened about her – though she couldn't have been more than
forty or so – as she bent down every few moments to the boy
and murmured to him to eat tidily, stroking his hair, adoring
him, asking if he were enjoying his extraordinarily unAmish-
like meal, as it seemed to me. She was devoted and anxious

about his well-being and contentment to a fault, completely
absorbed in loving and worrying about her son, but she took
the time to be well mannered and asked where I had come
from.

'England.'

She didn't respond to this with any greater (or lesser) interest than if I had said Pittsburgh, but nodded distractedly,
more interested in how her boy was doing. 'How is the weather
in England?'

It wasn't at all clear to me that she knew where in the world
England was, but she certainly knew, as all Americans do, that
the weather there should be referred to. I assured her it rained
a lot and she seemed satisfied to hear it. The world was as she
thought and there was an end to it. And where was she going,
I asked.

'Home to Libby,' she told me, and hugged the boy.

After a moment she seemed to notice that more was
required. She spoke shyly and quietly, rather rapidly as if to
get communication over and done with as quickly as possible.
She said no more than was absolutely necessary to say to a
stranger asking questions, but she was not unfriendly. She and
her family had been to her son's wedding to a girl from an
Amish community in Massachusetts. He was the fourth of
her boys to marry, and she had two married daughters: they all
lived with their wives and husbands in Libby. She spoke as if
Libby were New York or Paris; as if I couldn't fail to be familiar with the place. Then she clammed up, looking a little
flustered; demure and girlish, and slightly guilty, as if she had
already said too much to an outsider. She flushed even pinker
than before and dipped her head down to murmur at her son,
who nodded his satisfaction in answer to her queries and
grinned at me from time to time with hotdog-filled cheeks, like

a happy hamster. It was clear that any further curiosity would have been intrusive. For all my fascination, I couldn't find a way to enter into a real conversation with this woman so locked into her regulated contentment that any question about it from an outsider could only present a challenge. When I got back to my compartment and checked with the schedule, Libby was in Montana, just past Whitefish in Glacier Park, and we were due to arrive there at around 11 p.m. the next night.

I discovered that in spite of my luxurious sleeping accommodation, I was back on an old-fashioned train with a proper punishment smoking coach exactly the same as on the *Sunset Limited*, even down to the cigarette burns on the floor and the severe warning not to bring food or drink or to stay more than the fifteen minutes designated for smoking a cigarette. A kind of contentment came over me, a warm familiarity, a coming-home to the blue-grey fumes, the grime, the neglected scruffiness and a total absence of the irony and nostalgia of the glass smoking box on the *Empire Builder*. 'You want to smoke? Right, here's a filthy hole to smoke in. So smoke.' Much better. And here too was humanity and yet more opportunity for me to be a part of it. My eagerness to socialise had reached a critical low. Whatever it was about the human capacity for story that had engaged me on the first accidental journey had evaporated into a wish for stillness and silence as America passed by. I entered the smoking coach only because of my urgent need to smoke. I rather hoped it would be empty. I had no desire to break into a new social round. Apparently my increasing weariness of human company was not unique. In a memoir of train travel in 1878, Helen Hunt Jackson suggested that she had experienced a similar trajectory of social exhaustion:

Be as silent, as unsocial, as surly as you please, you cannot avoid being more or less impressed by the magnetism of every human being in the car. Their faces attract or repel; you like, you dislike, you wonder, you pity, you resent, you loathe. In the course of twenty-four hours you have expended a great amount of nerve force, to no purpose.

Far from being empty, the smoking coach contained the intensely sociable joys of Big Daddy. He was a bulging Southern gentleman in his early sixties, with the rolling accent and moustache of Rhett Butler, an elaborately floral embroidered waistcoat and a cowboy hat with a wide curved brim. His face was dark, deeply bronzed; he might have been black, or sunburned, it was impossible to tell. Perhaps it was just his name (from *Cat on a Hot Tin Roof*, I believe) that made me think he bore an uncanny resemblance to Tennessee Williams. He was loudly admiring a large black woman's T-shirt that had 'The Cardinals' emblazoned across her billowing breasts in cardinal red.

'That T-shirt is really something. I'd like one of those.' He turned to acknowledge me as I sat down, offering me his hand and his name. 'Big Daddy, ma'am. Those are very fine pants you've got on there. I do think highly of those pants.'

'Hey, Big Daddy.' The T-shirt woman squealed with laughter. 'You go on like this and you'll have a full set of clothes.'

Big Daddy was on his way to Whitefish, in Glacier Park, the Alpine skiing and fishing resort in Montana. He took regular holidays by himself, leaving his woman at home, he told me, allowing me to understand that he bestowed his charms wherever they might be wanted and that both he and those who succumbed to those charms generally found the outlay worthwhile. He was an ageing, old-time gigolo, still available to amuse. Once he heard I was a writer from England he chatted and charmed me with local information, telling me what I needed to know about the upcoming places of interest.

'Let me help you with your task, little lady . . .'

Shelby, for example, which we wouldn't be reaching until teatime the next day, was somewhere I should watch out for. Not that it was of any interest these days, but it was once famous for the gala World Heavyweight Championship fight between Jack Dempsey and Tom Gibbons, arranged for 4 July 1923. Thousands of fight fans hired trains to get them out west, then, a few days before the fight, Dempsey's manager Doc Kearns cancelled the match. The fans cancelled their trains and then at the last minute Kearns agreed that the fight could go ahead after all. There were 7000 spectators with tickets and 17,000 gatecrashers, pandemonium, of course, and while all the excitement of the bout was going on, Doc Kearns quietly slipped out of town with the $300,000 purse. Dempsey got nothing for his win over Gibbons, and four Montana banks went bust.

'And that's the story of Shelby, my deah. Now, soon we'll be crossing a bridge that a local man called Geary kept free of snow during the winter with his snowplough, the one and only snowplough in town. He was a rowdy fellow, this Geary, who liked his liquor, and one day after a real bender and whole lot of broken streetlamps he was hauled in front of the judge who gave him thirty days in the local jail for drunk-driving and banned him from driving for six months. When he got out he had to visit the probation officer to show he had changed his ways, so he got in his snowplough and drove there. "How did you get here?" the probation officer asked Geary. "Why, I drove here," says Geary. Well, Geary went right back to jail for another thirty days for driving without a licence. But by then the snows had arrived, and all through those winter days while Geary was back in jail, and while the driving ban was in force, every single train crossing the bridge had to run slow, real slow, at walking speed because the bridge wasn't being cleared of snow and ice, not being beautifully maintained by Geary who was in jail, warm and comfortable and well fed. And the snowplough being Geary's snowplough and the only one in town, no one else was permitted to drive it. The railroad company complained, but the law was the law.'

Big Daddy's entertaining stories came thick and fast. Strangely mythic, strangely inconsequential. A train guard was taking a smoking break on the seat opposite and enjoying the tales, nodding and smiling. Big Daddy grinned at him. 'Great job, you got, huh?'

The guard's smile turned sour. 'Used to be,' he grunted. 'Time was. Hey, don't get me started. Now . . . It's all run by *management* and friends of friends. It ain't professional like it used to be. These guys don't know how to run a railroad. They ain't professionals, they're businessmen and cronies. They sit in their boardrooms with charts and it's me who gets the customers shouting because they've oversold the train and it's late and it's broken down. Then they send you to charm school instead of fixing the problems, so you can learn how to calm the customers down. Keep everyone sweet but don't deal with the problems. It's the liberal way. The big liberal lie. They've taken over everything in this damned country. The government. The railroads. They've ruined everything with their big lie. The great socialist lie.'

His fury had grown to federal proportions.

'What big lie?' I asked.

'You know. The Big Lie. The Big Socialist Liberal Lie.'

I looked baffled and asked him for more detail, but he was at a loss to know where to start, it was so obvious. Hell, everyone knew about the Big Lie.

'They just tell lies. Socialist lies. Socialist double-talk. Political correctness. Like they don't say you have to pay higher taxes, they tell you you're making *contributions*. And they shoot their mouths off about gun safety and freedom when what they're actually doing is making gun law and restricting our freedom that was enshrined in the constitution of the United States of America. The right to bear arms. That's where our safety and freedom is ensured. Those are the kind of lies they tell, the socialists. The liberal lies that don't say what they mean. Hell, they mean the straight opposite of what ordinary folk understand by their words.'

He paused, as if waiting for applause, but no one seemed eager to support him, or urge him on further, though we listened politely. Neither Big Daddy nor the black woman in the Cardinals T-shirt seemed very interested.

'Hell,' he petered out. 'Don't get me going on the liberals. Just don't get me going.'

And he retreated into silence and soon muttered that his break was over and left. It was the first time that politics had come up on my train journeys.

By now it was early evening and my name was called over the tannoy system, summoning me for dinner, which occurs at a very early hour on the railroads. Lunch and dinner were served at set times and everyone had to reserve a slot and keep it. Lateness was frowned on. The dining car, if not the train, ran on a strict schedule. By nine it was cleaned and emptied, and if you passed through it there was always the head steward with receipts and a calculator totting up the takings, reconciling the pieces of paper. Paperwork seemed to be a

major activity in the dining car, and the diners themselves a bit
of a nuisance, to be dealt with as quickly as possible so that the
real business of adding and subtracting and keeping the ledger
straight could go ahead. I waved to my smoking companions,
and then made my way to the dining car. It turned out that
politics was going to be the theme for that evening, as if in
travelling west, we were also moving politically to the right.
The waiter seated me opposite a smoothly groomed,
respectable-looking middle-aged couple, who smiled politely
enough as I joined them. We said good evening and exchanged
regulation information on our origins and destination. In a
few moments a fourth member of our table was seated by the
waiter. I had seen her earlier making her way between the
seats through one of the coaches. She was a very slight woman
with unkempt grey hair, in her fifties, wearing tapered twill
trousers and a practical shirt with a leather bag strapped across
her body. She suffered from some medical disorder that caused
her continually to jerk and tic on a grand scale, and I remembered seeing her careering along the aisle of the moving train
like an irate windmill. As she began to speak, her words were
interrupted so that she could perform a wide arc with one arm
and a series of staccato twitches of her neck and head, seem-
ingly in a prescribed order. When it was done, the words could
come.

'I'm Glenys,' she said as she sat down neatly before per-
forming another set of ticcings and then relaxing. 'What are
your names?'

She was clearly much more used to being Glenys and taking
it for granted than were her dining companions. The couple
opposite looked alarmed; I tried not to, which amounted to the
same thing. Glenys had a proper understanding of her condition. She allowed her twitches full rein, to blossom and then to

die down before she attempted to reach for the salt, or put a forkful of food in her mouth. Her activities and conversation fitted into the intervals between her ticcing – or perhaps it was the other way round, and the tics took their opportunities as they may between the pauses in eating or talking. In either case, she and her condition had accommodated, and cohabited, as they had to, each giving time to the other.

'Are you on your own?' the man opposite asked Glenys, in a frigid voice that was too loud, over-carefully enunciating each word as one might talk to a foreigner or an idiot.

Glenys explained that she was having a two-day vacation in Whitefish, to see the mountains. She had never spent time in mountains, but she couldn't afford to stay at the resort longer than the two days, not on her fixed income from her disability pension. The woman opposite had absented herself from the table. That is, she was still sitting there, but she had withdrawn her social self from what was an impossible situation, apparently, so that her attention was entirely given over to her plate and the movements of her knife and fork. Her husband had another way. He glared at Glenys with unconcealed repugnance, as if he were looking at something that had landed by some mishap in our midst; something filthy that was without consciousness and had no capacity to see or look back at him. I have rarely seen one human being look at another with such naked disgust. For the rest of the meal, he addressed himself exclusively to me, as if there was no one sitting beside me. Glenys asked me where I was from and what I did. We exchanged information. She worked for an educational group which lobbied for special schools for the developmentally disabled, she explained. People I knew in England with disabled children were battling in the opposite direction, to get their children taught in the mainstream sector.

Glenys was firm, her position was radical and separatist. Disabled people were always at a disadvantage in mainstream schools where they stood out and their particular needs were not catered for. They were in a minority and inclined to measure themselves against a norm that was normal only by virtue of greater numbers and unachievable by them. Only schools that specifically catered for disabled children, where they were the norm and the majority, gave them the sense of their quality and rights in the world, and in both development and education children had been shown to perform much better in schools with specialist teachers and dedicated design rather than piecemeal structural adaptations. The move to close special schools and colleges down was, in her opinion, reactionary, regressive, a way of saving money, not a way of giving the disabled the best education and the ability to explore their full potential. She made a passionate case, all the while gesticulating and ticcing up a storm as if her strong feelings increased their intensity.

The man sitting opposite signalled to me. He caught my eye, attempting to draw me away from my sideways conversation with Glenys with a tiny repeated sideways wagging of his forefinger at just above the level of his plate, urgently indicating that what I was being told was completely in error, shifting his eyes, inviting me to follow them, in a direction away from Glenys, closing his eyelids against what was being said, and echoing the negating movement of his finger with a rapid shaking of his head. It was an extraordinary performance, quite as exotic and busy as any of Glenys's suite of tremors, and rather more alarming. I found myself just staring at him in wonderment for a moment. He was indicating to me, as if Glenys were blind, that everything she said was absolute nonsense, and that I shouldn't give any credence to it. When he spoke, it was in a lowish tone that was supposed to exclude the woman sitting on my left, as a doctor might speak in an aside to a responsible adult about a sick child who was present but not able to comprehend. Glenys was considered mentally defective, deaf and blind by this man who thought it was vital I understand the truth.

'Don't listen to her. This is the result of what happened in the sixties. The liberals and hippies and lefties let them all out, closed the institutions, and now they're on the streets, making trouble, a danger to society. Retards, loonies, drug addicts. Mental cases like . . .' – he tossed his head in Glenys's direction – 'who shouldn't be allowed to be in ordinary society. That's why normal decent people can't walk around freely and without fear any more. Those kind of people begging and sleeping in doorways, spreading diseases and demanding rights . . . You can't even have your dinner in peace.'

His voice, a whine of fury and frustration, matched the disgusted curl of his mouth as he corrected the misinformation I was receiving. I spoke politely.

'Sorry, but I was one of those liberals, hippies and lefties. As I remember it, what we wanted to do in the sixties was close the institutions and use the money saved to provide for local, humane care and education for people who were mentally and physically disabled, instead of locking them up and forgetting about them while they rotted for the rest of their life. In fact, nothing actually happened until the eighties when Thatcher and Reagan closed all the old asylums down, chucked the inmates on to the street and took the money and ran. They didn't put anything in their place, no system of care and no funding to rehabilitate or provide long-term treatment for the people they turfed out. It was the far right that filled the streets with people who had nowhere else to go, then walked away, not the left. When I was growing up in the centre of London, I never saw young people sleeping on pavements. It didn't happen until Margaret Thatcher was elected.'

Glenys and I now shared our dining companion's gaze of disgust. However, it was still only to me he spoke, since, leftie though I had been revealed to be, traitor though I was to what he thought of as normality, at least, in his eyes, I was not retarded. He was dreadfully disturbed by Glenys.

'No, no. It was the left who led the movement to close the institutions. Reagan and Thatcher were wrongly blamed for it. It's all in the history books. My god, where would we be today without Ronald Reagan, and Margaret Thatcher supporting him? We'd be under the thumb of Russia. We'd be ruled by communists. Is that the kind of existence you want?'

I gaped in astonishment.

'Oh, sure, you can look like that but I'm telling you. It was Reagan's Star Wars plan that scared Gorbachev into giving up his ideas of world domination. And you see what's happened? Now Russia is run by the Mafia. That's the Ruskies for you.'

This was a pointless conversation, but I was stuck in it. 'But the US has been run by the Mafia since the Twenties.'

Suddenly his wife looked up from her plate, and in an entirely neutral voice said, 'He thinks *they're* all right.' She looked down at her food again and he continued as if she hadn't spoken.

'And we've got traitors in our midst. Pat Buchanan has turned belly-up. He had this *epiphany* and decided that welfare was a good thing. Why the hell should decent hard-working people pay to keep *them* in benefits?'

'Just out of self-interest,' I tried, feebly. 'If "they're" left destitute what kind of a society will you hard-working right-eous people have to live in?'

'We ought to return to the agrarian economy.'

I tried not to laugh. 'But that isn't a choice—'

'Yeah,' he said, his face quite contorted with disgust and despair. 'It's too late now.'

It was enough. I waited for Glenys to finish her sweet and we left the table. There was nothing to say. I just shook my head. Glenys would have shrugged but it got all caught up in a great involuntary circular motion that indicated the whole world and everything that was included in it. When it was completed, we laughed and I went off for a cigarette.

We pulled in to St Paul's–Minneapolis at 10.25 p.m., dead on time. The train was taking on fuel and water, so we had a forty-minute break to stretch our legs, wander about the station and walk on solid ground. It was dark, and as I was walking back from the station building along the broad empty tarmac towards the train I heard my name.

'Hey, Jenny.'

It was Big Daddy. I went towards him.

'You like to dance?'

'Yes.'

'OK. I'll show you the *Sound of Music* routine I worked out. Remember when they are dancing on the terrace? I played it over and over on my VTR and worked out the steps. Here.' He extended an arm and took my hand gracefully in his. 'OK, just shadow me.'

He called out the steps in an undertone – step, step, back, step, and sideways step, step . . . We walked through the routine. A sort of minuet, between our extended arms, closing up and backing apart with the odd twirl, twirl, twirl in-between. 'Got it?'

We practised it two or three times. People on their way to and from the train stopped to watch.

'Yeah, you got it. Now.'

He began to sing the wordless tune of the dance and we did the routine in real time. Then, with more confidence, again, and finally, when we had a good crowd forming a circle around us in the dark night-time train station, with real sashaying pizzazz, ending with me swirling half a dozen times under his upraised arm. We dropped a bow and a curtsey to the applause and whistles of appreciation from our audience.

'Hey, you picked that up real good. By the time we get to Whitefish we'll get it perfect. Ready to shoot.'

'You're a good choreographer.'

Big Daddy smiled modestly. 'It's only one of my many talents, my deah.' He slipped an arm around my waist. 'Why not make a detour and spend a day or two in Whitefish? Who knows what dances we might choreograph together? We'd make a fine pair . . . of dancers.'

Stepping out in the night to perform a pas-de-deux on the platform at St Paul's–Minneapolis in the shadow of the *Empire Builder* was one thing, and quite delightful, but what about a weekend detour with a shameless new-world/old-world flirt in Whitefish, Montana? I liked the improbability of it. I was quite tempted by the spontaneity and irregularity of the idea – until I remembered how many hours there are in even a single day let alone two, and how easily charm turns sour, and that I am, for all my temporary keen listening and participatory interest in the world around me, deeply intolerant of other people, especially when the conversation flags and the cracks in the performance begin to show. To save us from me, to save us both the disappointment that more time than a quick dance routine requires would bring to Big Daddy and me, I declined the offer, but with something like genuine regret.

Grabbing experience was something of a habit I had

acquired when it was the watchword of the late Sixties. If someone handed you a drug, you took it, because it would be an experience. If someone invited you to have sex with them you did, again, for the experience. It was most important not to let anything pass you by. The drug or the sex might, and sometimes did, turn out to be bad experiences, but that was still valuable. For what? It was hard to say. To know life, or to know about life. But sex and drugs and forays into ancient eastern texts seemed to us at the time to be the main routes to experience. No one suggested that getting up at eight in the morning was an experience we needed to have (though to have stayed up all night smoking dope or dropping acid and then to greet the dawn qualified), nor that the experiences of going off to work day after day, or paying bills or phoning home, were essential to the full life. On the other hand, most of us ended up doing all those things eventually, so perhaps we weren't entirely wrong. It was a bit like the Duke of Edinburgh Award without the virtue. We took risks, and some people suffered very badly, but then you can fall off a mountain you're climbing for the experience. The war was over before most of us were born – that generation had taken risks without choosing to do so. It must have seemed mad to them that we were messing around with our heads and emotions, taking unnecessary risks when the world had just been made safe for us. But the world was not safe, of course. What most of us knew about was nuclear weapons, the Cuban Missile Crisis, the Cold War, and I was not alone in truly believing that I wouldn't live to old age.

That was the rhetoric. In practice, I was in the midst of depression, and every drug I took that was potentially dangerous was all right by me. While I have no doubt others were genuinely trying to expand their minds and have all the experience they could before kingdom came, I was in reality playing a kind of Russian roulette. I knew that I was the last person who should take acid or speed, that I sank too fast into depression without any chemical help to risk taking them. I took acid and I injected methyl amphetamine into my veins. I woke in the morning with a joint ready rolled so that not a minute would be wasted not being stoned. The speed was the most lethal in its after-effects, and therefore the drug of choice. But while it thrummed through my system it was extraordinary. I remember sitting in the flat in Covent Garden I'd moved into – a nursery land of drug availability – the first time I fixed. I sat on the floor with my back against the wall. There were half a dozen strangers, maybe more, in the room smoking dope, listening to music. The most extraordinary feeling came over me, once the initial rush of speed had coursed through my blood. It took a while to identify it, but eventually it dawned on me that I was at ease, comfortable, where I belonged, with people I belonged to – and what was astonishing about this feeling was that it was genuinely the first time I had ever experienced it so totally. Until then I had always been in the wrong place, with the wrong people, or never quite the right ones, never really with a sense that I belonged exactly where I was, that I wasn't just alien enough to be a watcher not a member of the group. I felt at ease for the first time in my life. Thank you, methyl amphetamine. See you soon. Very soon.

Actually, I was familiar with meth. When I was in Ward 6 of the Maudsley I was under the care of Dr Krapl Taylor, then head of the hospital. There are varying views about Dr KT's ministrations, but he was quite keen on experimental techniques. One of these was *abreaction*. A depressed patient was injected with methyl amphetamine and then goaded by a

therapist into a state of anxiety and distress. The resulting
explosion was supposed to be cathartic or something.
Psychiatrists go pale these days when you tell them that they
used this technique at a respectable psychiatric hospital. One
doctor who was actually on staff there just before I was a
patient said he had no knowledge that Krapl Taylor was using
such a treatment. So I knew about meth. I had it twice a week
when I saw my shrink, who then spent twenty minutes assur-
ing me that I was worthless in the eyes of Dr Krapl Taylor.
Being depressed I could only agree with KT's assessment. So
what's new? Can I have some more meth, I think I could get to
like this if you gave me a larger dose? In fact, I did finally
abreact – went berserk as required – but instead of shedding
my depression I lost quite a lot of blood from a slashed wrist.
The best-laid plans . . . Finally, after nine months, I wandered
into the drugs room and started to open the cabinet, while the
nurse in charge watched in open-mouthed astonishment. I
was just going to take myself a decent dose of meth. There
was a scuffle and I threw my clothes into a bag and left. I
headed for the Arts Lab in Drury Lane, sat in the café and
turned round in my chair to talk to the complete stranger
behind me.

'Do you know where I can get some meth?'

He grinned. Effortless, I had found the speed king of
London, WC1. Those were the days.

For a while my non-medical doses of meth continued to
give me a feeling of rightness in the world, but the come-
downs were murderous. They were my own depressions
doubled and blacker than night. Even so, I figured them worth
it. Meth was very easy to get hold of, the depression could be
sorted with another fix. I was never in any real danger from
heroin addiction. I lived in the kitchen of the Covent Garden

flat with a registered heroin addict, and my only experience of it (yeah, you had to try that too) just made me feel very ill. It takes time and effort to become a heroin junkie, I was in too much of a hurry. Speed was my speed. At least until the come-downs and the depression combined to make me take a large enough overdose of barbiturates to land me in hospital with plans to send me back to St Pancras North Wing – back to Go, Do Not Collect £200. That was when I decided I really didn't want to become a revolving-door psychiatric in-patient. I quit drugs, all of them, and decided to take the going-to-work-every-day experience – just for the experience, you understand.

After my dancing on the platform at St Paul's–Minneapolis and declining a weekend of delights and experience with Big Daddy, I slept like a baby rocked in untiring arms. I missed all the night stops – St Cloud, Staples, Detroit Lakes, Fargo, Grand Forks – and woke at 6.50 a.m. having just passed Devil's Lake, North Dakota. We were a mere twenty-five minutes behind schedule. The landscape had utterly changed. We had entered mile after mile, hour after hour, of non-stop prairie: my first view of prairie outside of the movies and those patronising, cutifying Disney nature films that caused a generation to grow up terminally anthropomorphic. This prairie was a thing to behold as the sun shone on red-gold grass and scrub. Brown, you might have said if you were being inattentive, but from my bed, gazing hypnotised out at the land, I caught infinite variations on the theme of orange, ochre, yellow and gold. What I didn't know until I went to the observation car and heard a couple of bucolophobic Chicagoans expressing what they thought of the landscape ('Hey, didn't we pass that fencepost a couple of hours ago?'), was that North Dakota is the butt of urban American jokes, and to Montanans the folk from North Dakota are what the Polish are to New Yorkers.

'But it's extraordinary. Vast. Beautiful,' I said to my neighbour who was shaking his head in pity at the lot of the North Dakotans.

'Honey, this land is flat, featureless and it ends in mountains. That's good. It keeps the inmates from spreading out into the real world.'

It was true that sitting there for an hour or two there is nothing to see but the grass and scrub, with occasional glimpses of the Mississippi winding and trickling through the land. Then suddenly you see a farmhouse. Just there, plonk in the middle of nowhere. Cows and horses standing about. Trees. Fences. Fences to keep the cows and horses in, I suppose, not to keep anyone out, because for 360 degrees around these signs of human life, and stretching to every horizon, there is blank nothing. No road; nowhere for a road to lead. Just empty space filled with wilderness. And how, I wondered, and continued to wonder for the next day as North Dakota became the grasslands of Montana, had these homesteaders decided that it was here, just *here*, in this actual spot, that they were going to build a house and a life. Why not a couple of hundred yards further along? Or back? Or to the right or left? What difference would it make? How could you ever make a decision? I imagined myself pacing back and forth trying to place my stake in the spot where I would build my house, but never managing to decide, because in the absence of defining detail, and assuming the Mississippi near enough by, absolutely any spot would do. And wouldn't you need, having travelled God-knows-how-far – from the East by wagon train, or from old Europe by ship – to feel that the place where you decided to settle was the most particular place you could find? Here is the perfect spot, your eyes and your heart sing together, recognising what and where it is you came all that way for, risked everything to find. But no, hang on, perhaps it's just a little to the left, or a mile and a half to the right. Well, let's assume that the pioneers and refugees had more practical minds than me daydreaming on a train, and had the good sense to get down and digging. Any place they hung their hat was home.

I gazed out of the window, a member of the audience for the moving picture that we were passing through, and started to see how it had all come about. The geography of movie America, the reason for all those celluloid dreams, rolled across the picture windows like a festival of film, freed from individual stories and script, but including all of them, making them necessary, inevitable. The genres had sped by. The industrial landscapes of Pittsburgh and Chicago, the railyards, the smoking factory chimneys, all spoke of fast urban tales of people doing their best and worst to make a living in a thundering black-and-white world. The poor and destitute, living rough, riding the rails, the dogged workers falling away from the civilised centres to the drab and dangerous peripheries, the corruption, the blind bland rich. The clichés jostled in my head as those movies had scrolled by until gradually they were replaced by the flat, featureless plains of Montana that caused the heart to pound in alarm at such endless space. For hours, for whole days, miles and miles of agricultural land, unrelieved by the slightest incline or hollow, each mile indistinguishable from the last, from the last hundred and the next hundred. This was the vastness that the pioneers had sought, the good living, the chance to do more than subsist. It was almost unbearable.

At breakfast I saw Glenys and joined her. She was sitting opposite a very small, wisp of an elderly black man, who still wore the natty clothes of his heyday. His face was creased and crumpled, but along with the feather he wore in his pork pie hat that had 'Indianapolis' written above the brim, he sported an embroidered waistcoat to put Big Daddy to shame, flared denims and a black leather string tie. This – I'm aware that I am forever describing Americans in terms of their likeness to movie or showbiz stars, but try though I might, this was inescapable – was Sammy Davies Jr revisited. Tiny, spry, fast-talking, and, in our breakfast companion's case, a little mad. He was as inclined to talk to himself as to us, so sometimes he was hard to follow, but he was, as his hat indicated, from Indianapolis, and he was, like Glenys, taking a long-waited-for vacation on his own. He was going to Seattle to, again like Glenys, see the mountains he had never been in. It is aston-ishing how many Americans tell you of longing for American landscapes but fail to get to them decade after decade. The remarkably untravelled lives of many of the people I met on the train quite pulled against the notion of a continent in flux, all its people on the move. Actually, for the most part, they seem to stay still and dream. Indianapolis, who was in his six-ties, I guessed, had only a few days away to see the mountains at last, even though he was retired, presumably because his funds were too limited for a longer holiday, but his train to Chicago to catch the *Empire Builder* had been so late that he had missed his connection. He muttered much of this out through the window, but Glenys had begun his monologue by asking where he had got on the train, so it seemed all right to interrupt his private recollections.

'So you had to lose a whole day out of your vacation wait-ing for the next train?'

He looked up and shook his head.

'Nope, this here is the train I was booked on. Amtrak flew me from Chicago to St Paul's to pick it up. I was waiting when it arrived. The plane was on time.'

I was impressed. He wasn't.

'Yeah, but the train was part of the vacation, and the reason I travelled by train is that I'm afraid of flying.'

I've rarely seen a man look so mournful, as he shook his head, dismayed at the memory of finding himself flying courtesy of the train company.

In the smoking coach were a new collection of people along with the old. Sitting in the near corner was a tired-looking woman with a body that had broken free of its youthfully contained voluptuousness and weary blonde hair with roots so badly in need of doing that it was almost half and half fair to black. Opposite her was a young man with severely cropped hair and dim, close-together eyes that I guessed not only tiredness had rendered unalert, but with a body that rippled with youth and fitness under his white T-shirt. I took him for a soldier. He was indeed a soldier on his way back to his base after a couple of weeks' leave. A woman called Martha, who I had met in line in Chicago station and who had immediately begun recounting in detail her adventures on the internet discovering her genealogy, and how everyone should do it, I should do it, and what, precisely, she had discovered, and who I had been avoiding ever since, was bending a willing acolyte's ear, as indeed she was whenever I came across her. She talked on and on and on. When she finished with the importance of finding one's roots, she moved to canonical books by women and feminist history. She was unstoppable, as if her every word was of everlasting interest and it was her duty to induct any lone female (and, because of the loudness of her voice, anyone nearby) into her world of historical self-justification. I wondered now, though, if perhaps she was manic, from the way she shot out the words as if they were all queuing and jostling to be said and couldn't wait their turn. Next to her, but turned firmly away, was the conductor on another break, telling a man next to him almost word for word about the liberal lie. Martha finished some exposition about the invisibility of women in the historical record by blaming 'the usual suspects'. Uncharacteristically, she paused and looked around the coach.

'Ha,' she gloated. 'The joke went over their heads. No one got the reference to *Casablanca*. *The usual suspects*.'

'I never saw that movie,' the soldier said, trying to be helpfully dumbed down.

'That is so sad. We've become ignorant of our own culture. Movies are very important . . .'

And she continued with a lecture about the educational and social value of film. But Martha's cultural understanding was stuck in the Forties. She clearly did not know that the film the soldier hadn't seen was not *Casablanca* (which he could hardly have missed if he were an avid TV watcher), but the more modern cultural must-know *The Usual Suspects*. Thankfully, no one cared to explain the gap in her knowledge and Martha was allowed to remain satisfyingly superior.

'Were you in the Gulf?' the tired woman asked the soldier.

'Yes, ma'am.' He spoke quite neutrally. He was a soldier describing where he had been, not venturing an opinion. He seemed too archetypal to be true.

'My son was in the Gulf,' she said, looking quite haunted. 'I watched it happening on the TV all the time. I never turned it off, slept in front of it, ate in front of it. The doctor put me on tranquillisers and said I had to turn off the TV and stop watching the war. But I couldn't. It was like I had to to keep my son alive. And, my god, when that stuff about friendly fire came out . . . Jesus, friendly fire, killing our own . . .'

'Yeah,' the soldier said, without any kind of expression on his face. 'My sergeant said watch out for friendly fire. He said friendly fire kills you worse than enemy fire.'

There was a small pause while we took this in, but no one indicated their appreciation for his exquisite irony. I looked at him a little harder, but I couldn't see anything in his face that knew the weight of what he had just said. The eyes stayed dim, the voice flat.

The blonde woman nodded. 'It's all the stuff they don't tell you. Like when they killed JFK. God, I cried and cried over that. I loved that man. We still don't know what really happened. They kept the truth from us.' She spoke with raw passion and a grief that dated back to 1963. 'I'm telling you, if we knew what we don't know, we'd be angry.'

The young soldier nodded, slow and solemn. 'Yes, ma'am, if we knew what we don't know, we'd know more.'

And for me it was one of those moments when, like the transition that occurs when an oil and egg-yolk mixture suddenly emulsifies into mayonnaise, the texture of human existence cohered and thickened. I have no idea if life does this sort of thing accidentally or because it has an independent sense of humour and it knows you're listening. Whichever, or whatever else, the humanity of humanity was on a roll just then on that train, and it wasn't going to stop until I did. It was altogether a day of rich textures.

Later that afternoon another stranger, Annie, seemed to be having the same thoughts as me about the arbitrariness of the homesteads.

'Now why did they put that house right there?' she

wondered aloud, as we both happened to be staring out of the same window while we puffed on our cigarettes.

Annie was from New Orleans and on holiday from her regular life. She had six kids aged from thirty-three down to ten. She was a single mother, black, and used to be a cook but had retired, earning extra money by doing a little babysitting now. She told me about her twenty-one-year-old boy who was diagnosed as hyperactive. He still lived at home, needing full-time attention, but the older children took it in turns to have him sometimes so that Annie could have a break.

'The boy has trouble with angritude,' she explained.

She took him regularly to classes to help him deal with his emotional ups and downs. They wanted Annie to become a volunteer and work with other troubled kids.

'You got to listen to kids. It's no good shouting. I grew up with my grandmother shouting and screaming. I cried a lot. No need for that. There's enough hatred in the world without having it in the family.'

While she was away she called her son twice a day. He resented her leaving him. Her other kids were good with him, but if he was having a tantrum they couldn't cope with, they'd get her on her mobile and she'd speak to him.

'Sometimes it takes two hours of me talking to him before he can calm himself down. He needs to hear someone speaking quietly to him, and he needs to talk himself and be listened to. Then he's all right. Hey, life is like a train, it goes round and round.'

'And it's always late.'

Annie laughed. 'Yup. And why the hell *did* they put that house just there?'

Human life in all its inescapable difficulty and the astonishing human capacity for somehow coping with or enduring it was positively parading itself on the *Empire Builder*. By mid-afternoon we were at Havre, another water stop where passengers could get out and air themselves. Taking advantage of a regular captive audience, the platform at Havre sported a large signpost explaining how the town got its name when two rivals in love fought over a local beauty. After hours of fisticuffs the loser stormed off shouting, 'You can have'er.' Every American town likes to have its mythic founding story, but Havre, I felt, just hadn't tried hard enough.

'Dumb, huh?' a voice said in my ear as I finished reading it. 'I hear you're a writer.'

A man in his late thirties or early forties stood beside me. He was short and stocky, in regulation baseball cap, jeans and a T-shirt. As ordinary-looking a man as you could imagine. 'I don't mean to intrude, but hearing you're a writer, I've got a story for you.'

I lit another cigarette and waited, trying to project a look that said I was interested but I wasn't going to get in any way involved in his life no matter how terrible his story was. It was clearly going to be pretty terrible, because the ordinary guy's eyes had taken on an intense and fiery look as he prepared to relate, yet again but never often enough, what had happened to him.

'I was OK until nine years ago. I led a normal life working as a joiner in a local firm. I lived at home. We were a regular family. Then my mom died. I got bad feelings about it, but I carried on. Then five years later, when my dad died, I went berserk. I got suicidal. Real crazy. Putting a gun to my head. Playing Russian roulette and stuff. I packed in the job and went to live alone in the woods for a long time. I got crazier and crazier out there in the woods, and then one day I realised that I had to get help. I saw a doctor, a psychiatrist who put me on Prozac, thirty milligrams twice daily. It was depression, he said. That shit hit me hard. In a month my teeth were chattering so bad that they broke. My teeth actually shattered to pieces because they rattled so bad. I thought my brain was going to be shaken to a froth. If I was crazy before, I was twice as crazy on the fucking – excuse me – Prozac, and it wasn't even my own craziness. When I finally saw a dentist, the state had to pay out seven thousand dollars to fix my teeth, I'd done that much damage to them. But they should have paid me a lot more. Damages. I should have sued them for what that stuff did to me. Prescribed by a doctor. I was trying to get better and it ruined my life, with the shakes and panics and what not. They still haven't gone away completely.'

'How do you live now?'

'I'm an artist, like you. I carve sculptures out of wood. I live alone, and I have my work and fifteen acres of land my dad left me. I manage OK on a day-by-day basis, but I'm not the same man I was. I lead a very isolated life. I stay very quiet. If I didn't have my sculpting, I don't know if I'd be OK. I guess I'm still depressed. It all preys on my mind, what happened to me and how I felt and everything. It goes round and round in my head, you know, the whole thing. My mom and dad and the pills and the depression. I think about depression twenty-two hours a day, every day. Every day of my life. I try to get it into my work, but I'm a visual artist. I can't write my feelings down. People should hear about what happened to me. About the Prozac and depression. You're a writer. So you can write my story.'

By the late afternoon the unchanging landscape in the distance ahead of us seemed to be coming to a conclusion. We were approaching the outskirts of Glacier Park, which was the far edge of the prairie and the beginning of the Rockies. The great plain just came to an end and the jagged snow-topped mountains rose abruptly like a retaining wall. The train commenced its climb of the foothills just when the sun began to set and as we headed into the new landscape, rising towards the snow level, the daylight went out. We had to take the beauty of the Rockies and Glacier Park on trust. The man sitting next to me in the observation car sighed at the last dying rays of the sun.

'Just when there was something to see, there's nothing to be seen.'

I laughed and said I supposed we'd have to take the train in the other direction to see the Rockies in daylight. 'Holidaying?' I asked.

'Yes, kind of. I'm recovering from brain surgery. I'm sixty-seven. I was an engineer. When I retired I started to get these seizures. I reckon it was because I was bored. Nothing to do apart from walk the dogs. The wife still works. So they operated. Said I had to lead a quiet life, but I figured it was the quiet life that was killing me. So I'm taking trips around the country by train. Just for something to do.'

'What do the doctors say?'

'That I shouldn't.'

He looked gloomy as he spoke, though his features had a natural downturn to them. Then he changed the subject, asking me about how things were going in Northern Ireland. He was Irish by descent. He'd supported the IRA for a long time, but now he was beginning to think he'd been wrong.

'I want our side to be good, but they turn out just to be terrorists, the way they behave, the way they treat people.' He shook his head. 'It's all wars. It seems like people just don't want a quiet life.'

'You don't, either,' I said.

'No, you're right. But I don't want to be dead more.'

At dinner life let up a little as a rather upmarket elderly gentleman in a good suit of clothes expressed delight that I was from the UK and regaled me with the pleasures of British television. Imported programmes from Britain were all he considered worth watching on US TV, especially the crime dramas. Through three courses he told me about his favourites and asked me about upcoming series that had yet to be shown in the States. He lovingly listed the programme names with the relish of a connoisseur: *Morse, Cracker, A Touch of Frost, Bergerac, Midsomer Murders, Poirot, Prime Suspect, Miss Marple* . . . did I know them, were there any he had missed, he wondered anxiously? And Oxford, Manchester, Jersey, Denton, Badger's Drift, St Mary Mead: were they just as they were portrayed? Morse, he had heard, though the episode had not yet arrived, had revealed his first name. Was that true, no, don't tell him what it was. And there was a rumour that Morse was going to die. Had I heard that? It was just terrible. How could they do such a thing? And there didn't seem to be a date for a new series of *Cracker*. But Jack Frost, Inspector Frost of Denton police, was still all right, wasn't he? Could I at least assure him of that?

I went to bed early, my head reeling with the intimate instant lives of others, strangers who popped up next to you, told you everything you needed to know about themselves and then waved as you or they moved on. You acknowledged people you'd spoken to with a nod and a smile as you passed them again in the aisle or at the bar or in the smoking coach, but you didn't have to speak to them just because they'd told you about their despair or their sickness or the looming shadows of their lives. Nor did they require that you tell them anything about you. The niceties were over once you had said where you were from and where you were going. It was OK by them if you wanted to tell them more, but it wasn't compulsory. You could stay as private as you wanted to, and when they told you about themselves, even terrible things that brought tears to your eyes, you weren't expected to make a long-term commitment to them. They told for the sake of telling, you listened because you were there.

I also went to bed early because I had to get up early. In the middle of the night, at Spokane, the *Empire Builder* split in two. One half went to Seattle, the other half, my half, went to Portland, Oregon. Unfortunately, the smoking coach went with the other half of the train to Seattle. There would be no smoking from Spokane until we reached Portland. The next stop after Spokane was Pasco at 5.23 a.m. There would be a few minutes while the train waited at the station. I set my alarm.

No one got off at Pasco, and a couple of very chilly-looking travellers got on in the steely, freezing dawn on the far foothills of the Rockies. The tired woman whose son had been in the Gulf was the only other passenger standing on the platform smoking. We looked at each other, puffing and shivering, and laughed.

'Did you put your alarm on, or did you just wake up and decide to have a cigarette?' I asked.

'Alarm,' she rasped.

'We're the last of the serious addicts.'

'Dying breed.'

We concentrated on smoking while stamping our feet to keep out the chill air. I managed the best part of two cigarettes before the conductor called out, 'Suck hard, ladies, we gotta go. That oughta hold you till Wishram.'

Incredibly, in spite of what everyone knows about US trains, in spite of my own experience of being hours late on the previous two trips I had taken, in spite of the *Empire Builder* having travelled 2256 miles since I boarded in Chicago, we pulled into Portland's Union station at 9.55 a.m., fifteen minutes ahead of time.

Just Like Misery

If it was Sunday lunchtime, it had to be Portland, Oregon. By Monday breakfast I would be in Sacramento, California; by Tuesday suppertime in Denver, Colorado. Then I had to spend the night in a hotel I had booked near the station and catch the bus at 6.15 the following morning – Wednesday – to Raton in New Mexico, to arrive twenty minutes before it was time to pick up the 10.56 a.m. *Southwest Chief* that would deliver me to Albuquerque by Wednesday at 4 p.m. – half a week away from Portland.

This was my social visit to Bet and her hero. Five days in real America with real Americans. Instead of just heading round the States in a moving corridor, I had a destination, people to meet me at the station, a house to stay in for five days that didn't move, didn't shake or rock or go any place at all. In England nothing would induce me to go and stay with perfect strangers for five days, but this was a journey, a

contrivance, and it seemed like a good idea to renew a previous accidental meeting that offered a new insight into an
America I didn't know. What made me think it would be all
right was that I liked Bet, and had enjoyed her company on
the train. You meet someone you like, you arrange to see
them again. What could be more reasonable than that? More
normal? Perhaps it was an attempt to give up being a stranger.
At any rate, to see if I could give it up.

When I called Bet from London and proposed the visit,
she sounded delighted. What was more, she and the hero had
just bought a trailer, and I could stay in it, a place of my
own, while I was there. So I wasn't going to be on exactly
rock-solid foundations during my time off the train, but I was
delighted at the idea of living in a trailer in suburban New
Mexico for a few days, and, of course, of having a bolt hole,
as well as not having to feel too bad about being in my hosts'
hair day in and day out. For all the apparent normality of the
visit, the trailer made the five days I planned to spend with
these very generous perfect strangers seem less insane.

'Stay a couple of weeks,' Bet urged. 'More. A month.'

'No, really, I have to get back on the train and finish the
journey, and I have to be back in New York by the end of the
month.'

'Just the five days, then. Well, you can always come back.'

Meantime, the glancing acquaintances of train travel continued. In the waiting room at Portland, before the train arrived,
a well but quietly dressed, unshowily good-looking man in his
mid-fifties smiled at me and asked the regulation question.
He was delighted to hear that I was English. I was intrigued
by him because he was the only executive type I had come
across so far on these travels. He was an estate lawyer, he told

me in a quiet, slightly anglicised, cultured voice. Eugene was taking the train to Sacramento from his home in Rochester, NY, because he had a meeting there first thing in the morning and it was cheaper and simpler to take the overnight train than to fly out the previous day and book into a hotel for the night. He didn't strike me as someone who chose very many cheaper options, so I took him to mean that he preferred to travel this way. By the time the train arrived, he had quoted Pliny at me on the subject of serving bad wine to one's guests, told me that there had been a great cultural falling away since the eighteenth century and that we had passed from the Golden Age, through the Silver Age, beyond the Bronze Age to something a good deal more leaden. He was, he said, a Yale man, and an active but old-fashioned Christian (there was nothing happy-clappy about Eugene), working in his spare time at trying to save the Book of Common Prayer. Cranmer had done for prose what Shakespeare did for poetry. Eugene was a different kind of American from my other train acquaintances, alarmingly wrapped up in lost worlds and boastfully ill-at-ease in the present one. He had been married for thirty-six years, he said, and then his patrician manner softened.

'We dated every week for every one of those thirty-six years, as if we were lovers. We were always lovers . . .' They had five children who were now grown up. In fact, he was well into his sixties, a decade older than I had taken him for. 'I missed the Sixties,' he said. 'But I am having a good time in *my* sixties.'

He wasn't speaking salaciously. He meant that he had started to find life enjoyable again. One evening five years before, he was waiting for his wife to appear for a drink in a bar on their weekly date. She always did her hair and make-up

and wore an elegant dress, as she had when they were courting. 'We were always courting.' She never arrived that night.
She collapsed and died of an aneurysm on her way to meet
him. For a moment Eugene's eyes looked blank. Then he
lifted his chin slightly. He was getting over it. It was time, his
children told him, to think about remarrying. I had the
strangest feeling as he said this that he was looking very
closely at me. The train came, and we agreed that we might
have a drink that evening before dinner in the observation car.
As it turned out, I had other concerns that made me forget
our vague arrangement.

The journey from Portland to Sacramento passed in a blur
of discontent. The *Coast Starlight* was intended to bring back
the American traveller and overseas tourist to the trains, with
a pastiche of rail travel of days gone by. It was clearly
designed to be the New World equivalent of the *Orient
Express*, with all the printed matter, logos and furnishings
echoing art deco. It was a luxury superliner of a train, much
more glossy and well appointed than either the *Sunset Limited*
or the *Empire Builder*. In keeping with the class values of days
gone by, first-class passengers – or rather *guests* – defined as
those with sleeping accommodation, had exclusive use of the
Pacific Parlour Car, an observation coach with upholstered
rotating armchairs by the panoramic windows and a bar of its
own. There was no mixing of the classes on this train. First-
and coach-class passengers met only in the dining car.
Flowers, embossed stationery and branded soap in the sleeping compartments completed the trying-too-hard-in-the-
wrong-areas feel of the train. And as for the usual other place
of miscegenation, the smoking compartment – my first investigation after I stashed my bag in my room – well, there
wasn't one. The *Coast Starlight* was, it turned out once I

found myself trapped in its swaying comfort, a no-smoking train. There was no place for the bad guys to congregate; for the young, the poor, the phobic, the wealthy, the old to discover that they had at least addiction to nicotine in common. More to the point, there was nowhere for me to smoke. Although the specially produced brochure ('the *Coast Starlight* with a tradition of excellence harkening [*sic*] back to the glory days of the "Streamliner Era" of the late 1940s') assured me that I was on 'Amtrak's hottest train with the coolest scenery . . . offering some of the most spectacular scenery in the west' with a 'Crew that makes the magic happen' and unequalled views of the Cascade Mountains, Crater Lake, the Klamath Falls, Mount Shasta in all its 14,380-foot glory and the Sacramento Valley, I concluded that the only way to survive the 650-mile, 16-hour, cigaretteless journey, was to sulk. I couldn't just sleep through the agony because there would be brief puffing opportunities at the nine stops between Portland and Sacramento, but that wasn't smoking, that was damage control. A cigarette is a ritual of pleasure that takes its own time, involves the entire body (posture, arm and hand movements, facial expression, tilt of head, cross of legs) and is at its most gratifying when smoked either in meditative solitude or as a buffer against social nakedness. It is not a thing to be snatched at in a moment of someone else's devising. The whole idea, once you are an adult smoker, is that whatever you happen to be doing, you can pull a cigarette out of a pack, light it and enhance the moment. Everything is made better, the good as well as the not so good, with the addition of a cigarette in the hand, the inhalation, the exhalation, the tapping of ash, the grinding out of the stub. The point of the body is made clear by smoking. Smoking is an art form that combines the separate capacities of the parts of the body and fulfils the meaning of the whole. The chastely limited satisfaction of gratifying the physical requirement for nicotine is quite far down on the list of the desirable effects of smoking. However, it is true that once the virtuous outside world outlaws smoking, the nicotine craving surges to a critical level and every minute of every hour is spent thinking about cigarettes and longing to scratch the itch in the blood and muscles with a fix. The entire Cascade mountain range could have erupted into a synchronised ballet of exploding fire and smoke, and it would only have put me in mind of the lack of ashtrays on the train. Crater Lake could have opened up and swallowed us whole, and my first thought would have been to wonder if under such special circumstances it would be permitted to smoke in the Parlour Car. When I was young and the world was in the grip of the Cold War, the question of what one would do if the four-minute warning sounded was on every pubescent's lips. The answer was almost invariably that we would grab the nearest member of the opposite gender and have the sex we were unwilling to die without experiencing before we were blown to smithereens. In those days, four minutes seemed like plenty of time for the short, sharp, explosive and by all accounts pleasurable experience we had only heard tell of. But for a long time now, though the question is no longer asked (the warning likely to be much longer, or much shorter than four minutes), my answer would be to have a final smoke. Even the harshest of authorities appeared to agree with me. No one is expected to face a firing squad without the lingering taste of tar and tobacco flavouring their last breath. What if the choice was to be between never having a cigarette again or having that last firing-squad fag, and of course the firing-squad? Well, I would have to think very carefully about that.

Have I conveyed the shock and dismay I felt at learning I was on a no-smoking train? Barely, I think. If there had been an international airport in Salem, the first stop after Portland, I would have been off the train and booking a flight back to the UK. The hell with meeting people, sod being an anonymous traveller, a stranger to myself and everyone I met, I wanted a cigarette, and more to the point, I wanted a cigarette whenever I wanted it.

I managed a few puffs at Salem, and then slept my way through the afternoon. I woke when my alarm went off to alert me to a stop at Eugene–Springfield just before I was due to be called for dinner over the loudspeaker. I managed a few inhalations before the conductor hustled me back on the train. I asked him when we were due to arrive at Chelmut.

'Eight-o-seven, ma'am.'

'Good, that'll be just about when I finish eating. Then I can light up, inhale a little nicotine and sleep until six thirty tomorrow morning, when, thank god, we'll arrive in Sacramento. I've got a six-hour wait for the Denver train, so I can smoke up a storm.'

'Well, ma'am,' the conductor told me with an inscrutable expression, 'unfortunately, they've got a law against smoking in Sacramento.'

'That's OK, I'll stand on the street and smoke. The weather's fine in Sacramento.'

'No, I mean there's a law against smoking on the sidewalk in Sacramento. They're very advanced in their thinking in that part of California.'

I was not feeling very companionable when I arrived at my table. Neither, it seemed, was the small, round, elderly man who sat opposite me. We nodded a brisk greeting to each other and then proceeded through our dismal salad and halfway through the steaks we had both ordered without a word being said. This was a first and I was grateful. A silent fellow-traveller. Although we were at a two-person table, he showed no sign of wanting to begin a conversation, and was concentrating hard on his dinner. I was in no mood for learning about anyone's life, no matter how fascinating. I'd had it with interesting strangers. I would have been quite happy to eat and stare at the scenery passing by. But it was dark. Looking out of the window simply reflected my own face back at me.

It's very hard to sit through a complete meal with others in silence, though I'd had a certain amount of practice at it when I was fourteen. Although I spent my days riding the Circle Line, during my sullen silence while living with my father and stepmother, Pam, I nonetheless had to eat. It helped that the evening meal ('tea') was arranged to be at the same time as the immortal rural family radio saga, *The Archers*. There wasn't much conversation to be had, apart from comments on the doings of Phil and Jill and their brood on Home Farm. I, of course, despised *The Archers*, and sat with *Lolita* on my lap, trying to read it until it was snatched away by Pam or my father, either because reading at table was rude or because it was deemed a dirty book, and in any case having your head in a book was an unhealthy habit. Then I had nothing to do but stare icily ahead, eat as fast as possible and ask to be excused from the table, when permission was given with relief. I was dying to talk, but I had been locked into a silence by the secret deal Pam had made with my mother, the ineffectualness of my father, and by my own rage and sense of strangeness and dependency. Awful meals. I remember them as cold damp food (lettuce, tomato and cucumber and a slice of wet ham laid on a plate with salad cream available for those with exotic tastes) and icy atmosphere.

I have always liked best to eat alone with a book in front of me. When I was little I would take a plate of something to my hiding place in a corner behind two armchairs and sit cross-legged, reading and eating. The next best thing is the convivial conversational meal. Table talk. Easy suppers with people laughing and arguing. Silent tables chill me. The last silent table I sat at was in a monastery I stayed at a few years ago. The monks were silent, and the rest of the company was on retreat. You nodded to your fellow diners as you arrived at the table and then kept quiet for fear of disrupting their med-itations. Getting the salt or the water jug from the other end of the refectory table was a matter of eyebrow raising, point-ing and mime – and not complaining when you got the mustard instead. I like silence, but silence and food in com-pany is a very bad combination in my view. And as for meditation, the only thing I managed to think at these monk-ish meals was how no one was talking and how everyone had their own special, and increasingly disgusting, way of shovel-ling food into their faces. A little talk helps you forget the purely physical aspect of eating. Perhaps that's what the silence requirement in the monastery is for, to remind us of it.

'Going all the way?'

I was quite relieved when he spoke. 'No, just to Sacramento,' I replied.

'My name is Joseph.'

Joseph was spherical and shy, an inoffensive, reticent man, mostly bald, not at all at ease, I thought, with strangers. I was, of course, quite wrong. Joseph was naturally timid, but he had learned to take himself in hand. He lived on Paulet Island, off the coast of Seattle, and had kids in San Diego and

San Francisco. He was on his way to visit them and his three
grandchildren, the youngest, just one month old, he had
never seen. Between bits of information, Joseph chewed his
steak conscientiously. I was pleased that there was nothing
especially interesting about Joseph. Just a nice old widowed
grandfather on his way to visit the family. No story, no insight
into the secret heart of humanity. I could cope with that. My
enthusiasm for the remarkable story that everyone had to tell
was already seriously on the wane. Joseph required nothing
more of me than to take a brief polite interest in the eventless
routine of a quiet life. I felt perfectly safe in asking him if he
was retired.

'Yup. Retired and living in suburbia. I was born in the
Bronx. In Hell's Kitchen. Where I live now is very quiet,
very quiet. Just front lawns and empty streets apart from the
cars going to and fro. People keeping themselves to themselves. Suburban life is much too unfriendly for my taste.
You don't meet people. I don't have a car. I have a bicycle
with a basket on for my shopping. I was an engineer.'

'Ah,' I nodded, relieved that my assessment of him as nar-
ratologically safe and bland was confirmed.

'Uh huh, weapons and space. I worked on the Apollo
engines. I guess the stuff I made is still up there, going round
and round. But I'm a professional dancer now, since I retired.'

In spite of Joseph's clue that he was the only cycling shop-
per on Paulet Island, I had been lulled into relaxing. I was
only half listening. I did a double take.

'Pardon?'

'On cruises. I'm a dance host.'

I looked at him harder, but nothing I could do in the way
of squinting and refocusing could turn podgy Joseph into
Gene Kelly, Fred Astaire or Shirley MacLaine. But I did see

the eyes take on a confident gleam and bald round reticent
Joseph begin to warm up as he explained what he had done
with his life these past ten years or so. In return for being
available as a nightly dance partner to a great surfeit of older
single women on board pleasure ships, Joseph got free cruises
all over the world. He'd never been out of the US before he
began his new career, but in just the past couple of seasons he
had been to Egypt and Australia, 'dancing,' he said with a
delighted smile, 'all the way.' But it wasn't easy. It wasn't the
sinecure it might seem to the uninitiated. This was by no
means a cushy number. There were no days off in the dance-
host business. Seven nights a week he was on duty. And he
had to look smart to a very high standard, wear a uniform of
white patent shoes and a blue blazer (the cost of which came
out of his own pocket) to show he was a member of staff. It
was necessary because single men who went on cruises could
be weird.

'You know, looking for moneyed women. You get a lot of
wealthy single women on these cruises. Mostly they're on
their own, spending their husband's life insurance. They want
fun. They don't want to stand around and watch other people
dancing. They paid good money for a good time. But they're
a prey to fortune-hunters. So the cruise companies employ
respectable retired single men like me – you don't get any
wages, but the trip and the food is for free – to keep the single
women company without them having to worry about what
we're after. Of course, there are strict rules and we're carefully
vetted. No drinkers or gamblers. And you have to have diplo-
matic as well as dance skills. Some of the girls can get very
possessive, you know. You've got to be careful about that.
You have to treat them all equally, and be seen to do that. The
other ladies notice and complain to the purser if a host dances

too much with one particular woman. It's completely against the rules to get emotionally involved with the passengers. You get into any kind of relationship, or get caught slipping out of anyone's cabin, and they put you off at the next port. Doesn't matter where it is. It happened on my last cruise. They put one of the dance hosts off the ship, because he'd been fooling around with a passenger and someone told the captain about it. Right in the middle of nowhere. A million miles from America. God knows if he ever got home. You've got to be very, very careful.'

And did he know how to do all the dances?

'Oh sure, it's part of the qualifications, along with being presentable and being able to talk pleasantly.' Joseph was beaming with pride now at what he had achieved with his life in retirement. 'My late wife and I used to go ballroom dancing. We got medals. I took a refresher course when I decided to sign on as a dance host. I can do them all. I myself am not too crazy about the cha cha or salsa. But you got to do them, and do them well. Me, I like to tango. Tango is my favourite. But you've got to be able to handle everything, and some of the ladies aren't the best dancers. You help them round the floor. You make conversation, and make them feel that you are enjoying their company. I get to travel and see the whole world, but I think I'm being useful, you know, as well. I help people enjoy themselves without worrying that they are being taken advantage of. That's not a bad thing, is it? It's a good life.'

Dinner was over and that was Joseph, who had spent his working life with weapons and space ships, and now twirled lonely women around a peripatetic ballroom in white patent shoes. There was not the slightest possibility, I realised as I stubbed out my last cigarette of the evening on the platform of Chelmut station, of coming across anyone who led the kind of uneventful and routine life that the vast majority of humanity were supposed to lead. Wherever these hoards of the normal were, they didn't travel by train. Or not on my trains.

In bed I watched the moon swinging erratically in the dense black night as the train curved and snaked down the West Coast. The stars were within reach, bright circles, so close that they appeared to hover like torchlights just above the level of the treetops. The bed swayed gently from side to side as our caravan moved through the night. And aside from the scratchy nicotine need in my belly I felt right then so content that I didn't want the trip to end. I was entirely detached from everything. From life back in England. From family, friends and lover. I felt I was nobody's, and nobody was mine. Like the stars: suspended, just passing through landscape and nightscape and by people, or those things passing by me, and there was little distinction. It was delicious, but I also badly wanted a cigarette.

We arrived at Sacramento at 6 a.m., half an hour before schedule. Amtrak trains are only late, apparently, when you are in a hurry. Six in the morning is too early to arrive anywhere. But the conductor had knocked on my door and warned me to get myself together, and there I stood with my bags on the grandly spacious concourse of Sacramento train station. The no-smoking signs were everywhere, and I had been warned that even the air was protected against my vice. Eugene turned up beside me. Apparently, six in the morning is too early to arrive even if you have got somewhere to go.

'My appointment is not until nine thirty. Would you like to have breakfast?'

We put our bags in Left Luggage and found an open diner

a block or two away from the station. It was just far enough
for me to light up and smoke a cigarette. Eugene didn't
smoke, but he didn't mind me smoking. It did no violence to
his libertarian views.

'Let me know if you see a policeman,' I said, feeling cagey.
'It's against the law to smoke even in the open air in this land
of health and never-say-die, I'm told.'

Eugene laughed. Apparently, the conductor had been
having me on, but I was prepared to believe any no-smoking
rumour going.

The diner was a bright Formica and chrome canteen,
already busy with workmen who brought in their own mugs
for coffee at a discount and had piled their plates with hash
browns, sausage and egg. I piled mine up with the same at the
counter, being famished and particularly partial to American
breakfast, stopping to ponder between over easy and sunny-
side up. I decided on over easy because I liked the idea of
saying it. I once wrote a short story called 'Over Easy'
because the phrase appeals to me so much. Eugene had waf-
fles and maple syrup. At six in the morning in a strange city,
in the pearly Californian light, we were comfortable with each
other, like old acquaintances. We talked more of books. He
asked me who I wrote for and was pleased when he heard the
name of a respectable literary journal he had seen. Although
our styles were quite different, I could speak his language, as
it were. And I was not married. I was possible. I suspected
that Eugene took his children's wishes very seriously.

'Are you sorting out someone's estate down here?' I asked.

'No, I've got a doctor's appointment.'

'Oh.'

'I'm going blind.'

Dear god, more story. Eugene had a hole in his macula, at

the centre of his retina. He was already blind in one eye and now the other was deteriorating. He would be completely blind within a couple of years. He was doing everything he could to prevent this happening, but all the doctors he had seen had told him that nothing could be done, and that he should begin to prepare for living without his sight. Finally, he had come across a specialist in Sacramento who performed an operation that was said to work. He was having his initial examination today and if he was suitable they would operate. It was an extreme measure because the post-operative proce- dure was arduous. It involved the patient being tipped forward so that his head was facing the ground and remaining in that position with as little movement as possible for three weeks. Gravity and immobility aided recovery. Eugene acknowledged that this was an awful prospect, as much as anything because he wouldn't be able to read, but it was his duty, he said, to save his sight if he possibly could. This pro- cedure might not work and if that was the case then there was nothing left to do. Then it would be his task to accept the sit- uation and learn how to be an effective blind man. Eugene presented his situation starkly and without drama or emotion. Somewhere in all this was a kind of muscular Christianity, but behind that, I suspect, a Stoicism of the ancient sort that I imagined he would admire. Marcus Aurelius was surely on his list of good guys.

What was more, in his careful account of his diagnosis and prognosis, I caught the note of someone laying his cards on the table. Of making his situation quite clear before going any further. He had a very pleasant house, he told me, and he was semi-retired. Once again an unlooked-for change of direction in my life beckoned; sort of picked me up and played with me the game of unconsidered possibilities. Mrs

Ivy League Eugene in my late middle age, five stepchildren, a well-appointed house in Rochester, NY, regular concerts, visits to European cultural centres, time and room to work in a civilised and mature relationship. Of course, in my current real life I had time and room to work, as well as something rather more than a civilised and mature relationship. I lived in a European cultural centre. My home in England was fine and I prefer CDs to going to concerts. Still, I slipped into the possibility of a new existence as, in the changing room of a frock shop, I would try on a dress of the kind I would never wear, just to see who I would be if I wore such a thing. We got on to politics. Eugene praised the eighties as the dying hope of a lost civilisation. Thatcher and Reagan were last-stand heroes of fiscal sanity. Thatcher, in particular, he admired, for her single-minded belief in free-market economy. I itemised the damage her single-minded belief had done to the British health service, affordable housing and state education. Eugene shook his head against my soft, wrong-headed and unthinking leftist attitudes and explained that the poor could only benefit from a strong independent economy and became feckless if supported by the state. This was a civilised disagreement, not like the occasion at dinner with Glenys and the awful man who was so upset by her. Eugene and I argued politely, even enjoyably from our mutually irreconcilable positions, but it became clear that the wedding was off. I took off the life in Rochester, NY, and let it drop to my feet, and Eugene gave up his dinner parties with his acerbic English novelist wife. We veered into talk about London and the theatre, and other harmless topics, but the edge was gone. I hadn't seriously considered myself as Eugene's consort, but now that our unsuitability was so clear, I had just a momentary twinge of disappointment, as if I really had lost something that had come into existence and died all in a fleeting moment. With a degree of regret on both sides, we finished our breakfast and, when the time came for him to go to his appointment, wished each other good luck. I hoped the eye operation was successful and he trusted my book would turn out well. I also wished very much, though I did not say so aloud, that he would soon find the sort of person he was looking for. I didn't think it would take very long.

I had three hours before the train to Denver was due, so I followed the signs that pointed to 'Old Sacramento', forgetting, for a moment, that I was in America. That's how much train travel insulates you. 'Old Sacramento' meant, of course, 'New but Distressed Sacramento'. It was the old part of town that had been suffering from inner-city blight for decades. In frontier days, the handful of streets had indeed been the original site of the town, but for a long time since, the area had been derelict and a hangout for junkies, the homeless, the criminal. But all that had been swept away by a city council who knew the value of investment in history. Old Sacramento had been pulled down and rebuilt as a replica of a chocolate-box American West. You've seen it in the movies – though they were more likely to be Audie Murphy oaters than Sam Peckinpah meditations on the passing of the old. Of course, it was only the frontages that were rendered out of date. By-laws and health directives required that the interior of the buildings provided late-twentieth-century safety and comfort, however much timber clad the modern building materials, and shopkeepers were not going to risk tourists missing items for sale with out-of-date lighting or old-fashioned displays. You clattered along the boarded, porched sidewalks complete with horse-retaining rails, but entered bright air-conditioned emporia selling cheap, tatty replicas of items that were once desirable mainly for their practicality: durable hats, boots, leather bags for cowboys to improve their peripatetic existence, now remodelled in shoddy materials and badly but equally suitably made for the life they would lead in the backs of wardrobes. Subsistence supplies had changed, too. Barrels of flour were replaced by Perspex containers keeping popcorn warm. A slug of whisky was more likely to be a Tequila Sunrise. A lunch of just-off-the-hoof steak with beans became toasted goat's cheese and oakleaf salad. Old Sacramento turned out to be theme streets of tourist shops. Heritage with fries. But signs (done as old 'Wanted' posters) boasted proudly of the restoration of the deteriorated and decayed 'historical district', at the sweeping away of inner-city blight and the reclaiming of the past for the edification of visitors. Of course, the past was not so much reclaimed as sanitised and sold, and it is startling how quickly these bright new versions of history become tawdry, as the gilding wears off and reveals the paper-thin profit motive. Apparently, if you tidy things up in order to sell crap, the crap wins out. Glum-looking men and women wearing western outfits greeted me with weary bonhomie, welcoming me into their empty, pointless shops. I slouched around, killing time before I could return to the interior of a train that was in every way more of a destination than any of this, staring at stuff made of plastic that lit up, or made a sound, or turned out to be something it didn't look like, and came away, eventually, with a small rubber replica of a brain, the size of a walnut, which was guaranteed to swell to twenty times its size when placed in water.

'Why do you make sexist assumptions?'

I had just asked the woman sitting next to me at dinner if

she was a nurse. She was travelling with two other women and I was sharing their table for lunch. The three of them were on their way to a convention of franchised sales representatives who bought and sold to their friends and acquaintances a large sea-green capsule that was filled with dehydrated extract of vegetables. It was, apparently, the latest way for West Coast would-be entrepreneurs to supplement their income. The three were a group of gay women in their late twenties who all had other jobs. The woman sitting next to me worked, I was told by her friend opposite, in a medical facility.

'Are you a nurse?' I asked.

Which brought down the accusation of sexism by her friend who seemed to be in charge of testing the world for wrong thinking.

'Why don't you ask if she's a doctor?' she snapped.

'Because why would she be selling vegetable capsules in her spare time if she had a doctor's salary? Are you a doctor?'

'No,' the woman next to me said. 'I'm a nursing assistant.'

There was a short silence.

'We believe in what we sell,' the one in charge berated. 'It's a complete supplement. One capsule gives you all the nutrition that you would get from the recommended daily intake of fresh fruit and vegetables.'

'Good,' I said. 'I hate vegetables. So if I have one of these a day, does that mean I won't ever have to eat vegetables again? I'll take a lifetime's supply.'

'You don't seem to be a very serious person,' I was told. And it was true; except for in the area of eating vegetables, which I seriously do not like to do.

I was aware that I should have taken more interest in the veggie-for-life-selling lesbians on the way to their feel-good convention, but I had suddenly come over profoundly

uninterested in all things vegetable, lesbian and feel-good.
The smoking coach beckoned and then my new sleeping
accommodation. The *California Zephyr* was a satisfyingly
dog-eared change from the *Coast Starlight*, with ageing
rolling stock and worn upholstery. And it had a smoking
coach as shabby as any I had seen. I smoked a couple of cigarettes in it, keeping my eyes on the increasingly empty
landscape to avoid being drawn into any conversation. Then
I padded off to my bed and slept until 5.15 p.m., when the
train drew into Reno, Nevada.

Back in the smoking car the sun was setting, but it felt
more as if the light was dying. Outside the desert passed by,
grey-green, sparse, bleak and getting bleaker every moment.
The sunset should have been beautiful, slipping through
pastel shades from pink to blue to beige, but it only increased
the sadness of the landscape and brought out that dying-of-
the-light desolation that lurks in some corner of me waiting
for the physical environment to match it. The coach was
empty apart from a man with a face as long as my gloom, who
sat opposite me, saying nothing. I was halfway through my
cigarette before he spoke.

'I hope it's not cold in Winnemucca.'

His voice was as doom-laden as his face. He wore a suit
and tie and lace-up shoes. A regular guy. A salesman, perhaps. We were due to arrive in the improbably named
Winnemucca at seven forty-five that evening. I had no option
but to ask why he was worrying about the temperature. He
nodded his approval at my question.

'I left my coat on the door knob at home. Clean forgot it.'

'That's a nuisance. You'll have to get a new one when you
arrive.'

He sniffed. 'Stores will be closed by then. That's not all. I left the car in the three-hour car park. The wife was going to pick it up after work, but when I got on the train I found the spare keys in my pocket, so she won't be able to. I'm away for three days. It's better not to imagine what the parking fine's going to be.'

'That's terrible.'

'Yes. And I left my travel bag in the car,' he shook his head and then looked at me with real distress as it all came together in a single dreadful fact. 'You know, I can put up with only having white socks to wear, I don't like it, but I can tolerate that if I have to, but what I can't even bear to think, what is really too awful to face, is having to spend three whole days using a hand-operated toothbrush.'

I began to feel much better. He was a gold-mining consultant, he told me when he could get his mind off his many tribulations.

'There's still gold in the Sierra Nevada, but it's all dust. The nuggets they mined for in the Gold Rush days are long gone. There's still plenty of money in the dust, but only if you can afford to collect it. It's not a game for individuals any more. Just recently they moved an entire mountain – I mean a real mountain-sized mountain – and sifted it, every last ounce of earth, to get out the gold dust. Then, because of the environmental lobby, they remodelled it. They rebuilt the whole damn mountain back where it had been. This is the landscape of gold and gambling. That's all that happens here. Sifting through the dust and playing on the tables. I don't remember the last time I brushed my teeth by hand.'

It was dark by the time we arrived at Winnemucca and it looked decidedly cold, I was sorry to note. That night we were passing through Salt Lake City, invisible in the dark. By the early morning we would have passed through the towns of Provo and Helper in Utah. Before reaching Denver we had to cross the Colorado Rockies in the daylight, and it was the most stunning part of the whole trip. Visually, it was extraordinary, chugging at a slow, careful speed around the mountains, carpeted at that height with snow, along a twisting track only just wide enough for the train, so that through one window was sheer rockface while through the other, if you dared look out, you stared straight down at an apparently diminutive ribbon of the Colorado River winding through the canyon two thousand feet below. And then there was the thought of those who made, and often died making, those tracks, blasting away the mountain to make a ledge for the rails or a tunnel through the solid rock. Human life was no impediment to humanity's will to press on. It was one of the most precarious and moving journeys I have ever made. Absurd really, to look at implacable mountains and decide to go straight through them. But perhaps not so absurd when you consider that the men who blasted and sweated and died were for the most part Chinese or Irish labourers working for a pittance, desperate for whatever work they could get, while the entrepreneurs followed on in moving staterooms making corrupt deals with the politicians. The usual background to humankind's most monumental achievements.

We approached Denver, spiralling down from the top of the Rockies, as the sun set. Denver proudly calls itself the 'Mile High City', but we dropped down into it like a plane making its grand and gracious descent towards a runway. Except that this runway was a whole city, flooded, sparkling and twinkling with light, spread out in front of us for half an hour or more before we were finally down at ground level.

'Ladies and gentlemen, boys and girls,' the conductor breathed over the loudspeaker. 'Isn't that a beautiful sight?'

Which was considerably more than could be said for Raton, New Mexico, when I arrived there after a three-and-a-half-hour bus journey that began around six in the morning. I hadn't slept much that night, being quite unaccustomed to the six-foot bed that remained perfectly still and the oceanic pleasures of the black jacuzzi that mysteriously was plumbed into a corner of my hotel room. I tried to enjoy both, but being in transit and geared quite differently, I found them only delicious distractions that I didn't want to become accustomed to. They were not what I was presently about so I rather wanted to get them both over and done with and on to the main business of moving on. I've never been able to take pleasure as it comes. I need warning and practice. In any case the edge is taken off the joy of a luxury room, giant bed and bubbling bath when you know you have to stagger out of bed at five the next morning to catch a bus to a godforsaken spot whose name you can't remember except that it has something to do with rodents.

Raton (pronounced Ra-*tone*, though I can't help but think of it, even now, as Rat-on) wasn't much to write home about. The station building was a squat, square, concrete and asbestos affair, though the stationmaster clearly took pride in the concrete planters on the platform, which were profuse with fiery red and orange flowers in the otherwise grey surroundings. The single track cut through the flat drab landscape extending right and left into empty infinity. If destiny in the form of gunslingers was on the train heading your way, you could see it coming for miles and watch the speck in the distance grow into looming inevitability.

The train came through Raton once a day, every day of the year, including Christmas, and every day, including Christmas, the uniformed stationmaster, a man of quiet if slightly amused efficiency in his thirties, was there to greet it and wave it off. He greeted the half dozen or so of us off the bus, checked our baggage on to his trolley and told us that the train would be a couple of hours late. No one was pleased. We had got up early and now found ourselves with the choice of waiting in the blazing sun or the un-air-conditioned station building. On the other hand, Raton in the midday heat did not look promising to explore as we peered at the empty featureless streets we could see from behind the station. But people lived there. Surely they had lunch, or drank in a bar?

'It's a pretty quiet town,' the stationmaster told us. We nodded grim agreement. 'But there's Bertha's Tea Rooms.'

People fanned themselves like eighteenth-century courtiers who had inexplicably found themselves in the wilderness. They decided it was safer to keep still than venture into the blank unknown of Bertha's Tea Rooms in Rat*one*. I more or less agreed, but Bertha sounded European enough to allow smoking in her tea room, and I really fancied sitting at a table, drinking tea and smoking in a public place. I hadn't done that since I left the UK, so I asked for directions. A young woman in jeans and a T-shirt with a large backpack strapped on to her said she would join me. We collected orders for doughnuts and Danish from several of our less intrepid fellow travellers, then we trudged off into town. It turned out that the shops were more shut down than just shut. It was a hopeless sort of place. We passed a cinema, but it was closed, and had been for a while by the look of it. It seemed that people in Raton had better things to do than go to the movies, though what those things might be was hard to imagine.

Bertha's Tea Rooms, however, were open, though there was only the one room, with plastic tables and chairs, and a handful of customers who seemed to have been specially sent from a Hollywood agency to play the role of regulars hanging out in a smalltown café, reading the local paper, throwing the occasional comment back and forth, and raising their heads in unison as my new friend and I opened the door. Bertha was behind a counter piled not just with regulation jelly doughnuts but with pastries and biscuits that would have been at home in any tea room in southern Germany.

'We've found the jewel of Raton,' I murmured to my companion as we ordered a plateful of delicious home-baked goodies and coffees.

Caroline was nineteen, and, she told me, had just finished college and was on her way home to a small town in Illinois. I asked what she had studied and she looked a little cagey.

'It was a theological college.'

We both waited to see how I would react.

'Are you going to be a priest?'

'No. I trained for missionary work. I'm planning to go overseas to work as a missionary after I've spent some time back with my parents.'

'Where will you be going?'

I wondered what part of which dark continent still welcomed missionaries.

'France.'

That dark continent.

'France?' I spoke too loud, and too astonished. She was startled. 'France, Europe?'

'Yes. That's where they want to send me.' Caroline looked nervous now. I tried to get the surprise off my face.

'I didn't realise there was much call for missionaries in France.'

'Yes,' Caroline said dubiously. 'I was sort of surprised when they told me. But I guess there must be a need or they wouldn't send me.'

I wasn't at all sure that she knew where France was, but I suppose that just the fact of it not being in America justified the sending of a mission. She was from a fundamentalist family, who were pleased that she had followed in their footsteps. This was a new encounter for me.

'So you believe in the whole creation thing?'

She nodded.

'And evolution? And genetics?' I felt weary as I said it.

'It's wrong. God made the world just as it says in the Bible.'

Caroline was nineteen. I know I've said that already, but I had to repeat it to myself.

'Seven days? The whole shebang? What about fossils?'

'Well, we're taught that God put fossils on the earth when he made it.'

'For what? For fun? To tease? To trick us?'

'No, I think the idea is,' she thought hard, back to her lectures, 'that God made the world already old, with all its history already made. That's what accounts for the apparent age of the world.'

'But why would God do that?'

'Well, you have to have history, don't you?'

We finished our coffee and cakes and began to walk back to the station with the doughnuts for the others.

'You don't have any qualms about converting people to your beliefs?'

'I shouldn't. I'm sure what I believe is the truth. But, you know, I have been a bit worried about being a missionary. I don't know if it's right to go to other parts of the world and tell people what to think. Even if I believe it's the truth, I'm not sure I've got the right to tell people twice my age what they should be doing. I haven't really sorted my feelings out about it. It does seem odd for me to go to France and tell them to change their ideas.'

I was both dismayed and encouraged by Caroline. Not the world's most independent thinker, but still, perhaps because she's young, perhaps because ideas can still impinge on belief systems in the young, she's wondering about the nature of what she's planning to do, of the notion of one group of people having a truth that they are entitled to impose on others. It wasn't much, but it was something. Or better than nothing. And anyway, I figured that France would be able to withstand the persuasions of Caroline, and even, possibly, teach her a thing or two of its own.

Bet, Mikey and her hero lived in a small, four-roomed one-storey adobe house in a suburb of Albuquerque. I immediately gave up hope of seeing Albuquerque itself, which might have been Jacksonville the way Bet shuddered, 'We never go into the city. It's all drugs and young people, these days,' as the hero drove us rapidly through it in his big blue Dodge four-wheel-drive on the way home from the train station. This wasn't the immaculate suburb of exquisitely green front lawns I'd seen in Phoenix. It was less uniform, less affluent, more utilised, with the front spaces of the houses serving more practical storage functions for the extra trucks or cars that wouldn't fit in the garages. Bet's space was gravelled. A trailer stood in front of the garage.

'There's your new home,' Bet said, pointing to it as we drove up. 'We're real proud of it. We just bought it this summer.'

'Huh,' grunted Hero.

'Ah, take no notice of him.'

'Sure, don't worry. But if you wake up one morning in the woods, ma'am, don't be concerned. It's just me taking advantage of the hunting season. Which is why I bought it.'

'Ignore him.'

'Hey, Jenny, you won't mind being surrounded by bears and cougar. Don't worry, I've got plenty of guns. Just give a yell and I'll come running. I'm only kidding.' Hero smiled broadly. 'You make yourself real comfortable. Just make sure you're gone before the hunting season's over.'

'I thought I'd stay for four or five days,' I said nervously. 'But if it's difficult . . .'

'No, I'm pulling your leg. You don't want to take me too serious. You're real welcome. I'll head off for a few days after you leave.'

He didn't mind my coming to stay, but he had been genuinely worried that I would be around for a month or so and wreck his hunting plans. The trailer was new: his treasure, his hunting lodge and his den. But my promise of staying just five days reassured him. Perhaps he was also worried about how things would go with Mikey.

The single-storey house was cramped and dark. All the curtains were drawn, and they stayed drawn when we went in. Jim, Bet's hero, went straight to an old armchair in the living room and turned on the TV. Bet showed me into the cluttered kitchen, which was the real communal room. Only Hero and sometimes Mikey used the front room where the TV was always on and the curtains always closed the better to see it.

There was nothing ambivalent about Bet's pleasure in having a visitor.

'This is so *great*. Can't you stay for longer? I thought you'd be staying a month.' No wonder the hero was anxious. 'Well, what about making it a couple of weeks? He can still go off with his pals on a hunting trip if you stay a couple of weeks. He's only kidding you, really.'

Actually, he wasn't, and I was glad enough to have a reason not to stay longer.

The floor and the shelves of the eating area of the kitchen were piled high with the overflow of Bet's train memorabilia, which also lined the walls of the hallway and snaked into a tiny room at the back which Bet called her study. Bits of track, old train and station signs, timetables, model engines, postcards and other mementoes were piled precariously on top of each other. In the dim light the dusty disorder made the place look like a junk shop. A small circular dining table in the kitchen provided a slightly less chaotic island in the middle of it all. There were three kitchen chairs and one wheelchair set around it.

'Never mind his hunting lodge. This is my guest bedroom,' Bet said, showing me to my sleeping quarters in the all-purpose everyone's-dream-come-true trailer. 'I've never had a real guest. You're the first. Well, the kids come, and the grandchildren, though not to stay, but I've never had my very own guest before.' She was as excited as a schoolgirl. She clutched me on my shoulder and gave me a little shake. 'Hey it's so *great* you've come to stay.'

By now I was beginning to panic. What was I doing in the home of these strangers, just one of whom I'd met on a train journey? Why had I put myself in such a situation? I couldn't remember why I thought it would be all right to do it. It

could only be because I had completely forgotten who I really
was. The coming five days loomed ahead and stretched out,
elongating like a dark unfriendly cat settling down for the
day. *Five days*. I imagined each night, each day, the hours, the
minutes, and my heart rose into my throat, making my breath
come in short gasps.

'Are you OK? Look, here's your bed. Jim made it up this
morning for you. He's really pleased you're here. He's glad
I've got someone to spend time with. Now let me show you
where everything is. And Mikey's really excited. He'll be back
soon. He can't wait to meet you.'

I was soothed by the interior of the trailer, which was
another version of my cabin on the freighter and the sleeping
compartment on the train. A small, highly ordered, ship-
shape living space, where everything could be done that
needed to be done, life could be lived, but with not an inch of
space to spare. The double bed was built-in to the width of
the trailer at the back. At the foot of the bed to the right was
the kitchen – a sink, a fridge and a gas cooker, an electric
kettle and cupboards above and below stacked full of cleaning
equipment and dry food.

'We keep it ready to go. You help yourself to anything.'

Bet opened canisters and we peered in to admire the contents: biscuits, breakfast cereals, Ryvita, tea, coffee, sugar,
and she pointed to tins of pilchards, pot noodles, luncheon
meat, corned beef and soup.

'You just take whatever you want. Treat the place like home.'

Opposite the kitchen was a table with benches on either
side where I could sit and work, and at the front was a
diminutive bathroom with chemical loo, a basin and a shower.

'Jim's hooked it up to the mains water and electricity.
Everything's working. It's your very own palace.'

And it was. My doll's house home for the next few days delighted me. I'd once written a novel about a wild old woman, presumably a forward projection of myself, who took to life in a mobile home, and, until I learned about the trouble and expense of caring for the hull, I entertained serious fantasies in my late twenties of living in a narrow boat on the Regent's Canal. The precisely formulated, limited space attracted me just as when I was a child I loved diminutive dolls' houses, farmyards and play houses, or that dark triangular space of my childhood behind the two armchairs in the corner, where I spent so many hours, keeping away from the raging fights between my parents, being what they called 'moody' and reading or playing out dramas of my own devising. And the trailer was, of course, outside Bet's house, a separate space, a retreat, just like ships' cabins and train sleeping compartments, a place away from everyone. Bet was the best and most enthusiastic of hosts. I was the worst of guests, wanting, before it even started, to hide away in my trailer against the conviviality and the talk, the addition of me to the family, quite unable to make the move from amiable stranger in control of my own sociability, to the responsibilities of a guest in the family house.

Bet was completely herself, but lighter-hearted than when we met on the *Sunset Limited*. She wanted to talk. She drew me back to the kitchen table, settled down with a large gin and tonic and told me about her life, her difficult childhood with her alcoholic mother, her youthful wildness, settling down with Jim and making a family which, when it was young, she herded from army base to army base all over the world – Germany and Japan – without ever setting foot outside the American-ness offered by the enclosing camps. She didn't consider herself well travelled, or travelled at all. Like

Jim, she had gone because America had sent her to make war
or keep peace. Now, the three older children were married –
no divorces in Bet's family – and earning livings as clerks and
tree surgeons, and all lived quite nearby. She told me about
the youngest, Mikey, who in his late twenties, not having
found what he wanted to do, had finally settled on being a
policeman and was in the middle of training when his accident happened. A pure accident, if that is possible. Bet, at
any rate, accepted it as such. The woman who ran into
Mikey's stationary car couldn't have avoided it, and Bet felt
no resentment that she was hurt not at all. Mikey was in a
coma for weeks and it was more or less accepted that he was
going to die, even by Bet, when he suddenly came round, his
right arm and leg paralysed, his speech profoundly slurred,
his short-term memory all but destroyed, his mental age
retarded to a nine-year-old. But he was alive.

'Oh, Jenny, it just broke my heart, but we got our baby boy
back, and now he's going to stay a baby for ever. You could
say we were lucky.'

Jim spoke very little. He broke into large amiable grins
when teased for his silence at the table by Bet, or sat low-
slung in the near-dark in front of the endless daytime game
and talk shows on the TV. If he seemed morose to me, it was
likely my own anxieties being projected. There was no obvious tension between Jim and Bet; she chattered and he
remained quiet, they had different ways of getting through
life but neither expected, or even appeared to want, the other
to be more like themselves. They were as solid a couple as any
I've come across. Quite different in style, but understanding
and tolerant of each other. Each of them knew the burden of
sadness they both carried and let the other be the way they
had to be to get through it. Though Bet's high-strung

neurosis showed itself as tense and fidgety, with a need to drink and talk sadness away, Jim seemed the more troubled because he was the least able to express it. His quietness was not restful, just as his hours in the armchair with a can of beer and the TV blaring did not seem an expression of relaxation but of suppressed anger, of feelings he had no idea what to do with except control like the military man he had been. He was a professional soldier, and had served unquestioningly in postwar Europe, Vietnam and the Gulf War. He had retired because it was coming up for mandatory and because he needed to be home to help Bet with Mikey. Once a day he would go off in the Dodge to the nearby base where he would sit and chat with old comrades and buy cheap cigarettes for him and Bet from the commissary. It was his club, his male home. He'd run a wholesaling business after he came out of the military, but it hadn't worked out. He wasn't a business- man. Now he and Bet lived well enough providing they were careful on their pensions, and Mikey had his own disability allowance. Still, whenever he was at home, I had the impres- sion of an explosion continually not occurring. Jim came alive, however, as if he had been charging during his daytime silence with his on-switch flipped, when Mikey returned home in the late afternoon from his day at the sheltered work- shop. The ambulance would pull up and Jim was already outside with Mikey's wheelchair, grinning and joking with the driver and joshing Mikey, standing back as he made his slow, lumbering way out of the back of the vehicle with the aid of a walking frame.

'Hiya, Mikey,' Bet chirruped when Jim wheeled him into the kitchen, as if he were making a rare and delightful sur- prise visit, and was not just coming home as he did every day, and would be for the rest of their lives.

'Hey, Mom, how ya doing?' Mikey shouted, playing back at her, and chuckling his pleasure at seeing his mother and father and the kitchen all there, still unchanged, still welcoming their long-lost boy home.

Mikey was delightful. He entered a room, took a deep breath into his heavily overweight belly and bellowed a great 'Hi', smiling long and hard into your face, then roaring with laughter, and you were lost in the gaiety. It worked such a charm that, whenever things went a little quiet and a silence fell between people, Mikey would bellow, 'Hi, how ya doing?' Like a comedian's catchphrase, it was irresistible and touching, that and Mikey's sweet need to keep everyone happy.

'Oh, Mikey,' Bet laughed, all sadness and fondness.

'Hey, son, how're *you* doing?' Jim said.

'Well, I'm doing just fine,' Mikey would shout, like the punchline of a joke, and the hilarity would shimmer around the room.

God knows what Mikey had been like as an undecided youth or a trainee policeman, but as a damaged survivor he made magic. It took a little while to understand his speech, but once your ear was in, you compensated for his slowness in getting his syllables out, his heavy arrhythmic sentences and his stuttering difficulty in articulating words. It even added to the fun, knowing what was going to come ('Well, I'm doing just fine.' 'Hey, Jenny, will you marry me?' 'When are we gonna eat?'), and then its eventual arrival, just as expected. I learned quickly to make fun of Mikey's little ways and to avoid responding to them as tragic symptoms of a broken body and mind.

'Come on, Mikey, spit it out.'

'Just . . . just . . . just . . . you w . . . wait. Donut be in su . . . su . . . uch a god . . . d . . . d . . . dam hur . . . hurry.'

'Watch your language, young man,' Bet would say severely.
'Huh, sorry, god . . . god . . . goddam it.'

Mikey was like Udi, he wouldn't let you not love him. It was a gift.

But Mikey was no less aware of his affliction than we were. We joked and he joked about the dozen exactly similar radios he had in his room and the multiple copies of his favourite CDs, which he bought over and over again on his Saturday outings with Jim to the mall to spend his week's wages because he forgot he had them already. He stubbornly refused to listen to Jim when he told him he had the new Santana, and insisted on getting it again, because he had no recollection of the pleasure of getting what he wanted the first time, and then the next. If everything felt new, nothing felt old and safe and regular. He forgot that he had eaten and demanded another pizza because he was genuinely hungry, if not for food then for satisfaction. That and the fact that he couldn't exercise had made him considerably overweight. Often he tried to do things for himself that took two or three times as long to do than they would if someone did them for him, but you stood back and let him. Sometimes, though, the frustration would mount up, he would be too slow making a coffee, lighting a match for my or his mother's cigarette, or getting to the loo in time, and he would crash down the mug, sweep the matchbox on to the floor, or slam the door shut on himself in his room, cursing darkly in a way that Bet couldn't stand. Mikey knew exactly what had happened to him, how he had once been, that he could once drive cars and go out with the boys, meet girls, get drunk, have sex, make plans, fail exams because he didn't care, not because he couldn't write, and stay out wherever he wanted for as long as he wanted. He remembered in his grown man's body that he had once been a grown man in other ways before he had been condemned to play the lovable child for all his life. When he shouted his anger at Bet, Jim responded immediately.

'Don't ever talk to your mother like that.'

Mikey, of course, got over his tantrum quickly enough, forgetting it had happened, but for the rest of the evening Jim would be sunk deep into his armchair, his hand over his forehead, half covering his eyes, while a game-show host urged his contestants to ever higher peaks of hysterical, squealing excitement.

Jim was particularly pleased that I got on with Mikey. It was what had most worried him about my visit. Right at the beginning we had established that he and I had different views of the world. While driving back from the train station Jim had made some passing remark about welfare and liberal pinkos, and I decided I'd better establish my credentials and leave it at that.

'Listen, Jim, I'm so liberal pinko, I'm virtually blood-red. But we'll manage to coexist for the few days I'm here, won't we?'

'Sure, so long as you don't try any of your communist world domination tricks on me.'

'It's a deal. Not a domino will fall. I'm so wishy-washy liberal that I'm prepared to coexist with you.'

'Just for five days, right?'

'Yeah, just for five days.'

But his real concern was how I would manage with Mikey. He feared, I think, pity, sentimentality or an open expression of sadness. Once it turned out OK, he relaxed, pleased that Bet had someone to talk to, taking off on his own to the base for longer periods because he felt that she had company. But I was not the best of company, staying for long periods, when

Mikey was at work, in the trailer, reading, avoiding Bet's engulfing need to talk, to have the company of another woman, to go over and over the childhood pain she had experienced. I listened for as long as I could, but it was never enough. Jim, full of love for Bet as he was, had stopped listening years ago. Not that Bet stopped talking to him, but he switched off and you could almost see the words slithering around and over him as he sat at the kitchen table thinking his own thoughts or not thinking them. On the second morning of my visit I woke with my eyes pouring tears and feeling as if knives were being turned in the irises. When I staggered into the kitchen from the trailer, Bet found some drops which we tried at the kitchen table, and then, my eyes red raw and streaming, not much improved, she continued with her monologue while I held paper tissues to my face, using up an entire box as each got drenched. She was concerned, but whatever was happening to my eyes had happened before, I told her, and having established that I didn't have to be rushed to hospital, her need to talk reasserted itself, and I sat, weeping and flinching in pain, while she continued with whatever story it was she was telling me.

The same morning I received a letter from England. It was proofs for an article I'd written just before I left, and I had given Bet's address to the editor to send them to me for checking. I was quite pleased to get something that looked like work to keep me in my trailer. That evening, early, I took my hosts out to eat. We went to Bet and Jim's favourite Tex-Mex restaurant. It was in a local mall. Mikey liked it. They knew him well there and joked with him easily. The food was neither here nor there, except there was plenty of it, and as Jim said, 'It ain't fancy.' Always a plus in his eyes. We had to eat very early because the final game of the World Series was on TV that night. Baseball, American male ritual, Jim and Mikey in front of the TV eating chips and popcorn, drinking beer.

When we got back, Bet snapped on the small TV in the kitchen to see how the preparations for the game were going. What I know about baseball is nothing except that it functions quite like religion for American men. I even had to be told, with eyes rising towards heaven, that the World Series was baseball and not football. I worked out for myself that 'world' in this case meant just the USA, revealing what Americans really thought of themselves. The men were in the kitchen, Jim explaining that the final was between the Raging Somethings and the Wild Whatevers, when disaster struck. The Wild Whatevers were owned by Ted Turner, and the commentator said that Turner and his then wife, Jane Fonda, were in the stadium to watch their team.

'Shit!' Jim barked, and Mikey looked up astonished to hear such language from his dad.

'Oh, Jesus,' Bet groaned.

'What?' I asked. The atmosphere was thunderous.

'Turn it off,' Jim said.

'Jim, it doesn't matter. Just watch the game. You always watch the final of the World Series.'

'I'm not watching anything that bitch is watching. Hanoi bloody Jane. I don't want to see her ugly traitor's mug on my TV set. Turn it off.'

'You're not going to watch the game?' I asked.

'I saw men die in Vietnam while Miss Ho Chi Minh Fonda was prancing around in Hanoi encouraging the Commies to kill American soldiers. She should have faced a firing squad. She ain't going to show her face in my home. Turn the frigging TV off.'

It was the first time I'd heard a real person use the word *frigging*.

'But she was young. Even the GIs thought it was a bad war.'

'I don't know what kind of war it was, except my country asked me to fight and if necessary lay down my life. I didn't see Hanoi Jane risking anything. Or she thought she wasn't. But I tell you there are people even now who wouldn't go to any picture she was in, not even to spit at the screen. We won't forget. She deserves a bullet for what she did. She'll never be forgiven. How dare she sit in the fancy seats of the World Series final under an American flag? She used to burn it.'

'Turn that bitch off,' he ordered Bet.

'Don't be silly. Mikey wants to watch. Jenny's never seen the World Series. Just don't look at her when she comes on screen. Come on, let's pop some corn.'

Jim made a popping noise of his own and stomped out of the kitchen into the darkened lounge. The noise of a quiz show blasted out of the large TV, drowning out the commentator on the kitchen set.

Mikey, Bet and I watched the game with the sound down low. Mikey tried to explain the finer points of baseball to me, while Bet got intermittently excited and punched the air at some unfathomable thrilling moment. We all felt slightly guilty and treacherous, aware of Jim's powerful sulk next door, but equally committed to common sense and doing what all America, except Jim, was at the very same moment doing. I watched the game in much the same way I watched the test card as a child – waiting for something to happen. So far as I could see it was rounders but so slow it made cricket look like an extreme sport. Men in ridiculous clothes posed and gyrated and almost invariably produced no-balls, and so had to begin the posing all over again. When a ball *was* good, someone ran a few yards to the next base, people cheered, the commentators did arcane arithmetic and the whole sequence began again.

'Excuse me, does anything else happen in this game?'

Mikey and Bet looked at me reproachfully.

'It's a great game. You don't understand.'

The camera picked out Ted Turner and a matronly, most unrevolutionary Jane Fonda cheering their team on. At the mention of their names by the commentator, the TV in the next room rose several decibels.

'Hey, Jim, keep it down.'

But he couldn't hear over the yelps of glee as someone gave the correct answer to a question that was worth a whole laundry room full of white goods.

'How do you like the trailer?' Jim asked the next day.

We had made a trip to Santa Fe, Mikey took the day off work. Santa Fe was, according to Bet, 'where the artists all live', but wandering around it seemed more full of posers than last night's baseball. Hampstead on a bad but sunny day. In fact, there was the Georgia O'Keeffe museum, which might have been interesting, but when I mentioned it I got a distinctly cool response from my hosts. We went to the tourist shopping street, and once again I found myself staring at modern parodies of cowboy boots and modified saddle bags with mobile-phone holders. I managed to get them to the strangely jolly cathedral, all light and colour, the Mexican influence overriding morose Catholicism. Though the Catholicism fought back. A notice informed the congregation that the holy bones of the tepidly virtuous St Thérèse of

Lisieux would be arriving to be venerated on the New Mexican leg of their American tour. Bet lit a candle for Mikey. I just lit a candle in the belief that there ought to be as much light as possible in the world.

'The trailer's wonderful. Love it. A great place to work.'

'Yeah, I can't get her out of it. I think she's hiding from me,' Bet complained, only half joking.

'No, honey, she's like me, busy doing nothing. I got nothing to do and I'm still only halfway through it. Hey,' Jim said to Bet. 'I've had a great idea. You like Jenny, I like Jenny, Mikey likes Jenny. You like Jenny, don't you, Mikey? Why don't we keep her?'

'Yeah,' Bet agreed. 'Good thinking. How we gonna do that?'

'Hell, no one knows she's here. We can keep her in the trailer. It'll be just like *Misery*. You know, that movie about the writer? We lock her in one night, and I'll take it off on my hunting trip. We'll go way out in the woods, and I'll just shoot deer and let my hair grow until the search for the missing English Commie lady writer blows over.'

'Just pinko, Jim.' I tried to join in with the game.

'Nah, it's no good,' Bet said. 'She got a letter yesterday. She told her boss our address. She must have known we'd decide to keep her for ourselves. They'll know she was here.'

'That's OK. We can say she was here but she left after a couple of days and we don't have any idea where she's gone. Did you see *Misery*, Jenny? You remember James Caan was a storywriter and . . .'

I'd seen *Misery*. I thought it was quite funny. A nice take on the folly of writers' best hopes and worst fears. But during the drive back to the empty suburbs of Albuquerque, Bet, Jim and Mikey took on a more shadowy reality in my mind.

As if they'd turned inside out, an underlying darkness gleaming glossily on the surface. The veneer of joking affection was replaced by a mythic malevolence, and an overriding will to action. My vision adjusted. Rationality, which I had held on to so far, receded, and I began to see only the gothic underbelly, the monsters that are created by lurking unresolved pain and disappointment; the underworld of decent normality, of suburban vacancy, of the ordinary turning to horror, that American movies understood so well. I passed from America-in-the-movies into movie-America, just as Buster Keaton had wandered dreamily from his seat in the cinema to slip through the screen and become part of the celluloid action.

When I got back to the house, I tried to walk the fearful feelings, the absurd feelings away, through the wide empty streets that went nowhere. I found myself in anywhere and everyplace, the empty space of modern American living, and I recognised it with an increasing chill in my heart. The movies were my only guide to these depleted suburbs, the bedrock from which the contemporary monsters of America emerged. In the cinema I had seen Freddy Kruger and his ghastly peers stalk these unending, dangerously clean, lethally clipped, vacant, peopleless, inhuman streets, free to pick and choose among the near identical residences which front door (always closed except to enter or exit the car) to storm, to which blankly normal household he would announce his beastly reality. Now I saw how these films came about, how they couldn't not have sprung into the head of anyone who walked along the antiseptic avenues, as I did, looking for signs of life. I walked for what seemed to be miles, but house after house stood mute, a clipped bit of lawn, a car or two, maybe a truck or a trailer, but no shops or bars or cafés appeared where locals could meet, greet and gossip. There was no sound of kids, no sight of the young, mixing and injecting life and play into the emptiness. It was uncanny. So safe that danger echoed with every footstep. Hitchcock, John Carpenter, Wes Craven and Stephen King understand this vacuum, this white hole available to be filled with all that is darkest and murkiest in the human psyche. The new gothic landscape, a heaven that whispers hell in all its neat, inhumane silence.

By the time I was back inside my trailer – now hovering impossibly between a haven and a threat – I was feverish with unreality, or, as it increasingly seemed to me, clearly observing the reality that I had until now failed to see. I have never been mad as such, by which I mean that I have never thought myself someone or somewhere other than I am, not heard voices informing me of truths inaccessible to the rest of the world, not seen visions that bore no relation to what was happening in the sight of everyone else. At any rate, whenever any of these things did occur, it was usually in my twenties and directly attributable to a very carefree use of drugs. But I do know a kind of madness that lies low in the mind, half-buried in consciousness, which lives in parallel to sanity, and given the right circumstances or even just half a chance, creeps like a lick of flame or a growing tumour up and around ordinary perception, consuming it for a while, and causing one, even when not at the movies, to quake in fear of the world and people and what they – I mean, of course, *we* – are capable of.

In the dark, that night, I had no doubt that the joking threat of kidnap was no joke at all. As a matter of fact, even in the cool sanity of this present moment, I suspect that there was something more than just a tease, but that night in my head the threat combined with Jim's evident fury, Bet's need

for company and the wish of both for a sympathetic soul to
keep Mikey happy, and whatever portion of cool sanity I pos-
sess couldn't be seen for dust. I spent the night in lonely
terror, like all the children who had been spirited away in
grim folk tales, like James Caan in *Misery*, like Tony Last at
the finale of Evelyn Waugh's *A Handful of Dust*, condemned
for ever to read Dickens to a madman in the jungle. I *believed*,
by morning, that I would be consumed by these emotional
cannibals I had unwittingly set myself among. They would
refuse to let me leave. I would be secreted by them.
Imprisoned. Sequestered. Killed. The waking nightmare
lasted into the daylight. When I say I believed this to be the
case, I mean that I absolutely knew it to be my situation. I
knew also that it was ridiculous. That I was in a *condition*.
That I might be pleased these kind and generous people with
whom I had little in common liked me enough to joke about
wanting to keep me. But knowing that was nothing like as
powerful as knowing that I was enmeshed in a horror movie
that had come to life. The horror, of course, was my horror at
having got off the train; at joining the parade instead of letting it pass me by. Even for five days. I felt that I was dying
and made it easier on myself by letting myself think that
someone out there – instead of me – was doing the killing.
That day, in order to shake the horror off, I read books (Zizek,
for God's sake, on fantasy), I worked on the proofs, I lay on
the bed breathing deeply, fighting for calm, but the fear that
I would never leave that place remained. I wasn't due to catch
the train until after lunch the following day. Until then I was
trapped in anxiety: until the moment when I was due to leave,
I couldn't know for certain that they would let me go. They
just don't take me to the station. They keep me away from the
phones. There is no other form of transport to get myself to

the train, no passing pedestrian I can appeal to for rescue.
They just drive me away in the trailer and I am lost. Getting
to the train became crucial. And the more I tried to feel the
absurdity of my fear, the more my fear told me that such
things happen, that craziness occurs, that I might well be
captured and . . . and what? Killed? Kept as a friend for lonely
Mikey? Punished for having an easy life? It didn't matter
what. The sense of threat was everything. An engulfing black
cloud descended over me, and made a nonsense of all
attempts at rationality or efforts at distraction.

I gave no indication to my putative captors of my state of
mind, I think. I am rather good at keeping my madnesses
private. I kept to myself as much as I could, but I ate with the
family, laughed with Mikey and listened to more of Bet's stories of her childhood. Yet all the while the bizarre threat
remained. Several times Jim and Bet reminded me of it.

'Hey, ain't it great having Jenny living with us all the time?'

I laughed along with them. I dreaded the coming night
when the fantasy would gain full control and the terror of
abduction grow massive. During the night my heart beat so
hard I thought I might die of it. In the morning all I could
think of was catching the train, but that I was dependent on
Jim getting me to the station on time. He might simply disappear to the commissary. What if he took me but contrived
to be late enough to miss the train? What if he kept taking me
to the train, every day, and I kept missing it, day after day, and
we all began to live in a pretence that they were letting me go
when it was perfectly clear that I was in fact imprisoned? I
feared the politeness of a nicely brought up child who does-
n't dare be rude enough to say to the stranger offering her a
lift to oblivion that she doesn't want to get in the car with
him. I thought of suggesting that I get a cab to the station,

but I knew my hosts wouldn't hear of such a thing. I would be trapped by good manners into an eternity of out-of-town Albuquerque. In fact, I had the phone number of the daughter of a friend who lived in the city and worked at the university, but I didn't phone her. The phone was in the kitchen and I didn't want to be overheard. You remember that scene in the movie? And I feared too that I would blurt out my panic and reveal myself to a sane stranger to be ridiculous, as well as hear my own absurdity as I spoke the words. 'I'm afraid I'm being kept prisoner here . . .' So idiotic, she would send a doctor to me, and in consultation with Jim and Bet it would be decided that the best thing would be for me to stay where I was, on calming drugs, and wait until the madness passed over. It would, of course, take for ever. I would never be free, I was their prisoner. No, no, I'd remember as the fantasy took off, the point was that I would be revealing myself to be paranoid, in a state of unreality, but all scenarios led back to the pit of fear I had dug for myself.

What all this was about was that I had got off the train. I'd stopped moving, meeting and withdrawing from people. I was grounded in a house with a family, and I wonder if Jim and Bet hadn't made their *Misery* joke whether I wouldn't nonetheless have generated the fear all on my own. Just five days, not even a week, and I was beside myself with despair that I was trapped, that I would never get away from people. To be a stranger on a train is to be inside a private anonymous bubble of one's own, waving at other passing bubbles; to be staying in a house with a family was to be engaged in a way that I found nearly intolerable, actually dangerous. And when the partial safety of my separate trailer was taken from me with the notion that it might become a gaol, full-blown panic ensued. The people I know at home I trust to let me keep a certain distance, to withdraw when I need, to need a degree of withdrawal themselves. Bet and Jim and Mikey I didn't know and couldn't trust to give me leeway, or to want it. The people I know at home I trust up to a point, but not enough not to need to feel I can withdraw. Bet, Jim and Mikey I didn't know or trust even to that point. I knew exactly what I was doing when I put myself on a train. I forgot myself, or mistook myself, when I got off it.

The final morning was spent in a haze of anxiety, added to by a flurry of will-we/won't-we-get-her-to-the-station jokes, and by Jim taking off with a teasing grin to buy cigarettes at the base at around midday, an hour and a half before my train left. I did the only thing I know to do when panicking about something that might, but probably won't, happen: I fast forwarded. I put myself past the time of danger, into the future, and had myself seated safely in the train moving away from Albuquerque. It's always worked a treat so far.

It worked, for example, when I was coming out of my last major depression in 1984. I'd spent three months sitting on the sofa, immobilised by the worst episode yet. But as you do, though as you don't believe you ever will, I was beginning to come out of it. I went to Vermont to stay with a friend and spent the final two days (having been warned against it) alone in New York before flying back. I'd never been to New York and I walked for miles around the only city I would recommend during a depression – the energy level buoys the most leaden of moods. I wandered around the park in the late summer sun, and settled on the grass to listen to a jazz band. A Japanese man began to speak to me. Well, I thought, strange city, strange times, go with it. That old grabbing-experience habit again, not quite guttered. We walked around the park and he told me that he had just returned from

Edinburgh where he had been researching the use of lithium
in pure depression rather than only bipolar illness. I kept a
straight face, but was most impressed at my capacity to attract
the appropriate professional. I asked him questions and then
he was impressed.

'Are you in the field?' he asked.

'No, I just take a lay interest.'

Soon we were talking about diagnosis, and as we sat on a
bench he explained to me the set of ten to fifteen questions
psychiatrists use to diagnose and assess depression in patients.

'Like what?'

He asked me the first and then waited, as if we were playing a game, for my answer. After six or seven he began to look
at me more carefully, by the final question he looked very
serious.

'A severely depressed patient is expected to give certain
answers to half the questions. You have given them to two-
thirds.'

'Oh, I was just trying to put myself in the mindset . . .'

He was not convinced. Nonetheless, he told me he was
meeting a Japanese friend at Columbia and then going on to
the best Japanese restaurant in New York. Would I like to
come along? He was a round-faced, amiable man in his early
thirties, who spoke gently and smiled kindly. Here I was in
NY, I was being invited to eat great Japanese food with two
Japanese people. Why would anyone in their right, or righting, mind, turn such an offer of spontaneous experience
down?

We picked up the friend who had a car. As soon as they
met, everything changed. I was put in the back of the car
and the two men got in the front. They spoke to each other in
Japanese, and addressed not a word to me. I began to

wonder . . . One Japanese bloke in a strange city is another
person; two, it turned out, became a cultural phenomenon. I
was ignored, geisha-like in the back of the car as we
approached the bridge.

'Um, where are we going?' I asked.

'Restaurant's in New Jersey,' my friend barked and then
continued his incomprehensible conversation with his friend.

My friend in Vermont knew I was in New York, but no one
knew I was in New York in the back of a car with two complete strangers whose language I couldn't understand, heading
for the wilds of New Jersey. Now it crossed my mind that I
had not behaved with caution. I thought of asking to be let out
of the car before it crossed the bridge, but decided it would
force the issue, and I didn't want to know quite so definitely if
I was really in danger. I sat in the back, listening to the two
men in intense conversation – about how to rape and murder
me, or about the funding of psychiatric research in
Edinburgh? – and I ran through the newspaper files in my
mind for reports of rape and murder by Japanese men abroad.
I came up with nothing. I decided to sit it out and fast forward
to them dropping me off at my hotel after a pleasant meal in
New Jersey. It didn't make me feel good, so I forwarded further to my arrival at Heathrow the following night. This was
good because it also took care of my mild flying anxiety. I
stayed very calm and decided that sooner or later death was
inevitable and that now was as good . . . Perhaps I was not
quite as over the depression as I thought.

The meal was good. It was ordered without reference to me
by my companions in Japanese, which they continued to
speak to each other. They did not once talk to me. I picked at
this and that, trying not to think of it as my last meal. Finally,
a credit card was produced, I offered mine and it was flipped

back at me. I followed them out of the restaurant back to the car. I felt a little better after we crossed the bridge back to New York, but only for a moment.

At 11.30 on a Saturday night my friend's friend stopped the car at the subway in Harlem and said goodbye.

'Don't forget you get the A train. It must be the A train,' he said in immaculate English and he left us standing.

It was a warm night, but that wasn't why my friend was sweating. Saturday night in the subway in Harlem was not where tourists were supposed to be, especially ones with expensive Japanese cameras around their necks. He was paralysed with fear, but there was no chance of getting a cab. There is nothing like someone else's panic to induce calm, I find. I led him gently down into the subway, to his doom he supposed. While we waited for the A train, large young men with blaring boom boxes stood and scanned up and down the platform. My friend was now saturated with fear, but it occurred to me that all these dangerous-looking guys were no different from the kids I taught at the Islington Sixth Form Centre. In fact, they might have been very different, but it's always good to find a familiar point of view. Anyway, I was depressed, I had just escaped rape and murder and I had a man with me who was much more scared than I was. I stayed in charge, put him on the train and we clattered along under the pavements of New York until we got to a stop that my friend knew was near a jazz club he'd heard of. He jumped up and left with a slight wave of the hand. What the hell. I got off half a dozen stops later, still unmolested, at Central Park where, at midnight, there was not a cab in sight. I had no idea where my hotel was – because I am the only person in the world who, having no spatial sense, cannot orient herself in New York City. I was lost, and not feeling so brave any more. Finally I saw a cop. I asked him for directions to my street.

'I can't work it out.'

He looked down at me with wonder.

'Carn't? Carn't? You *carn't* work it out?' He was doubled up with amusement at my accent.

'Listen, that's how they talk where I come from.'

He shook his head in wonder and chuckled as he wandered off, quite failing to set me in any direction at all, let alone the right one. And yet, here I am, a couple of decades on, alive and well enough, because moments later a cab drove by, stopped and took me to my hotel, once I had convinced the driver that I really didn't want a drink, just a ride home. And the next night I was indeed walking through the arrivals door at Heathrow, just as I had pictured on my way to New Jersey with two perfectly strange strangers. Fast forwarding. The same thing, I suppose, as I did when I was a kid, imagining myself dead. The technique has never let me down.

Seated safely in the train moving away from Albuquerque I shook my head against the power of my fancies. Not that my friends hadn't had fancies of their own, but what we rely on, and what usually works, is that people have fancies but also the capacity to control them so that they do not spill over into reality. It doesn't always work, some people lack that capacity, but society depends on it mostly working in order to function. Mine had run too far amok in my mind, though not out into the world. They had kept theirs under control, only letting a little sadism spill out. I wonder, though, if I had not controlled my fears even as much as I did, whether theirs might not have edged closer to reality. So we depend on each other.

I arrived a few hours later back at the oasis in Phoenix. John and Maria had no idea what had been going on, but once again left me to my own devices by the pool. It was a place of refuge, but what I wanted very urgently was to be back home. My trip had come to an end. I would have to continue on the train back to my starting point in New York to get the return flight, but it was now just space to be crossed, not a *journey*. And the idea of the planned four or five days in New York and Long Island with a writer friend was more than I could contemplate. I called the airline. Could I bring my flight forward? I could at a price. I paid it, and then went to bed and sobbed with relief.

What State I'm In

Journeys come to an end before they end, just as they begin before they begin – with the arrival of anticipation. I was as good as home. I had put my curiosity about the human race, us, me, them, back where I was most comfortable with it: in my study at home. When I was there again, I'd do some thinking; right now, I had a trip from A to B to take to get me there. John got up at 4.30 on Wednesday morning to drive me to Tucson train station. I waved him off gratefully and he, equally gratefully I imagine, drove back to bed in Phoenix, while I settled down on a bench to wait for the *Sunset Limited*. It would take me to New Orleans for the night of Thursday, then I would catch the *Crescent* early Friday morning heading up north and get in to Penn Station, New York at 2.10 on Saturday afternoon. I had just an hour or so to wait for the train, plus an added hour for how late it would be. As far as I was concerned, I was heading home. My journey was done, even though there were three and a half days and an Atlantic flight before I'd be in my study. I wasn't watching, listening, waiting. I was travelling to a destination. Game over.

'I heard you speaking to your friend. You sound English. And you look Jewish. My two favourite peoples on the planet are the English and the Jews. The English gave us our blessed language. The Jews gave us the Book. I thank you, ma'am.'

The speaker was an elegant tramp sitting on a bench opposite me with the rising dawn glowering over his shoulder through the waiting-room window. Spread on either side of him was his breakfast, a thermos, sandwiches and biscuits, which he had been eating and drinking absentmindedly while leafing through unruly sheaves of papers perched on his knee. He wore an ancient but once good, long raincoat, a pair of very worn but sturdy walking boots laced with string, a flat tweed cap, and had a well-aged, open, but still bulging satchel propped between his feet. He sat straight and was long-legged, in his late sixties, perhaps.

I nodded an acknowledgement that he was right about my English- and Jewish-ness and smiled weakly at the reasons for his reverence of both.

'Jack W. Grey.' He bobbed his head. 'I would be honoured if you would share my breakfast.'

He held out a packet of digestive biscuits. I wanted to say, I'm on my way home, I'm not being a curious traveller any more, I'm no longer on the lookout for interesting encounters with eccentric types – perhaps I wasn't really in the first place. I swear, I'll just stay put once I get home. Not go out. Stay in. Keep quiet.

I took a biscuit and thanked him.

'Ah, your lovely accent. What do you do?'

I have often answered this question with the information

that I am a biscuit packer in the Peak Frean factory. At the look of blank boredom that comes over my questioner's face on hearing this news I'm inclined to embellish.

'I work on the Fancy Assorted Tins line. It's so much more demanding than you might think. First there's the responsibility to the product. A Fancy Assorted Tin is *designed*, you know, and not just on the outside. It isn't at all superficial. Each biscuit type has its place in the overall scheme and if the packers don't concentrate it would be easy to ruin the whole thing by slotting a careless jam whirl in the coconut cream section. It only takes a moment's distraction and the whole pattern is destroyed. And then again think about the nature of the tin of biscuits. It's a Special Occasion product, people bring out their tins of biscuits for Christmas, give them to people for their wedding anniversaries. Imagine the disappointment in finding that half of them, or even one, just one Viennese Dainty say, were broken. The whole illusion is smashed, the luxurious becomes the tawdry. Packing biscuits is not just packing biscuits. There's a whole social and cultural aspect to it . . .'

Usually, my listener is casting about desperately for an escape route, but I get to the point where I convince myself of the importance of my work. Why shouldn't biscuits be packed with the same sense of accountability and obligation to others that scientists and social workers bring to their tasks? It isn't important what you do, it is the attitude with which you proceed through the world that matters. But the burden of persuasion is generally lifted from me by the sudden departure of my new acquaintance. Sometimes, as a change from biscuit packing, I explain that I am a retired member of the cult disco-dancing troupe Pan's People, or, if the questioner is of the right generation, of the high-kicking arms-linked Tiller

Girls. This involves explaining that the life was by no means all glamour and late night supper parties. People imagine that it's non-stop fun, fun, fun, but no. I go on to tell of the sheer sweat and labour required of precision dancers, the rehearsals that continue until the feet bleed, the exhaustion, the staying up night after night sewing fallen sequins back on to one's costume.

But this morning I had no stomach for distancing daydreams. I gave up and allowed another interesting character into my trip.

'I'm a writer.'

'And I'm a poet.'

Of course he was. He riffled through his papers in the satchel and read me his poem about being in San Francisco in 1967 and how everything was changed in 1997:

What do dyed hair and plastic flowers
Have in common? Only the beauty is real.

Jack told me he had read this to some young people while he was waiting at another station recently. Thinking Jack was out of earshot one young man had said to another, 'That man's poem was awesome.' I congratulated him and thanked him for reading it to me. More and more pages came out of the satchel and were declaimed in the manner of Ginsberg and his chums. The stationmaster wandered into the waiting room and then wandered out again. I short-circuited the reading of his entire works by asking him what kind of travelling he was doing. Jack was doing pretty much what I was doing: travelling around America on the trains. It was some kind of annual salute to Kerouac and the boys. At home in Minneapolis he lived with his Polish-born Jewish wife Emily, the mother of his three children. She had been shipped out of Poland as an adolescent in 1938. Their marriage had been long, passionate and artistic.

'I still to this day, old as we are, worship at the shrine of her breasts. I kneel before those ruined works of art of nature and take them in the palm of my hand and caress them. On my knees, with my face nestling between them, I tell her, "These empty hanging sacks I have loved and have fed on just as our babies fed on them for life and strength."'

I said I was pleased to hear it. Did she accompany him on his Dharma Bum travels?

'She understands about my need to be free sometimes. I have to tell stories in poetry and I have to travel. She says to me when I leave, "If you meet a woman on your travels, you can fuck her, but don't read her our poem."'

'It is one you wrote?'

'No. It begins: *Had we but world enough, and time . . .*'

'Marvell.'

'Ah yes. It goes on—'

'But you promised not to recite it.'

'Yes, I know, but perhaps you are to be something different.'

'No, really, I'm not.'

There was a pause.

'My greatest conversation on this trip was on the bus from Vashon to Tacoma with a man whose wife is Greek Orthodox. He is of Protestant roots – something like Emily and me, although she is Jewish. He knew about the Second Crusade around the year 1205 which diverted and sacked Constantinople and Hagia Sophia church. His work partner was with him – in computers – very alert and laughed etc. He said nothing, but he liked my talk so much, he scribbled as I spoke. That's rare. I think he had a Polish-Irish-Catholic name. One of them left a briefcase when they got off. I asked the bus driver to wait and I ran after them. "That shows what a good talk can do!" he said.'

I explained I had to go outside on to the platform to smoke.

'I don't smoke, but I will come with you. You must give me your address in London where I can write to you.'

Back in London, I got several fat air-mail letters from Jack W. Grey. Photocopies of letters he'd written to other people and to newspapers, excerpts from his journals, messages from Emily and his favourite poems by himself and others, including one by Frances Cornford because 'women I like like this'. One segment of letter ended: 'Since I met you in Tucson and talked with you several hours that day, what do I think of you now? I've been around drunks (what's the difference in the drunk and the alcoholic? – they both drink the same but the drunk doesn't have to attend all those meetings). So AA saves their jobs: I ask them after a year of no booze and a medal: how often did you think of a drink? – "about each 15 minutes". So I think of you each day.'

I didn't have the courage to reply. The letters have stopped.

When the *Sunset Limited* finally came, I spent a good deal of time in the smoking coach, puffing up a smoke screen and, I must admit, hiding from Jack W. Grey, who told me as we were separated by the conductor towards our different destinations that he had a lot more to say to me. The ugliest man in the world sat opposite me, or perhaps it was just my mood. In a deep southern accent he was talking to an elderly black man who was completely silent and seemed to be paying no attention. I – no longer on duty – was not listening to what was being said, but suddenly the black guy shook his head and said, 'Ol' Catfish died, huh?' What goes round comes round, round and round.

Next to me a man was explaining about law and order.

'In Singapore, they whip the fingers off thieves. North Africa it's the complete hand. They know what they're doing. One thing I can't stand is people who hit on kids. Those pae-dophiles, I'd take a baseball bat and break every bone in his body from the elbows down.' Several men were nodding fer-vent agreement.

'Yeah, this chicken-shit community service. Some kid got caught spraying graffiti in our town, and you know what? They made him *and his father* do twenty-five hours' commu-nity service. A couple of years in prison for the kid, that would do it.'

Apparently, I had been listening, because I wondered aloud what kind of society they would like to live in.

'What do I want? I want to mess about on boats and drink plenty, play pool and fight. Hunting in the hunting season and gambling in Vegas during the winter. That's my kind of society.'

There was a good deal of agreement and chuckling with this vision of the good life, which was not entirely unlike Karl Marx's vision of the perfect life.

'I like the way they run the trains,' the man who approved of North African justice told me. 'You make trouble, they put you off. Doesn't matter where it is. Just stop the train and throw you out.'

The last time he was on this train they had stopped it and put a drunk out into the desert three miles from El Paso. Not, he assured me, that they don't temper justice with mercy on Amtrak. That same journey there was a paraplegic in a wheel-chair who put his hand up a nun's skirt.

'The conductor didn't throw him out, he just gave him a warning and a good talking to. Next time, he'd be out on his butt, wheelchair and all. Another trip there was this real simple guy. Like a retard, you know? Well, there was this hooker working the train looking for tricks, and the retard just kind of fell in love with her. He didn't get what she was. They put her off the train for soliciting, and the retard, Jesus, he wept and screamed for her. He wanted to get off right there and find her, he pushed the emergency stop and the train screamed to a halt, and he howled and howled to be let off. They couldn't stop him shouting and crying. He went crazy. In the end, they went to the next town and called the cops. They took him in, just to calm him down they said.'

A plump, middle-aged Amish man came and sat down next to me. An elder, I suppose. He prepared his pipe with slow enjoyment, all cheery and ruddy smiles on his wide country-fresh face.

'Good day to you. Where are you from? Ah, English. I met another Englishman just the other day on the train. He was German. I spoke to him in German but he couldn't understand what I said. He spoke German, but not Old German. We speak Old German. He couldn't understand. Do you speak Old German in your area?'

'An Englishman?'

'Yes, a German.'

I concluded that English meant European. Or perhaps he thought England was in Germany, or Germany in England. His information about the world outside his community was very limited. It was the first time he had been away from his home. It was just him and his wife.

'I promised Mother that we would travel, but there has always been work to do. Mother said, now we must have our holiday. The children are grown and we can take a week off from work to see the world. So we left. We are having a very good time.'

The ugliest man in the world was telling his new friend how he had stomach cancer, and that it was due to Agent Orange used during the Gulf War. He had also been shot in both shoulders and got a shell in his thigh. When he got back to the States, he had to be hospitalised and drugged to deal with his aggression.

'Listen, I'm not aggressive, or I wouldn't be. All I want is for those sons of bitches to say they're sorry. I just want them to pay attention and apologise to me.'

I'm listening and listening. Although I've had it with other people, I can't stop listening. Sit still and listen to people talking, especially strangers, and what you hear is everything there is to hear. You gather in statements of how things are, the way of it, what it's like. The details vary a bit, but the tone becomes as familiar as the sound of the wheels running over the track. Every word is banal, corny, expected, a story a thousand times told, but every word is true. People may have learned to talk like the movies, but the movies learned everything there is to know from them. Each of them. I love it, and I can't bear it.

Next door to my sleeping compartment a family – mother and father in their thirties, two small kids – stayed shut up in their 'family room' next door to my sleeping compartment, apparently working through all the possibilities of togetherness. Through the wall the children whined and cried, being bored and restless, the mother encouraged them to play nicely, the father told them off, the mother shouted at the father, the father shouted at the mother. Sometimes it grew quiet when the children, and therefore the adults, were content for a while.

Then another explosive argument or fight. The adults yelled, the children wailed. Things quietened down again. The father came and went collecting food and drink from the bar. The mother soothed and told distracting stories and slammed out of the room. I lay on my bunk listening.

Back in the smoking car, a young man in a suit was working at his laptop – the first I'd seen used on the trains. It turned out he was trying to track the route of the train as it went along. He had never travelled by train before. He was amazed.

'I'm trying to find where we are. I didn't imagine I ever wouldn't know what state I'm in, but the land goes on and on and you lose any sense of where you are at all.'

For hours and hours we had been passing unchanging fields of sugar cane. I had a sense of void. Of being empty of content. This was the discovery I made (again). This was the real experience of experience. Vacancy. I listened and took in. I talked, I reacted. But I was in fact no more than an outline containing dark space. I had no feeling of substance, inside or out. As if I were an empty shell made of thin sugar. Nothing that happened, or had ever happened, accumulated into something solid, into anything I recognised as a – for want of a better word – self. If I thought I would hear clues that I could put together to make a picture of the world, of myself, I was quite wrong. Words and experience just fluttered about, like windblown butterflies. But at the same time, I was astonished by people, by what they have to say, how they live, how the planet exists with so much nonsense and so much endurance. I was touched by what I saw and heard, but when I stopped nodding and talking and smiling and grimacing, there was nothing inside, or nothing other than emptiness. Emptiness was all I could identify as I watched the miles of sugar cane through the window. The old Circle Line trip I used to take was a clearer indication of the blankness of the circle. Blankness outside as well as in the empty centre, and fellow travellers sitting in unassailable silence. If the experience of being no one was what I had been after, I had succeeded in so far as such a logical impossibility is achievable. But being no one sometimes feels like nothing at all.

I spent the night in a hotel in New Orleans, keeping still, not thinking, just waiting for the next train. The *Crescent* would get me back to New York. New York would get me back to London. London would get me back to keeping still and quiet and the fantasy that if I listened to silence and no one, I might hear something interesting. Who knew what? Something about nothing, maybe.

The *Crescent* had a new, cruel twist on the smoking theme. There was no smoking car, but there were smoking *periods*, when addicts were allowed to light up in the bar. I'd forgotten about the other good thing about being at home. I could smoke as much and as often as I wanted. The shift system was explained over the tannoy by the steward who enjoyed giving out the news.

'Howdy, folks, for those of you without the self-discipline to quit, we have special designated times when you can feed your addiction. These are: 9.30 a.m.; 12.30; 4.30; 7.30 and 10.30. Smoking is absolutely not permitted anywhere on this train except in the lounge bar and only at the stated times. The smoking periods last for twenty minutes. Your cooperation is appreciated. Have a nice journey.'

I boarded the *Crescent* at 7 a.m., so it was two hours before there was any point in making my way clutching my cigarettes to the bar. Actually, it was only an hour and a half before I was sitting in the bar waiting for lighting-up time, because I

didn't want to be late and miss one smoking second. I was not
alone. A bunch of anxious faces were walking like ghosts
towards the small lounge bar, all of us early. We found seats at
the tables in the clean conditioned air that was being vacated
by non-smoking breakfasters. The bartender came round and
placed a foil ashtray at each table. A clock ticked over the bar.
Slowly. No one spoke. We just waited. At 9.29, the steward
arrived. He checked the clock and he looked at his watch, rel-
ishing his moment.

'Not long now, folks,' he crowed. 'On your marks . . .
lighters at the ready . . . go!'

We lit up. Brows smoothing, breaking into smiles and sigh-
ing contentedly as we exhaled the first lungful. Twenty
minutes is plenty of time to smoke a cigarette, but not to
smoke two. You have to rush the first and light up again
immediately. But you had to smoke two because there would
be no more smoking for two hours and forty minutes. All the
pleasure was absorbed by anxiety. The steward watched us
contemptuously.

'Hey,' someone called out to him. 'What's the schedule for
sex on this train?' The steward smiled. He'd heard it all before.
'Suck it on up, guys. Time's passing.' And time passed. 'OK,
that's it. Put 'em out. Let's get some clean air again.'

It was a strange system. The lounge bar after twenty minutes of concentrated smoking by all the smokers on the train
was a thick fog, much worse than if a couple of people had
been sitting there all day and lighting up from time to time.
When the non-smokers returned, they choked on the air that
even the smokers found unpleasant. Everyone was unhappy,
except for the steward. And so we trooped back and forth,
every two hours forty minutes, by mid-afternoon familiar
faces, taking the same seats, raising our eyes at our helpless

situation and our craven need. I was just getting through the time as best I could. Going home. My journey had ended before the circle was completed. I'd had it with the tedious, stunning, clichéd, sentimental, heart-rending, banal truths of my fellow travellers and myself.

By 10.30 and the final smoke of the day, we were somewhere or other, South Carolina. For the fifth time that day I sat opposite a woman who smoked deep and hard as she swayed her head in time to something she was hearing through the headphones clamped over her ears. She had the remains of a double whisky in front of her. When the Marquis de Steward called time on our final smoke, both she and I stabbed out our cigarettes but stayed where we were. There was no point in moving, and there was at least the smoke-laden air to breathe.

The woman was in her forties, untidy in a sensual kind of way, good-looking but weary. She sighed profoundly and then looked up at me.

'Going far?'

'New York,' I said. 'Then back to London.'

'I'm going back to Virginia, to my home. My husband's meeting me at the station.'

She looked at me hard, to see if I understood what she meant. I understood that she was going to tell me.

'Complicated, ain't it?'

'Usually.'

She still had her headphones on and moved her head in time to the silent music. 'You like country and western?'

I nodded. I do, I love the perfectly formed two-minute stories of heartbreak. I admire and respect the unashamed sentiment. The whine of human love and loss. Banal and true enough. The whole journey might have been a country and western album.

She pulled off her headphones and handed them to me.

'Listen. This is so great. Just listen to the words. Want a drink?'

She called out to the bartender for two whiskies. In my ear a high-pitched male voice complained in a simple but catchy rhythm and even simpler rhymes about heartbreak, about love gone wrong and life never going right again. She told me his name was Aaron Someone. Her face was the template of emotional suffering, her drawn eyes and taut cheeks twitching slightly with the effort of holding the pain in, the corners of her mouth curved into the faintest smile of sad self-knowing. I drank the whisky fast when it arrived.

'Do you hear what he's saying? Listen to the words. It's so *true*. I've been married for nineteen years. It's my third. It was good for a long time. But for fourteen years now, I haven't been able to break down the walls between us. It's like we live on different planets. I don't know what went wrong. We couldn't *talk*. I said I wanted to get away. Have some time alone. It was cool with him, so I took off. Stayed in New Orleans. You see, I wanted to . . . find myself.'

'And did someone find you?'

It slipped out. I wished it hadn't. Her eyes focused sharply on me. She looked awed. 'How did you know?'

How could you not know? I handed Aaron Someone back to her and she put him back on to her ears.

'Wow, that's real smart of you. You understand. Yeah, someone found me. I met a man. I hadn't intended to. I truly had wanted to be on my own. But there was this young guy. Younger than me. A lot younger than me. But really wise, you know? Like he really knew what was going on in me. He was a lot older in his head than his years. We didn't have sex. Not full sex. I wouldn't allow it. I was worried about Aids. I mean,

I don't know him, and I have to go back to my husband. But we were so close, just those few days, and no sex, but so close, it was like we'd known each other for ever. It was like he was my other half. My missing half. He says he wants to be with me. You know, all the time. But I don't know. I want companionship, you know. He says it's love. The real thing. And it was amazing how he knew what I was thinking. I'd start to say something and he'd finish my sentence. It was scary. But, I don't know. I said no. I said I was going home. He was so charming. It scared me how charming he was. I'll go home and see. I'll wait and see. If it's meant to be, it'll happen. He knows my name, and how to find me. If it happens, it happens. That's what I think. Right now, I can't wait to get home. I don't know what I want. I don't know who I am.'

The last two statements were sung – in tune I imagine with Aaron Someone who was having very similar difficulties.

'Wow, these words. They're so *true.*'